For Anne Kaufman

About the Authors

Jesse Feiler has written a number of books about FileMaker, Mac OS X, the Web, and new technologies; his books have been translated into Japanese, Chinese, Polish, German, Spanish, French, and other languages. His most recent book is *Special Edition Using FileMaker 9*. As director of North Country Consulting, he has designed and implemented a variety of solutions for small businesses and nonprofits in fields such as production, marketing, the arts, printing and publishing, food service, and construction. He has taught and consulted widely on nonprofit governance, and he is the founder of ChamplainArts.com—a listing of cultural events in 2 states, 2 countries, and 2 languages.

About the Technical Editor

Jim Bumgardner is a senior technical guru at Yahoo! Music, a teacher at Pasadena's Art Center College of Design, and the creative mind behind CoverPop.com and CrazyDad.com. An expert in graphics and music software, Jim makes mashups, software toys, and experimental user interfaces using Flash, JavaScript, PHP, and other tools.

Contents at a Glance

v

Contents

Acknowledgments

Roger Stewart and Carly Stapleton at McGraw-Hill worked tirelessly to help move this book along. Carole McClendon, at Waterside Productions as always contributed her skills and expertise. Jim Bumgardner's technical edits were invaluable; you will notice several code snippets and specific suggestions from Jim that I'm happy to be able to pass along.

Introduction

Few developments in the world of computers have been embraced as quickly as mashups. The most common mashups remain those that build on the various mapping APIs, but dynamic combinations of data from multiple sources or in multiple formats (the basic definition of a mashup) are all over the Web. Part I of this book provides an introduction to the world of mashups.

Mashups require you to know a little bit about a number of Web technologies, and that is what you will find in Part II. Long books have been written about each of the technologies described in the chapters of Part II, but what you will find here is guidance about the specific parts of those technologies you are likely to use.

In Part III, the technologies are put together to build mashups. The first chapter of this part of the book introduces the basic steps common to building all mashups in the book. Then, you will find pairs of chapters: the first introduces a specific API (eBay, Google Maps, Flickr, and so forth), and the second builds on the technologies of Part II and the specific API to create a mashup.

The code described in most chapters is available on the author's Web site (www .northcountryconsulting.com—the Downloads link is at the right of the page, just beneath the bio), as well as on the McGraw-Hill Web site (www.mhprofessional.com, or more precisely, http://www.mhprofessional.com/product.php?isbn=0071496270). The downloadable code is in self-extracting ZIP archives and is organized by chapter. Because the examples are built from chapter to chapter, make certain that you are using the right chapter's code: the mashup from one chapter will have only a fraction of the code as the same mashup in a later chapter.

Note that most of the mashup code requires you to register to use the API involved. (This is described in the book.) The code that you download will not run until you replace placeholders such as `myAccountName` with your actual account name.

Part I

Introducing Mashups

Chapter 1

Welcome to the World of Mashups

How to...

■ Sell Things with Mashups

■ Provide Information with Mashups

■ Create Art with Mashups

This chapter presents a few of the thousands of mashups you can find today on the Web. No one knows how many other mashups live behind corporate firewalls, but, chances are, the number is large. The mashups in this chapter were chosen to show the variety of the world of mashups. Some of them are proofs-of-concept, others are works-in-progress, and others are experiments. Others are actual, live products or marketing tools.

Mashups often provide visualization of information, and, frequently, that visualization is in the form of interactive maps. The release of the Google maps API was a major factor in the interest in mashups, in large part because so much information lends itself to mapping. As you will see in later chapters of this book, new technologies grouped together as Web 2.0 and AJAX are the building blocks of mashups. In conjunction with APIs such as Google mapping, eBay, Yahoo!, Flickr, and others, you will soon be able to build your own mashups like the ones shown in this chapter.

AJAX (Asynchronous JavaScript and XML)

AJAX (Asynchronous JavaScript and XML) is a term first used by Jesse James Garrett in 2005. *AJAX* is generally considered to include JavaScript, XML, XHTML, DOM, and XMLHttpRequest, all of which are technologies developed in the 1990s, some of them in conjunction with Microsoft's Remote Scripting project. Despite this plethora of technologies, the principle is quite simple: a Web page can retrieve and display data without having to refresh or reload the entire page. To do this, the page needs to have its own programming logic (usually provided in JavaScript); it needs to be able to send a request for data (usually done with XMLHttpRequest); and it also needs to be able to load, and then unload, data to and from requests (usually done with XML, XHTML, and DOM).

The phrase "Web 2.0" was first used in 2004 by O'Reilly Media. *Web 2.0* refers to the Internet as a platform, as well as the growth of collaborative and sharing services, such as social networking sites, wikis, and the like. programmableweb.com is a primary reference to mashups. You can find mashups categorized by tags, as well as by technologies, on that site.

Sell Things with Mashups

Mashups can search a database for items that have known addresses. Figure 1-1 shows one of the most basic of such searches: a real-estate listing service (http://propertylistingmaps.com/site). This is a natural for mapping mashups, not only because the items being mapped are not movable (they are houses), but also because the data are already in a searchable database. The map has the controls you find in most of the mapping mashups: zoom controls; controls to move the map (including sensitivity to mouse drags); and a choice of a map view, a satellite view, or a hybrid view showing both. Markers indicate data points. In this case, you can click on a marker to open an info window with text, as is shown for the 927 Roble Av address. You can also hover the mouse over another marker (such as 888 Creek Drive) to display a pop-up window.

The legend in the lower-right of the map identifies two types of markers, based on when data were last updated. Mapping APIs let you customize markers to provide yet another level of information on a map.

| FIGURE 1-1 | Property Listing Maps |

A mashup is likely to be seen by a self-selected group of people (such as those interested in real estate in a certain area). This makes a mashup a good candidate for a service such as Google Ads. Scrolled out of view at the bottom of the window shown in Figure 1-1 are several such ads.

The real estate business certainly predates mashups, but other opportunities for mashups represent new businesses or new areas for an existing business to pursue. TutorLinker.com (http://tutorlinker.com/), shown in Figure 1-2, lets you specify an area and an area of skill to find tutors. This mashup uses the Google maps API, and it demonstrates the use of a link in an info window.

FIGURE 1-2   TutorLinker.com

Figure 1-3 shows another aspect of mashups. It lets you search an area for various items, but, as you can see from the tabs at the upper left, it will let you see listings from multiple sources such as eBay, Wal-Mart, Amazon, and Craig's List. Mapping, shopping, and comparative mashups are among the most common. Whereas the real estate mashup and the tutor mashup were designed to sell goods or services, mashups such as this are used either as a vehicle for advertising to people interested in specific products or as a way of generating referral fees to the mashup creator from services such as Amazon.

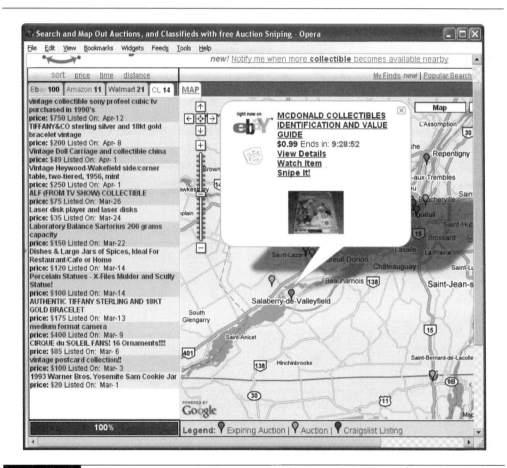

FIGURE 1-3   findnearby.net

Provide Information with Mashups

Mashups are an excellent way of presenting information from one or more sources. Figure 1-4 shows a mashup that uses several Web traffic services to analyze up to five domains graphically (http://attentionmeter.com/).

The information provided can be dynamic, as in the case of AttentionMeter. It also can be information in the public domain that you as a mashup creator organize and present, as shown in 1001 Fishing Holes in Figure 1-5 (http://1001seafoods.com/fishing/fishing-maps.php).

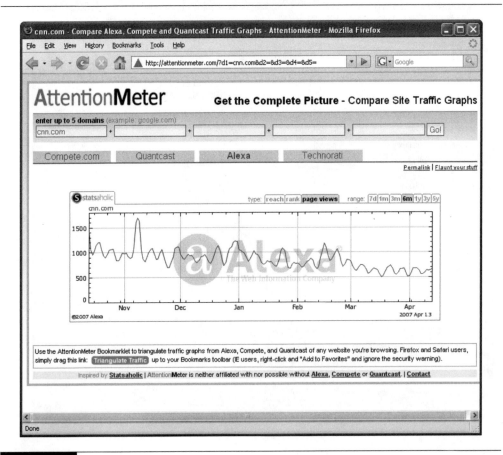

FIGURE 1-4   Attentionmeter.com

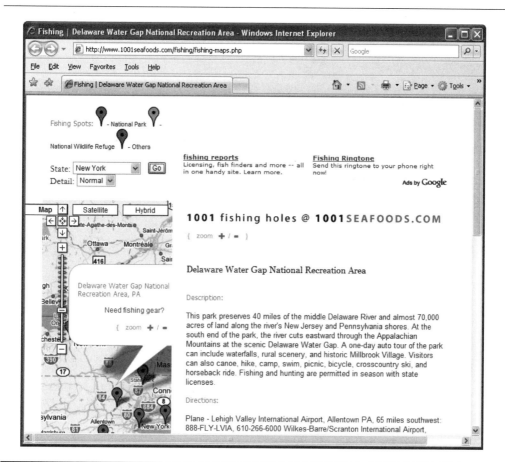

FIGURE 1-5   1001 Fishing Holes

The Harley-Davidson mashup, shown in Figure 1-6, takes this much further by providing company-specific information (dealers), as well as information of interest to motorcyclists in a mapping mashup.

OpenSecrets.org, a Web site run by the Center for Responsive Politics, keeps tabs on political contributions. The information provided on its site is designed to help organize that vast amount of publicly disclosed data in a way that makes it available to individual citizens, as shown in

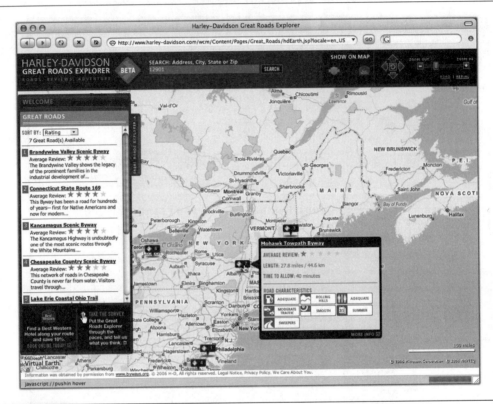

FIGURE 1-6 Harley-Davidson Great Roads Explorer

Figure 1-7 (http://opensecrets.org/travel/index.asp). As you can see, information on specific members of Congress is shown both in a tabular form and on a map.

All the mashups shown previously in this chapter have started from a user selecting information to be shown. Figure 1-8, from Epispider (www.episider.org), uses a different approach. The Epispider mashup reads various news feeds and automatically searches them for information about epidemics and natural disasters. It then creates maps, such as the one shown in Figure 1-8, that let you see what has happened in various parts of the world.

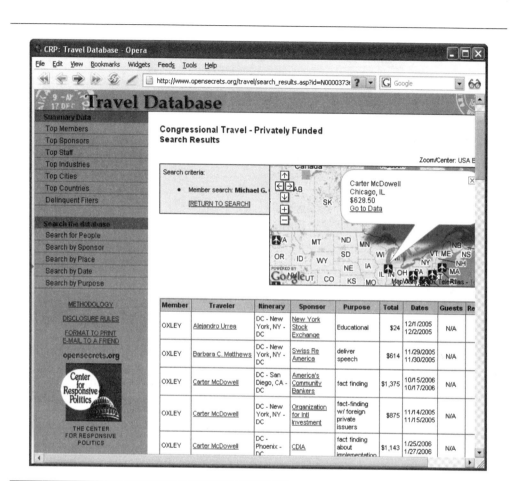

FIGURE 1-7 OpenSecrets.org Travel Database

Create Art with Mashups

The Epispider mashup displays whatever it finds in news feeds without the user controlling the search. The mashup designer specifies the news feeds and the rules for displaying information, and things run automatically from there on.

Artists have been experimenting with such techniques for decades (even longer if you agree with the Wikipedia citation that includes Mozart's 1757 "Musical Dice Game"). (Jim Bumgardner, the technical editor of this book, provides an earlier example. As Bumgardner

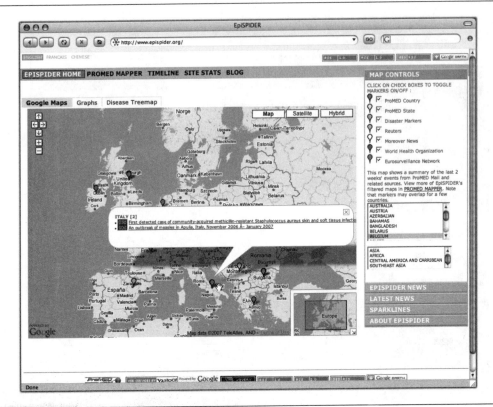

FIGURE 1-8   Epispider.org

points out, "An earlier example of algorithmic music composition was extensively documented by the Jesuit Polymath Athanasius Kircher in his 1650 book, Musurgica Universalis. Kircher described a box of wooden rods called the 'Arca Musurgica' and a related one called the 'Organum Mathematicum' (a few existing examples are in European museums) that was used to compose polyphonic church hymns by stitching together a collection of short musical phrases inscribed on the rods. Search for Kircher on my blog Krazydad.com for more info—I created some music using his data set [using Perl] a couple of years ago.")

Alexis Lloyd created The Ad Generator (www.theadgenerator.org/) as part of a thesis project at Parsons The New School for Design. It sets up rules for generating advertising slogans from randomized components of real slogans. The Ad Generator then searches Flickr for images relevant to the new "slogan." You can see one such "slogan" and its paired image in Figure 1-9.

FIGURE 1-9 The Ad Generator

Chapter 2

Understanding the Mashup World

How to...

- Describe a Mashup
- Build Your Own Mashup
- Make Money with Mashups
- Achieve Goals with Mashups
- Improve Productivity with Mashups
- Know How to Use Mashup Data Legally

In the previous chapter, you saw mashups from the outside, as a user would see them. In this chapter, you look inside mashups. First, you see a description of the process of building a mashup, and then you find information about what you as a mashup developer can do with mashups.

Describe a Mashup

Unlike many Internet standards and protocols, mashups did not emerge from a design process. Mashups arose as people combined existing standards and protocols in innovative ways. As a result, although many people know what a mashup is when they see (or create) one, a clear and unambiguous definition of a mashup can be elusive. As used in this book, a *mashup* is a Web page that uses Web 2.0 technologies, which may include JavaScript, PHP, and XML, to present information from a variety of sources or in a variety of ways where the presentation enhances the information.

As far as the user experience is concerned, a mashup is generally characterized by presenting specific information without forcing the user to click through various screens and URLs. The mashup—not the user—performs the synthesis of the data, so everything is presented at once. One way of describing mashups is to think of them as managing complexity.

This definition includes the two major types of mashups: *multisource* mashups and *presentation* mashups. Being able to describe a mashup helps you move on to the step of developing one.

Use Multisource Mashups

Many mashups combine data from two or more sources. For example, for a given ZIP code, a mashup can combine census data and economic data. A mashup could combine restaurant and movie theaters. The heart of a multisource mashup is the combination of the data sources in a logical way that adds value. The mashup developer's contribution often is the idea of combining specific data sources in a new and useful way.

Did you know?

All Those Mouse Clicks Take Time and Effort

The Web lets users click their way through an incalculable amount of information, following their ideas and questions wherever they may lead. As many people have noticed, this can eat up considerable time. Some of this is the same sort of time that would be spent reading books or magazines, or watching television, but much of the browsing and clicking time is spent getting to the information you want. Mashups provide a way to get to targeted information in a simple way. The world of mashups consists of a vast amount of data (basically everything on the Web) and mashups, which are the specifically targeted tools that retrieve just what you want, usually without any interaction at all (or perhaps a single mouse click to get started).

Use Presentation Mashups

A mashup need not combine two data sources. Instead, it can use Web 2.0 technologies to present the same data in two different ways—for example, in text form and on a map. The same principles of mashups apply here: the mashup does the work that otherwise would require a number of user interactions with various Web pages, mouse clicks, and the like. The mashup developer's role is to identify the most meaningful way of presenting the data so the mashup—like a multisource mashup—presents everything needed all at once without further interaction on the user's part.

Build Your Own Mashup

The steps for developing a mashup are fairly simple and apply to most mashups. These steps are discussed in detail in the later chapters of this book.

- Decide on Your Mashup's Objective
- Identify the Data and the Keys
- Get Access to the Data
- Regroup
- Design the User Interface
- Implement the Mashup
- Implement the Starting Page

Decide on Your Mashup's Objective

Even if you are building a mashup solely for the purpose of learning how they work, you should have a clear objective. Decide what you want to do, referring to the description of mashups. The goal is to present information to a user in as usable a format as possible. You need to know what the information is and what the user is likely to be looking for. The best mashups pull everything together, so the first Web page presented to the user has everything needed in a simple format with no further interaction required. This pulling together of information (or the presenting of it in several formats, such as maps and text) can answer a user's question, but the synthesis can also provide information and pose questions in the user's mind that go far beyond the user's initial query. In short, you need to get inside your user's head.

This means keeping your mashup focused as closely as possible on the issues and terminology of the user. Every time you think of an option to add or an extra button to put on the Web page, you are likely to muddy the mashup.

Identify the Data and the Keys

Whether it is one data source or many, a mashup relies on data, and usually a lot of data (although a small subset is what is delivered to the user). If there is not a lot of data, there is no point to a mashup.

Not only do you need to identify the data, but you also need to identify the specific item or items you will use to combine data sources or to display data in multiple formats (such as maps and text). In database parlance, such an item is a *key*. As you search for data to use in your mashup, you need to keep in mind the keys you will use, because your various data sources (and presentation techniques) must recognize the same keys. This is why so many mashups rely on geographical data: clearly defined formats for addresses are shared by many data sources. Names are poor keys for matching—not only do duplicate names exist, but there are also many ways of presenting the same name (with initials, last-name-first, and so forth).

If the keys do not match, you may wind up with a mashup that does not present any data, or you may wind up with a mashup that presents matched data that do not match.

NOTE   *You may find people who refer to keys as attributes, fields, columns, items, or elements. Because the idea of matching data sources based on certain matching values is a fundamental tenet of relational databases, the database term "key" is used for this purpose. All the issues related to keys that apply to databases apply also to mashups in this case, including the possibility of modifying one or more of the key values, so they do match.*

Get Access to the Data

You can gain access to data in three ways:

1. You can use an API to get data from a database or other online resource you do not control. This is done when your mashup runs. Much of the data used in mashups are accessed through APIs provided by the data owner such as eBay, Amazon, Flickr, Google, and so forth. You generally need to register to use the API, and your mashup

will include a registration code that is passed along when it runs. You need to abide by the conditions set for use of the API. These conditions might include a fee, but more often they contain restrictions on the use of the data, including a limit on the number of transactions you can perform from your mashup in a specific period of time. After all, your access of the data through the API involves your running transactions on someone else's computer.

2. You can get data from a resource you do control. It may be a database or it may even be a flat file or data that are hard-coded into your mashup. Because you control it, you may use an API call or you may read the data directly.

3. You can get data from a resource you do not control where those data are publicly available without the use of an API. An example of this is reading a publicly available RSS data feed. If the data feed is public, anyone can read it without using a proprietary API and without needing to register.

Regroup

This step is such a common one, it deserves to be listed here. If you cannot find appropriate data sources and a key, or if you cannot get access to the data you need, it is back to the first step: decide on your mashup's objective. If you are working with data you control or you can influence (such as is the case in a corporate environment), you may be able to work with people to provide you with the access you need or to make keys more usable. But, if this is not the case, there is no point in proceeding further.

Design the User Interaction

Mashups generally do not have a lot of user interaction or much of a learning curve. The whole point is to provide quick access to data (perhaps coming from several data sources or in several formats) without all the interaction that can waste time browsing Web pages. Typically, the mashup's user interaction has two parts:

1. A starting page lets the user specify the data to be displayed (a ZIP code, for example).

2. The mashup page itself displays the data.

Sometimes, the starting page can be omitted. This is the case where the mashup itself decides what data to retrieve (data from the last 24 hours, for example).

Implement the Mashup

Although from the user's perspective the starting page is the first step, in this book, the general process starts from implementing the mashup once the user data selection is made. From a practical point of view, this means implementing the mashup with hard-coded data until it is developed properly. Because the mashup itself is the heart of the process, and because it may use skills and techniques you do not have, it makes sense to start there.

Implement the Starting Page

Once the mashup works with hard-coded data, you can go back to develop the starting page and allow the user to enter data to replace the hard-coded data. Because you will know the mashup itself works, this implementation should be fairly easy.

Another reason to do the implementation in this sequence is this: if, in your development and testing of the mashup, you realize you need a different key or a different data source, you will not have to redo the starting page.

Make Money with Mashups

Every new Web technology brings with it this question: how can people make money with it? Because the Web and its data are largely free, making money directly from the Web is difficult. Major Web money makers are businesses that use the Web (as do iTunes, eBay, and Amazon), but their money typically comes from the old-fashioned notion of selling goods and services. Some of these companies are opening their APIs to mashup developers—in the hope of increasing their existing sales and customer base.

It is conceivable that mashups could be so powerful and useful that people would pay to be able to use them, but this has not yet occurred, and it is doubtful it will. Furthermore, many of the APIs set strict limits on how the data and the API can be used, making it more difficult to sell mashup access.

Still, money is to be made with mashups. Because mashups may well be a sales tool, rather than a for-sale product, this does not diminish the fact that money can be made. In some categories, if a company does not develop its own mashup-based interface or open its API to mashup developers, that company may be at a competitive disadvantage.

Therein lies another way to make money from mashups. Although the technologies involved are relatively simple, building a secure and efficient mashup requires many skills. In the list of development steps described previously in this chapter, the second step is Identify the Data and the Keys. If you are a specialist in a certain type of data, and if you know who the major players are and how to contact them, you are in a perfect spot to use your data-specific expertise to build a mashup or to consult with mashup developers.

Finally, the mashup pages (either the startup page or the mashup results page) are excellent vehicles for advertisements. The most productive advertisements on the Web (or in any medium, for that matter) are often those targeted to people who are interested in the content. If you have a mashup that maps political campaign contributions, a campaign consultant who works in a ZIP code requested by the mashup user might want to place an ad on that page, as might publishers of political journals, or even candidates.

Achieve Goals with Mashups

The Web itself, and mashups in particular, are assuming bigger and bigger roles in advocacy. The United States presidential election of 2004 was marked by aggressive use of the Internet, not only for fund-raising, but also for scheduling and communicating with supporters and the media. (It also marked the first time many people heard the word "blog.")

Many of today's issues are incredibly complex. Mashups can provide a way of simplifying abstract concepts and helping people make enormous amounts of data meaningful to themselves.

In one of the examples in this book, data from the U.S. Federal Election Commission is presented in a mashup for a selected ZIP code to which contributions were given or from which they were contributed. This allows individuals (and journalists) to quickly get to what interests them without having to sort through hundreds of thousands of data records.

People who are working to support various causes respond positively to low-cost ways of getting their message out. Mashups can fit the bill.

Improve Productivity with Mashups

Perhaps the most useful area for mashups is the least-known one. Mashups thrive behind the corporate firewall. Many of the problems that can bedevil a mashup developer disappear in the corporate world. For example, matters of API and data access are usually not an issue within a single entity. Even more important is, within an organization, many of the issues involved with finding keys to match data are easily resolved. As noted previously, names are particularly unhelpful in matching data records. Identifiers exist that uniquely identify individuals (such as a Social Security number), but these may not be public and they may not be able to be used for many purposes. Within an organization, however, unique identifiers, such as an employee number, can be available and can be used without any problem.

Because mashups can make it faster to find and present data, they may well emerge as the major productivity tools of the next few years. In fact, before long, mashups may be the primary way of presenting data in some environments.

Know How to Use Mashup Data Legally

Finally, remember to read the fine print on your API agreements and your data access agreements. Mashups typically use other people's data—either through API access or through access to a local copy. Data and collections of data are generally copyrightable, and wholesale coping of a database or distribution of data may not be legal. Sometimes, exceptions are noted in a copyright notice for a database. In addition, the law has an exemption for "fair use," but you need to know what is "fair."

Fortunately, although these are real issues to be addressed, you can easily stay on the right side of the law in most cases. If you use an API to access data, simply read the instructions and limits (before you write your mashup—making certain you have the right to use data is part of identifying the mashup's data). If you do not have the right to reuse the data in a mashup, you can pursue an alternate data source or see if you can work out an arrangement with the copyright holder.

If you want to experiment with large amounts of data (as is the case if you want to follow the examples described in this book), you may want to turn to data that cannot be copyrighted, which is the case of much government-collected data in the United States.

If you are working in a corporate environment, these public issues generally do not apply, although you may need to comply with internal policies.

Part II

Learn Mashup Technologies

Chapter 3

Know the Web 2.0 Mashup Rules and Design Principles

How to...

- Manage Multiple Technologies for Mashups
- Separate Data from Presentation
- Use Scripts
- Access Data with APIs
- Minimize Full-Page Loading
- Make Your Mashup Visible to Search Engines
- Use Object-Oriented Programming Techniques
- Adopt Standards

This part of the book focuses on the mashup technologies. You may want to go back and forth between chapters in this part and chapters in the third part of the book where full examples are given. In some cases, code used in the full examples is presented here to illustrate various technologies.

This chapter provides the high-level design principles and the ground rules for mashup technologies. The remaining chapters in this part of the book address the key technologies themselves. Because they generally share these design principles, the content of this chapter is not repeated for each individual technology.

Manage Multiple Technologies for Mashups

At first glance, the number of different technologies that can be involved in mashups may be daunting: what about the good old days when you created Web pages by typing in HTML? Many such hand-crafted Web pages still exist, but over the last decade, it has become increasingly obvious that the sheer volume of information people want to present on the Web cannot be accommodated with such old-fashioned technologies. For a twenty-first century information revolution, a reliance on so much manual labor is a major stumbling block.

 **It's Not Just About Mashups**

The technologies and design principles described in this part of the book apply not only to mashups, but also to the Web in general as it exists today. Just because these technologies are described in the context of mashups, do not make the assumption they are only used in mashups.

Dynamic Web sites have been around for years. Often powered by databases, they consist of relatively few Web page templates that are populated with data in response to user clicks and queries. Think Amazon, eBay, or Google—those Web pages are all created dynamically. Newspapers and other media outlets on the Web almost all use dynamic Web pages. No one sits there hard-coding HTML for the latest news about sexual escapades in Hollywood and world capitals: there is just too much of it. The stories are normally written and edited online, and the resulting text flows in one direction to the page layout software, then to a printing press, and, finally, in another direction to the dynamic Web site.

For mashups (and, indeed, for all Web pages), whatever is done to gather data and format information in response to a user query or request for a URL culminates in an HTML page. The HTML page is then downloaded to the user's browser and is displayed by that browser. There may be multiple data sources, as well as a variety of scripts and formatting mechanisms, but, ultimately, the results are displayed in a browser. Browsers are the windows onto the vast resources of the Web.

Knowing that everything results in a Web page in a browser brings some order to the world of mashups and dynamic Web pages. You can use any technologies you want—and as many of them as you want—but, somehow or other, a Web page for a browser must be the result. Remembering that simple fact can help you make your way through the multitude of technologies involved with mashups.

In the past, there have been many ideas about how to develop large-scale systems. The computing landscape is littered with large (even gigantic) development frameworks that required years of learning to be able to devote years of implementation to enormous projects that often never saw the light of day. The simplicity of the Web browser interface—the fact that everything ultimately must be a page displayed in a browser—has made it possible to design and implement large projects from a multitude of small components that are glued together by this simple principle.

The use of small components and specific technologies means you need to learn and understand how to use only those elements relevant to your project. The trade-off is you have more things to learn, but each one is easier to learn than an entire new programming language or a set of system specifications.

Not only is each one relatively easy to learn, but all these technologies share the basic principles outlined in this chapter. This makes it relatively easy to learn each new technology because they all fit together in the modern scheme of Web technology (which is sometimes called Web 2.0).

Separate Data from Presentation

The Web supplanted earlier Internet search and data display technologies, such as Gopher. Those technologies were character-based; the formatting was provided by the software displaying the data. When Tim Berners-Lee began working on the Web, he invented the HyperText Markup Language (HTML), which was based loosely on Standard Generalized Text Markup Language (SGML). A variety of reasons existed for not using an existing format, but most of them centered on the need for the Web to be as independent as possible of particular technologies—worldwide, in fact.

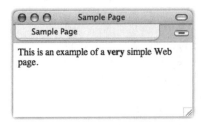

This is an example of a **very** simple Web page.

FIGURE 3-1   A very simple Web page

HTML was powerful and simple. It let you easily construct Web pages with basic markup language. Figure 3-1 shows a very simple Web page.

The HTML code for that Web page is shown here. It was created using *Dreamweaver*, a Web design tool with a graphical user interface. As shown in Figure 3-2, Dreamweaver consists of a window in which you can type text, much as you would in a word-processing application. The formatting is handled with standard text-formatting commands in the menu bar.

Dreamweaver automatically produces HTML code. The code created for this Web page is shown in Figure 3-3. Dreamweaver, like other graphical user interfaces for HTML authoring, lets you switch back and forth between these views as you create a Web page.

The problem that soon arose with HTML is that it combines data and presentation information together. For example, the text shown in the browser contains embedded formatting—the <strong> element, which causes the word "very" to be shown with strong emphasis—often interpreted by browsers as bold. (Another element—<b>—specifies bold text.) Leaving aside the issue of whether the Web page designer should be specifying a specific type style (such as bold) or a general styling instruction (such as strong), the fact remains that the Web page's data are inextricably bound up with the formatting instruction.

Browsers adhere more or less to standards, but cases still occur in which some Web sites in some browsers do not appear properly because different browsers interpret formatting tags in

This is an example of a **very** simple Web page.

<body>   550 x 114   1K / 1 sec

FIGURE 3-2   Creating the Web page in Dreamweaver

FIGURE 3-3   Dreamweaver's HTML editor

different ways. Nevertheless, the data—text in this case—are independent of the browser. For reasons such as this, a variety of attempts have been made to separate presentation information from data. Perhaps the most significant approach to this is the use of cascading style sheets (CSS) to provide formats for data on Web pages that are described not with specific formatting commands (such as `<strong>`), but with styles specified in a separate file. In this way, the presentation of a Web page can be changed by changing the style sheet while leaving the data untouched.

This matters particularly in cases where the Web page is constructed dynamically by an application server or other software. The code to generate the Web page has no styling information in it, and the presentation of the page can be modified simply by changing the style sheet.

Separating content from presentation information runs through modern Web production. The two skills—graphic design and what is actually programming—are separate. While some people are equally adept at both, for many other people they remain distinctly different skills (one right-brain and one left-brain, to be specific). This does not mean you cannot do both, but it does mean you must understand they are separate processes. (In some companies, such as Yahoo Music, three groups are working on projects: the designers, the data service providers, and a front-end engineering and programming group. In other companies, the front-end engineering and programming is often handled by the data service providers.)

As you look at the various technologies involved in mashups, it is worthwhile to consider whether they are focused on data or on the presentation of data. Rarely do you find a technology used for both.

Use Scripts

Scripts have been used for years now to augment static Web pages. Two types of scripts come into play: server-side scripts and browser-side (or client-side) scripts.

Server-Side Scripting

Server-side scripting consists of scripts that run on the server when the request is made for a Web page. Server-side scripts are triggered in a variety of ways. One of the most common involves accessing a URL that, itself, is a server-side script, such as a PHP script that might be accessed with `http://www.yoursite.com/ContributionsByDonorZIP.php`. When the Web server receives this request, it recognizes this is a PHP script and it runs that script. The output from the script is generally a standard, dynamically built, HTML Web page, which is then returned to your browser. The PHP code is normally not downloaded.

Because the server-side script runs on the server, it has access to the server resources that may include databases, other data stores, and communications channels you cannot access directly through your Internet connection. In general, the security level for the server-side script is determined by the process running it, which, typically, is an application server or whatever software is receiving your request for a Web page. It is normally not your security level as a visitor to a Web site.

Before designing a mashup to use server-side scripting, make certain the scripting language you want to use is supported on your server and the version is what you need. PHP 5, for example, was a major change from PHP 4 in many areas that affect mashups. (This book uses PHP 5 in its examples.)

Browser-Side Scripting

Browser-side scripts (also known as *client-side scripts*) are part of a downloaded HTML page (or they are in a separate file accessed through the HTML page). These scripts are run by the browser when the page is loaded. They run on the client machine and have access to the resources on that computer (subject to security constraints).

Browser-side scripts include *JavaScript*, which is the most widely used scripting language that can be included in HTML. JavaScript is supported broadly by most browsers on most platforms. Frequently, scripts are used to manipulate the interface, dynamically setting fields based on partial data entry or performing edits on data you entered. A script can run while the page is displayed and it need not access the server computer.

Before designing a mashup (or any Web page) that uses browser-side scripting, make certain the browsers your users will use support the scripting language. In the past, some users have turned off scripting support out of fear of virus corruption and, in the early days of Web browsers, because of the feeling that running scripts could degrade performance. Today, most people are used to scripts running on the Web pages they have downloaded, but in some environments (such as behind corporate firewalls), browser-side scripting still cannot be taken for granted.

Access Data with APIs

Since the dawn of the computer age, people have written programs to read data from computer files. There are two general ways of doing this: reading the data directly and accessing the data with application programming interfaces (APIs).

Did you know?

Accessors Come in Two Styles

Accessor routines frequently come in pairs. *Getters* are routines that get data and *setters* are routines that set data. Getters are typically functions. They return a result that is the data requested and, sometimes, getters also return an error message. Setters typically take a single parameter, which is the data to be set. Note, not all APIs provide accessor routines. Some APIs return data in a structure such as an XML document, which you must unpack yourself. However, as you see in Chapter 4, the XML data are highly structured and not dependent on position.

Originally, you had no choice. You needed to read the data directly. To do this, each data file came with specifications that told you where to find the data—the first six characters as an ID code, the next four characters as a region code, and so forth. (You can still find such documentation—and often you find the character positions identified as columns—a holdover from punched cards. You may even find data files with no more than 80 characters/columns in a record. This, too, is a holdover from standard 80-column punched cards.)

The problem with positional data is this: if anything in the data flow changes, all software that accesses the data flow needs to change. Rather than reading the data directly, you now are frequently able to access data using procedure calls—APIs. Such a procedure call, for example, `GetIDNumber`, can be delivered by the provider of the data. If the data flow changes, the `GetIDNumber` routine must change, but your code, which calls `GetIDNumber`, need not change.

In addition to providing a better architecture for accessing data, APIs frequently are used to implement security features with more sophistication than can be done with direct access. In the world of the Internet today, you often have no choice: you must use APIs.

People are still around who believe the increased processing time involved in calling an accessor routine, such as GetIDNumber, is not worth the saving in maintainability of the code. Computers are now faster than ever before: use APIs and accessor routines to access data.

Minimize Full-Page Loading

Like many contemporary Web technologies, mashups rely on high-bandwidth connections for their most impressive performance. Although we hope this is only a temporary situation, many, many people still access the Web through slow connections. Areas in many countries exist where no choice other than dial-up is available. Even where there are options, some connections (often including wireless ones) are much slower than the connection you may normally use on your desktop. As you design your mashup, consider how it will function in an environment with limited bandwidth.

Constructing Web pages with forms that need to be submitted to the server to display the next page is easy. Where minimal processing is involved, consider using browser-side scripts to keep the processing local and avoid going back to the server over a potentially slow connection.

In a similar vein, look carefully at your mashup to make certain you are downloading as much data as you need, but not more. Using a browser-side script can make sense to interactively hone in on the specific data a user wants to use before retrieving the data needed (and only those data).

Make Your Mashup Visible to Search Engines

If your mashup is designed for use in a controlled environment (that is, behind a corporate firewall or on a Web site known to your customers or colleagues), you do not have to worry about making it visible. You can announce its presence on a home page or in a newsletter.

But, if your mashup is designed for people to find it through a search engine when they are looking for tools to understand election financing or other specific issues, remember to make it visible. The data your mashup may use are not stored on the basic page. Those data will be displayed on a dynamic page as a result of user interaction, and dynamic pages may not be indexed by search engines. If they are, they may be indexed based on a snapshot in time that is not true for the page at another time. This issue of pages changing after having been indexed by search engines can apply to any Web page, but it is particularly troublesome with dynamic pages that may change in substantive ways every time they are accessed. In addition, text that is part of a graphic element or a Flash animation (such as a logo or a tiff version of a company name) is usually not indexed.

Make Your Mashup Web Page Visible to Search Engines

The simplest way to make your mashup page visible to search engines is to make certain that descriptive text appears on the page, just as you would with any other page. In general, a resource such as Google's documentation for Webmasters (https://www.google.com/webmasters/tools/docs/en/about.html) is a good starting-off point. You can augment it with other resources from other search engines because differences occur in the ways search engines work.

As you wander into this arena, remember, this is a real battleground. Your desire to have your page indexed by search engines is exactly the same as the desire by spammers, pornographers, and purveyors of malware to get their pages showing up on search engine results. The meta keywords tag, for example, fell out of widespread use because it began being used to deceptively bring people to Web pages that were not what they were represented as in the meta tag.

You can use a variety of strategies to make your page visible to search engines. A basic Web page that presents its information as static text generally has no problem being found. But when you move beyond that paradigm, you need to think about visibility issues.

Use Object-Oriented Programming Techniques

Object-oriented programming (OOP) is now the standard technique for developing software (although many people prefer other techniques). Originally developed in the context of large systems, OOP is now implemented by a variety of programming languages, including C++, C#, Objective-C, Ruby, Python, and Java. OOP is also supported in varying degrees by JavaScript, Perl, PHP, and other languages.

OOP lets developers create structures (called *objects*) that can communicate with one another and that can contain both programming code and data. This is distinct from other programming techniques, which focus on functionality and operations. Each object is clearly defined and, in most cases, you can develop applications by creating new objects and reusing old ones without necessarily knowing how an object functions inside itself or how it stores its data. This clear delineation of functionality and interfaces permits large applications to be built and maintained with much less effort than other programming techniques.

One of the attractions of OOP is the programming objects may be analogues of objects in the real world—customers, bank accounts, buildings, and so forth. This is not always the case (particularly with small utility objects), but it can help developers and users to understand the structure of systems as they are being created.

Even if you are not using an OOP language, as you develop your mashup, consider using the OOP technique in which objects are clearly defined and their internal workings are generally not exposed to other objects (although their interfaces that access the internal workings obviously are exposed to other objects).

Just as you can bring a sense of order to your mashup by remembering that everything it does must, ultimately, result in an HTML page to be displayed in a browser, you can bring a sense of order to its architecture by designing it in objects (or modules or components—whatever terminology you like). Design the objects and their functionality; specify their interfaces. Then, move on to implement them in the appropriate languages. As long as the architecture and the logic are correct, you will be on the right track. If you let yourself be distracted by starting to write code before you know how the mashup will be constructed, you may find yourself wandering down dark alleyways of rambling code.

NOTE   *You can find more about object-oriented programming in Chapter 5.*

Adopt Standards

Finally, adopt standards to make your mashup as usable and reusable as possible. Mashups that adhere to common standards should not have problems being displayed in various browsers. Their server-side code should not have problems running on various operating systems. In an ideal world.

In reality, a variety of standards exist—draft standards, revisions of standards, competing standards, and even competing implementations of standards (that happen to function in different ways). Standards for Web pages (the ultimate output of your mashup) have more or less settled down. Likewise, standards for the programming languages and development tools you are likely to use are reasonably stable. Where the issues relating to mashups arise are in some of the duplicative standards. Just as Web designers have gotten used to the related, but not identical, emphasis (em) and italic (i) tags, mashup developers are adjusting to technologies that overlap. Before adopting a particular technology for your mashup, the best strategy is to do some Web searches to see what similar technologies exist. Furthermore, if you are using an API, such as Google or Yahoo!, look to see what the other API supports. If a standard is supported by several players in the space you want to work in, it is likely to be more reliable in the long term than an API supported by only one player.

The one indisputable point is if you have a choice between using an existing standard and creating your own idiosyncratic technology, go with the existing standard.

Chapter 4

Use XML to Structure Data

How to...

- Understand XML Structure and Purpose
- Learn Basic XML Syntax
- Create and Use XML Elements
- Use Attributes to Identify Data Characteristics
- Avoid Confusion by Using Namespaces

Extensible Markup Language (XML) is the language used to describe data in many mashups and other Web applications today. Although XML has a superficial similarity to HTML and other SGML-based languages, it has no formatting or style features. The purpose of XML is simply to organize and describe data.

This chapter helps you understand the basics of XML, so you can use it in building your mashups. Remember two points as you read this chapter. First, you almost never create XML—you are using it as input to a mashup. Second, XML is almost never created manually by anyone. XML is designed so it can be read and parsed, if necessary by a human being, but those chores are normally done programmatically.

Beyond that, all you need to know is that XML is simple and its rules are strict. That makes XML a perfect tool for automated parsing of data.

Understand XML Structure and Purpose

XML is one of the foundations of mashups and other modern Web technologies. As noted previously, HTML was a wonderfully simple and powerful way to present information and hyperlinks in a platform-neutral manner. Its rules were relatively few, and the browsers that were built in the early and mid-1990s easily handled the text and formatting syntax of HTML—often in consistent and predictable ways.

Find More Information About XML

The primary source for information about XML is http://www.w3c.org—the World Wide Web Consortium. At the XML section you will find the language specification as well as links to other resources.

As formatting needs became more complex, and as people began to appreciate the need to characterize data not just in their formatting, a new language was needed. Whereas at one point, using HTML tags such as the header tags (H1, H2, H3, and so forth) was sufficient to suggest the logical structure of a document, that approach quickly became unworkable as the demands of stylistic formatting intersected with and sometimes conflicted with the needs for a formatting-independent description of the data.

XML is designed to describe data without any formatting rules applied to it. Style sheets are often used in conjunction with XML to produce a well-formatted document. But when it comes to mashups, XML documents by themselves are often used with the mashups, providing the interpretation and formatting of the data.

All this happens as the data and the formatting are separated in accordance with modern Web design principles. Several examples of XML documents show you how this separation of formatting from data works and how you can begin to use it in your mashups.

NOTE *This section shows you how XML is used. In the remainder of the chapter, you see how those uses are achieved.*

In Figure 4-1, you can see an example of an RSS news feed distributed in an XML document. The XML data contain no formatting information. The formatting of the data in Figure 4-1 is provided by the Opera browser (version 9.10) running on Windows.

The Opera display is interactive: clicking on one of the articles in the top pane shows you additional information and a link to the article in the lower pane of the window. In Figure 4-2, the same XML document is shown in Safari (version 2.0.4) running on Mac OS X. The formatting is different here. Rather than one-line summaries in the top pane of Opera, Safari displays the first sentence of each article and provides a Read More link to the article itself. At the right of the window, you can sort the articles, search, and limit displays to specific periods of time. If you compare the articles in Figures 4-1 and 4-2, you can see that the same articles are shown, although the order differs. Remember, all of this is happening to the same XML file, but the two browsers provide different interfaces and functionality.

Figure 4-3 shows yet another way of displaying the data. This time, Internet Explorer 7 is running on Windows. The functionality is similar to that of Safari. Instead of Read More, a right-pointed arrow lets you get to the hypertext link to the article.

Figure 4-4 demonstrates the functionality and display are determined by the browser, not the XML document. In Figure 4-4, you can see Safari displaying a different RSS news feed. Except for the data, this is identical to the window shown previously in Figure 4-2.

If you look at the source of the pages shown here (using the browser's View Source), you can see what is being displayed is not XML (which cannot itself be displayed in a formatted manner without external instructions). Instead, as you can see in Figure 4-5, which is part of the source code for the display shown in Figure 4-2, what is displayed in the browser is HTML generated by the browser parsing the XML data and mixing it with its own formatting for an RSS feed. (Other browsers, such as Firefox, display the XML data alone when you choose the View Source command.)

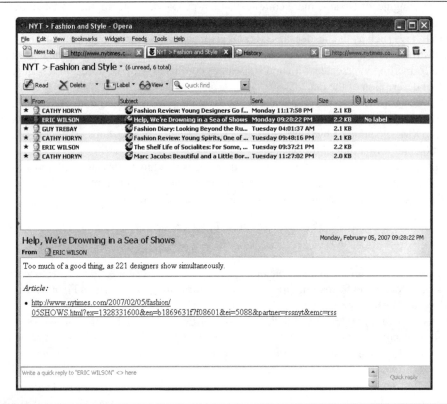

FIGURE 4-1   RSS news feed in XML shown in Opera

One aspect of the HTML source shown in Figure 4-5 that should be noted is the use of the <div> element, along with class, id, and name attributes. The <div> element lets you group HTML elements and code into an element that can be identified and addressed. The class attribute is often used with style sheets, the id attribute is unique in the document's namespace, and the name attribute may be unique (as it is in this feed), but it is not required to be so by HTML syntax rules.

Identifying elements in HTML and XML means scripting languages, such as PHP and JavaScript, can operate on them by using the identifying attributes. This becomes increasingly important in the following chapters.

Learn Basic XML Syntax

XML documents have two structures: a logical structure and a *physical* structure. The physical structure of an XML document consists of *entities*, which begin with the *root* or document entity that contains the entire document. That entity may contain additional entities in a strictly

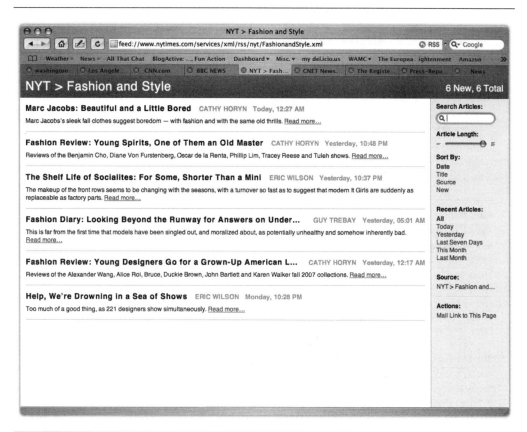

NYT > Fashion and Style

FIGURE 4-2   RSS news feed in XML shown in Safari

hierarchical fashion (that is, entities are contained entirely within other entities; you cannot have an entity that is partly in two entities).

In addition to the physical structure of an XML document, there is a *logical* structure, which consists of elements, tags, comments, declarations, character references, and processing instructions. The most important of these are the first three: elements, tags, and comments.

Below is an excerpt from an XML document. The components are described in the following sections, but you can get an overview of the logical structure of an XML from this excerpt. The entire document consists of an rss *element,* which begins with a tag on the first line and ends with a tag on the last line. All the content of the XML file is specific to the file and to its own *schema* (logical structure). Thus, the idea of an element and a tag is part of the XML specification, but the idea of a specific rss element is part of the specification of this particular type of XML document (an RSS feed). Everything in the XML file is an element, and elements may be contained within

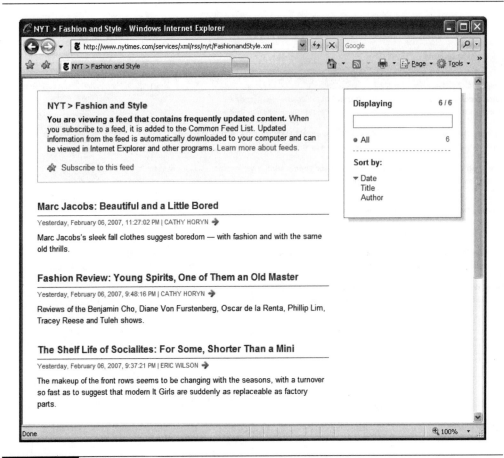

FIGURE 4-3   RSS news feed in XML shown in Internet Explorer 7

one another. For example, the rss element contains a channel element, and the channel element contains a title element and an item element (which itself contains another title element).

```
<rss version="2.0">
  <channel>
    <title>NYT > Art and Design</title>
    <item>
      <title>Room With a View of an Architect&#8217;s
        Retired Ideas</title>
    </item>
  </channel>
</rss>
```

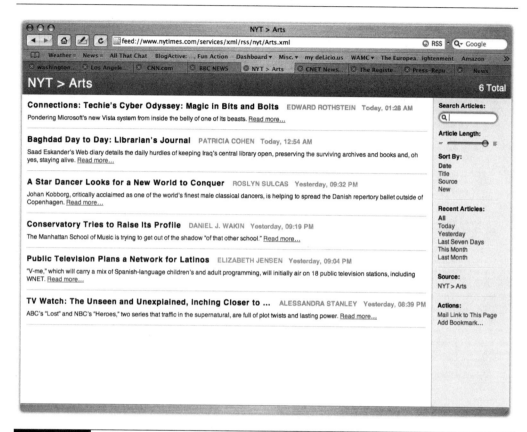

FIGURE 4-4   Different RSS news feed in XML shown in Safari

XML is stricter than HTML in that it respects capitalization, so the following two lines are different:

```
<Name>
<name>
```

XML elements sometimes appear like HTML, but they are different. In HTML, you can specify the beginning and ending of bold and italic formatting using code such as this:

```
<b><i>This is bold, italicized text.</b></i>
```

This line of code has four tags in it:

- <b> is the starting tag for bold formatting
- <i> is the starting tag for italic formatting

```
○○○              Source of feed://www.nytimes.com/services/xml/rss/nyt/FashionandStyle.xml

<script language='JavaScript'>document.body.offsetWidth;</script>
<div name="1/64/22922" class="read" onmousedown="return articleClicked(this)"
       articlesortdate="192518822" articlesorttitle="marc jacobs: beautif" articlesortsource="" sourceindex=""
       >

    <div class=articlefooter></div>
    <a class=articlehead href="http://www.nytimes.com/2007/02/07/fashion/shows/07FASHION.html?
ex=1328504400&en=421879eb53910613&ei=5088&partner=rssnyt&emc=rss" target="_self" >

       <div class="subject" title="Marc Jacobs: Beautiful and a Little Bored">Marc Jacobs: Beautiful and a Little Bored</div>

          <div class="author" title="CATHY HORYN">
             CATHY HORYN
          </div>

       <div class="date" title="Today, 12:27 AM">
             Today, 12:27 AM
       </div>
    </a>

    <div class=articlebody>
       Marc Jacobs's sleek fall clothes suggest boredom - with fashion and with the same old thrills.


          <a class="articlelink" href="http://www.nytimes.com/2007/02/07/fashion/shows/07FASHION.html?
ex=1328504400&en=421879eb53910613&ei=5088&partner=rssnyt&emc=rss" target="_self">Read more&hellip;</a>

    </div>
</div>
<div name="1/64/22920" class="read" onmousedown="return articleClicked(this)"
       articlesortdate="192512896" articlesorttitle="fashion review: youn" articlesortsource="" sourceindex=""
       >

    <div class=articlefooter></div>
    <a class=articlehead href="http://www.nytimes.com/2007/02/06/fashion/shows/06FASHION.html?
ex=1328418000&en=b17a70200d975fee&ei=5088&partner=rssnyt&emc=rss" target="_self" >

       <div class="subject" title="Fashion Review: Young Spirits, One of Them an Old Master">Fashion Review: Young Spirits, One of Them an
Old Master</div>

          <div class="author" title="CATHY HORYN">
             CATHY HORYN
          </div>

       <div class="date" title="Yesterday, 10:48 PM">
             Yesterday, 10:48 PM
       </div>
    </a>

    <div class=articlebody>
       Reviews of the Benjamin Cho, Diane Von Furstenberg, Oscar de la Renta, Phillip Lim, Tracey Reese and Tuleh shows.
```

FIGURE 4-5   HTML source for the RSS news feed in Safari (Figure 4-2)

- ■ </b> is the ending tag for bold formatting
- ■ </i> is the ending tag for italic formatting

In XML, starting and ending tags define elements. For example, in the RSS feed shown previously, one of the XML elements is a title. It consists of a starting tag, content, and an ending tag. Those tags are shown here on three separate lines for clarity:

```
<title>
NYT>Fashion and Style
</title>
```

The starting and ending tags in the HTML example are not properly nested for form elements. To be properly nested, they would have to be shown as:

```
<b><i>This is bold, italicized text.</i></b>
```

Here, an italic element is nested within a bold element. The original line of code did not show this formal structure because the two ending tags were reversed. (To be fair, most people would prefer the second HTML structure, but many browsers happily display the first version.)

In XML, you have no choice. You must terminate elements with an ending tag and you must properly nest elements.

You can employ one shortcut. If an element is empty, you can terminate it with a single tag. Thus, an empty description element can be written in XML as

```
<description/>
```

An empty element may have meaning—there may be no value for that specific element, but the element exists.

Figure 4-6 shows the raw XML from the RSS news feed shown in this chapter's previous figures. (The raw XML was generated by opening the RSS feed in an old version of Firefox that did not support RSS.)

Portions of the XML in Figure 4-6 are referred to in the following sections.

Create and Use XML Elements

Creating and using XML elements is as simple as creating starting and ending tags (respecting capitalization, of course) and placing text or other elements within them. Some XML documents require certain elements to exist, as is the case with various RSS news feeds. In writing mashups, you generally find you are a consumer of XML documents, and you need to parse them to extract data from the appropriate elements. Usually, you are not creating XML documents unless you need to do so for testing. (Parsing XML documents is discussed in Chapter 6.)

TIP *If you need sample XML for testing, you can certainly create your own documents. However, you may find this safer: take an XML document with the data you need to work with and strip it down to a much shorter version. The reason for this is deleting lines of XML (when done carefully) is safer than typing lines of XML, which might contain mistakes.*

In the RSS news feed shown in Figure 4-6, you can see several XML elements. As is the case in many XML documents, some elements have more importance than others (this has nothing to do with XML; instead, it is related to the content of the document). In the news feeds, the item elements are the main ones. They are part of the rss and channel elements, and they contain other elements, such as pubDate and author. But, in an RSS news feed, the items are the primary elements about which people care.

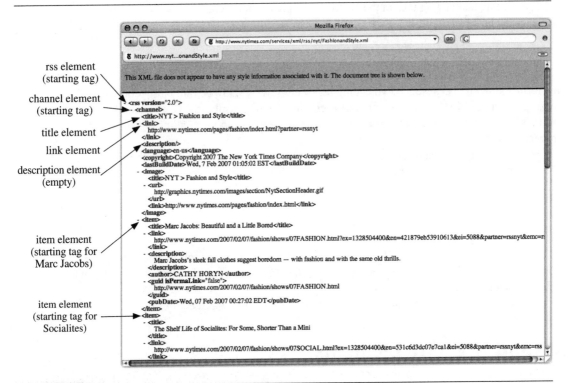

FIGURE 4-6 XML from an RSS news feed

Unlike HTML, where the elements are predefined (such as <b> for bold), there are no XML-defined elements. Each document can create its own elements that reflect the content of that document. In practice, common document types (such as RSS news feeds) have standard elements, so they can be parsed by consumers of the data, but these are not XML-defined elements.

Use Attributes to Identify Data Characteristics

Elements can have attributes as well as content. The first line of Figure 4-6 shows the starting tag of the rss element with an attribute:

```
version="2.0"
```

All attributes in XML are enclosed in quotes, as shown here.

The next line in the listing shows the starting tag for the channel element. All the subsequent lines shown in Figure 4-6 are within the channel element, and, because elements must be enclosed within a single parent element, all those lines are also within the rss element.

Next comes the title element. This element consists of a starting tag, content, and an ending tag all on one line.

Following that element is the link element. This one appears on three lines. (You might want to refer to the earlier figures that show these data formatted in various browsers to see how the data are displayed in various ways.)

The description tag is an empty tag: it is present, but it contains no data.

For an RSS news feed, within the channel are a variety of elements, such as title and link; following them are 0 or more items. You can see two items highlighted in Figure 4-6. One is "Marc Jacobs: Beautiful and a Little Bored," and the next is "The Shelf Life of Socialites: For Some, Shorter Than a Mini." Within these elements are additional elements, but because they are contained within item elements, you cannot confuse the titles, links, descriptions, or authors. As you can guess, these descriptive elements of items allow the browser to sort items by pubDate, author, and so forth.

Avoid Confusion by Using Namespaces

Elements are often named for the data they contain, which makes the XML document easy to understand when you look at it. Unfortunately, such simplicity can cause problems. Because no standard set exists of XML element names, many people can and do create elements with identical, meaningful names such as <name>, <owner>, <title>, and so forth.

You can prevent confusion by using a namespace for your element names. A *namespace* is simply a globally (as in the planet) unique identifier that can be combined with the element name to produce a unique element name. Typically, namespaces are identified by uniform resource identifiers (URIs), which may be uniform resource locations (URLs), but need not be. The assumption is this: if you control an Internet domain name (or have access to it), you have the mechanism in place to make certain that element names within it can be unique.

For example, if your domain name is http://www.yourcompany.com, you can enforce the rule that the <name> element means a customer name. If your domain name applies to a large company, you can qualify it down to a department or division level by using a URI, such as http://www.yourcompany.com/yourdivision/yourdepartment. Within that qualified name, you can control the assignment of element names. (Remember, although these look like URLs and actual Web addresses, they are relying simply on the uniqueness of the domain name to produce a unique string.)

You assign a namespace to an XML element by using the xmlns attribute of an element as in the following example:

```
<myelement xmlns="http://www.yourcompany.com"
<mysubelement> contents </mysubelement>
</myelement>
```

In this example, mysubelement is prefixed by the namespace http://www
.yourcompany.com, which is the default namespace for all elements declared within the element
with the namespace declaration.

You can declare multiple namespaces. For example,

```
xmlns:myprefix="http://www.yourcompany.com/subcategory"
```

is a namespace that you can use in an element such as

```
<myprefix:mysubcategoryelement>
```

Namespaces apply to the element in which they are declared, as well as all subelements.
They typically are declared at the root level of the document, but they can be declared anywhere.

Because you are normally not creating XML documents, you do not have to worry about
creating namespaces. But, when you are using XML documents, you must remember to properly
look for prefixes of element names, so you do not confuse similarly named elements.

Chapter 5

Use JavaScript to Script the Mashup Page

How to...

- Understand JavaScript Structure
- Use Local and Global Variables
- Create and Use Functions
- Use JavaScript Objects
- Work with Events
- Handle Errors
- Handle JavaScript Environmental Problems

JavaScript is an interpreted scripting language designed to add interactivity to HTML pages. Starting with its release for Netscape in 1995, JavaScript enabled Web designers to dynamically create or change HTML elements on pages, to perform data-entry validation processing, and to work with some of the then-new Web features, such as cookies.

Today, JavaScript is still used for those purposes, but it has taken on added roles that center around its low barriers to use and its capability to interact with remote scripts and servers. When you start using the Google Maps API, you will probably use it with simple JavaScript function calls.

This chapter neither addresses the routine Web-page authoring uses to which JavaScript can be put nor does it address standard programming syntax that JavaScript shares with other languages (for and while loops, if statements, and so forth). Rather, it focuses on the features of the language used most often in mashups. Those are the more programmatic features, such as the use of functions, handling globals and variables, capturing errors, working with events, and using objects.

Find More Information About JavaScript

A great deal of information about JavaScript is available on the Web. Any search engine can quickly find resources for you. Remember, JavaScript has been around for a while and has evolved over time. Some articles you might find with a search engine may be old and outdated, so be careful to look at the last date of updates. For a definitive guide to JavaScript, you can go to the Mozilla Developer Center at http://developer.mozilla.org/en/docs/Main_Page and follow the JavaScript link. Also, an excellent tutorial is at http://www.w3schools.com/default.asp.

Understand JavaScript Structure

JavaScript is like most programming and scripting languages: you can create variables, use controls such as loops and if/else constructs, and create functions. One of the most important features of JavaScript is the document.write command, which takes a parameter that is text to be output onto the HTML page in which the script resides. Thus, you can write the following code in JavaScript. (For more details on the actual syntax, see the section "Use JavaScript Objects.")

```
document.write ("Hello World.")
```

Place JavaScript Scripts in Script Elements

Scripts can be placed on HTML pages in script elements. The `type` attribute identifies the scripting language, as in the following code snippet:

```
<script type="text/javascript"
  document.write ("Hello World.")
</script>
```

Use Scripts from an External Source with the src Attribute

Script elements may have an src attribute in addition to the type attribute. If an src attribute exists, it points to a script located somewhere outside the file containing the HTML code. Such a script element is placed wherever you would normally place the script code on the page. Here is an example of an external script:

```
<script
  src="http://maps.google.com/maps?file=api&v=2&key=yourkey"
  type="text/javascript">
</script>
```

Note, the src attribute contains not only the location of the script on the Web, but also some additional information, such as the version number and the unique key that can be used to access it. This is the script you use for the Google Maps API.

NOTE *In this code snippet, as well as others in this book, the code has been adjusted to fit on the printed page. As a general rule, you can type longer lines of text into an editor for HTML, JavaScript, or other languages. Unless clearly indicated, do not worry about duplicating the line breaks shown in the text. Also, be aware that many of the code snippets for mashup APIs include unique identifiers and keys, which you must obtain before gaining access to the API. Text such as key=yourkey should be interpreted in this vein. Variables and phrases introduced by "your" should be considered as placeholders.*

Scripts Are Interpreted as They Are Encountered on the HTML Page Unless They Are in the Head Element

The script is interpreted, rather than being compiled. This means the script commands are executed when the page is loaded and as the script itself is encountered (in the simplest form of JavaScript scripting). Thus, if you have a paragraph element, a script element, and another paragraph element—in that order—the script is executed after the first paragraph element is processed and before the second paragraph element is processed. The user's Web browser does all of this processing.

Inline scripts (that is, scripts placed within the body of the HTML page) are processed when they are encountered. They may generate HTML code, which is then immediately processed by the browser. This is how many, if not most, JavaScript scripts operate. But, to do much more, you need to treat scripts as programmatic entities. Doing so almost always requires you to place them in the HTML head element, and to use variables and functions. When you start to use functions, you generally need to start to identify the elements on the HTML page that the function addresses.

You Can Use Semicolons to End Statements

Within a script, each line of text is generally interpreted as a single statement. If you have multiple statements on one line, you must separate them with semicolons. You may also use a semicolon at the end of each JavaScript statement, even if there is only one statement per line. Many people feel the explicit use of semicolons to indicate the end of a statement makes for more readable code (and compatibility with other programming and scripting languages you may be working on at the same time as JavaScript).

```
document.write ("Hello World.    ")
document.write ("Hello World.    ");
```

The semicolon is optional. But, in the following line of code, there are two statements and the semicolon after the first one is required:

```
document.write ("Hello. "); document.write ("Goodbye.")
```

Continue Quoted Text Strings with \ and Concatenation (+)

Quoted text strings that span more than one line can be continued from one line to the next using the \ character within the quoted text string. This is a somewhat dicey thing to do because it makes the code less easy to read. If you have a text string longer than what conveniently fits on one line, consider using a concatenation operator (+) to construct that text string from several smaller strings (this method is shown several times in this book).

For example, you can construct the text "this is the start of a long string that contains more text" by using the following code.

```
theString = "this is the start of a long string";
theString = theString + " that contains more text";
```

Use Spaces and Comments for Readability

Two JavaScript concepts make it easy to write code that can be maintained well. You can use spaces wherever you want to improve readability of code (although spaces within a quoted text string are treated as parts of the text string, as you would expect). Together with code that is aligned for readability, you should use comments—lines introduced by //—to document what you are doing in the code.

JavaScript Is Case-Sensitive

Finally, remember JavaScript is case-sensitive. Be careful how you capitalize the names you use for variables and functions. In HTML, you may not worry about this, but in JavaScript and XML (along with many other technologies used in mashups), you need to be aware of capitalization. Tracking down errors in code due to mismatched capitalization can be both time-consuming and frustrating.

Use Local and Global Variables

Variables in JavaScript can store data, just as in any programming language. Variable names must begin with a letter, an underscore, or a $. They may contain those characters as well as numbers and, of course, they are case-sensitive.

As is common in interpreted scripting languages (in fact, in many dynamic languages), variables are not typed: you do not specify whether a variable is to be used to store a number or text.

The best way to create a variable is to use the `var` keyword and follow it with one or more variable names. You can also assign values to the variables you create. Here are some variable declarations:

```
var i, j, k;
var i = 5, j = 6, k;
```

In the first line, three variables (*i, j,* and *k*) are created with no values associated with them. In the second line, the three variables are created, and values are set for *i* and *j,* but not for *k.*

If a variable is declared within a function, it is *local* to that function. A variable can be set and used within that function, but it has no meaning outside the function. If a variable is declared outside a function, it is *global,* and it can be used in any JavaScript code on that page whether or not it is inside a function.

In fact, you can create a global variable anywhere by simply using it:

```
i = 5
```

This creates a global variable and assigns the value 5 to it. Creating a global variable in this way can generate a warning message if you are using strict JavaScript rules. If you are declaring a variable, using the keyword `var` is best.

And, while considering good programming practices with regard to variables, here are some more.

- Always assign a value to a newly created variable. Without a value assignment, the variable's value is undefined. Set the variable to a valid value or to null. The value null is treated as false when used as a Boolean and as zero when used as a number. An undefined value is also treated as false when used as a Boolean, but using an undefined value in a numeric operation can raise an error. You can check to see if a variable is undefined, but initializing everything with some value is much better. Remember, null may be treated as false or zero, but it is a distinct value and can be tested.

- Do not use values for things other than what they are. In other words, zero is a value, but null is missing data.

- Place variable declarations together. For globals, a good idea is to place them at the beginning of the script. For local variables that are going to be used within a function, place them at the beginning of the function. You can create variables as you need them, but placing them together makes the code more maintainable.

- Declare variables for constants that might otherwise appear deep inside lines of code.

- Use semicolons to terminate JavaScript lines of code. It also increases readability. Furthermore, as you move from one programming language to another, you do not have to worry about when a semicolon is required. You use a semicolon to end every statement unless it is absolutely forbidden by the language in question.

- Use meaningful names for variables and functions.

- Begin functions with a comment explaining inputs, outputs, and assumptions.

- Use the comment operator (//) to provide additional information about a variable:

```
var mapHeight = 500; // height of the map before user adjustment
```

Create and Use Functions

Functions can make your JavaScript code more readable and reusable. Functions also are generally good programming practice. Programs and scripts quickly grow large, and, without careful structuring, they can become confusing and unwieldy. *Functions*, which are sections of code that can be executed from your main JavaScript code, often with varying data ("parameters" or "arguments"), are a key part of that structuring. Functions are similar to procedures in some languages.

As with any programming language, name your functions clearly, and be clear about what they are to do. You can implement a script with three functions called Func1, Func2, and Func3, but that will not be helpful when you come back to update the code.

JavaScript functions begin with the keyword function, the name of the function, a list of parameters, and the code.

Here is the simplest function—it has no parameters and no code:

```
function load() {
  }
```

You may want to create stubs such as this for functions you plan to implement later.

Here is a function that has four parameters:

```
function showAddress (address, addressText, icon, option) {
  if (!map ) {
    createMap();
  }
 //code deleted
}
```

If a function has no parameters, as in the first example, it still must have the (empty) parenthesis following the function name. In the second example, note the function showAddress begins by testing to see if a map exists, and, if it does not, it goes on to create the map by calling another function. The function names make it clear what is happening.

Functions are placed in the head element of an HTML page and are available to all JavaScript code on that page. They also can be placed in files with the suffix .js, which can then be included using the src attribute of the script element.

Functions are called by using their names and passing in any values needed for the parameters. Note, the createMap function shown in the second example takes no parameters, but it still has the parentheses in its invocation to indicate it is a function.

A function may return a value. If so, you can use the returned result in your code, as in the following example:

```
myVariable = myFunction (parameter1, parameter2);
```

The assumption here is this: myFunction returns a value that is then placed into myVariable. To return a value from a function, use the `return` statement. More than one value can be in a function, as this example shows:

```
function myFunction (parameter1, parameter 2) {
  if (parameter1 == "test") {
    return "test"
  }
  else  {
    return "not test";
  }
}
```

When the return statement is encountered, the value is returned and the function terminates.

Functions can also be associated with events that are generated as the HTML page is created (such as the onload event). They are called automatically as the event occurs without your having to explicitly call the function. This is described in the section "Work with Events."

Use JavaScript Objects

JavaScript supports objects, which means you can write your most structured object-oriented code in JavaScript. You do not have to use objects and, in fact, many JavaScript programmers use objects without realizing they are doing so. In developing mashups, you are likely to be explicitly using objects, so here is a brief summary.

JavaScript contains a number of built-in objects, such as strings, dates, Booleans, and arrays. You automatically create a string object when you use text. Thus, this code creates a `string` object with the name myString:

```
var myString = "test string";
```

Other objects are created using the new command. For example, to create a date object, you can write

```
var myDate = new Date ();
```

An object consists of methods and properties, both of which are accessed by their names placed after a dot and the name of the object. For the built-in string object, you can use the built-in method toUpperCase to capitalize the string, as in the following code:

```
myString = myString.toUpperCase ();
```

A string object has a *length* property. You can access it as shown here to find the number of characters in a string:

```
lengthOfTheString = myString.length;
```

As you can see, a *method* is basically a function that is part of an object (note the parentheses), and a *property* is a variable that is part of the object. You can create your own objects in addition to the built-in ones, but for most of your mashup coding, you work with the built-in objects. The objects you are most likely to use are basic ones, such as strings, dates, and arrays, as well as objects designed to work with the interface and with the HTML Document Object Model (DOM).

The two most important interface objects are window and document—they are the window and document in which the JavaScript is running. If you want to write some HTML code from inside a JavaScript, you use the document object's write method, as shown here:

```
document.write ("<h1>This is my heading</h1>");
```

If you are familiar with object-oriented programming, all this may be familiar. The biggest source of confusion to some people is where the window and document objects come from. The answer is this: they are there as a result of the document and window in which the JavaScript code is running. You do not have to set or initialize them.

The other built-in objects you may use are the HTML DOM set of objects. These include the document object itself and a variety of interface elements. Two of the most important methods of the document object are getElementById and getElementByName. They let you write JavaScript code that manipulates the HTML elements declared on the page using their name or ID attribute.

The examples in Part III of this book provide more details on the use of JavaScript objects.

Work with Events

JavaScript declares events that occur at various points as a Web page is created and used. Their names are often self-explanatory. If you use JavaScript to change the appearance of buttons dynamically, you may have used onMouseOver and onMouseOut. Likewise, if you are doing processing when a form is submitted, you probably used onSubmit. If you wrote JavaScript code to validate or edit user data entry, you may have used the onFocus, onBlur, or onChange events to trigger your editing.

Two other events are particularly important for mashups. The *onload* event is generated when a page is loaded. This is the point at which you normally check for browser compatibility. In the world of mashups, that may also be the time at which you interact with an external API or set up your variables. The *onunload* event may also be important because it is triggered when the page is unloaded, and you can use it to release memory and disconnect from an external API or close a database.

The syntax for an event is simple: you provide a function call for that event. Here is an example of a body tag that uses onload and onUnload to work with the Google Maps API. The load function is declared elsewhere in this script. The GUnload function is part of the Google Maps API, and it is included with the script element that accesses that API.

```
<body onload="load()" onunload="GUnload()">
```

Handle Errors

Compilers can catch syntax errors in languages they process, giving the programmer a chance to correct some errors before they occur. Interpreted and dynamic languages need to catch their own errors as they run—either by making assumptions about how to continue when problems occur or by executing error-handling routines you write.

Because mashups involve so many pieces of code that run on several computers, a good idea is to start with error-handing routines at the beginning. You may feel you are wasting time writing the error-handling code before you have even finished the first draft of your mashup, but this may save you time by catching the errors and showing them to you in a controlled manner.

The error-handling strategy in JavaScript is the common try/catch architecture. It consists of three basic parts:

- The *try* block consists of code you want to try to execute. If the try block generates an error, JavaScript follows your instructions in handling it.

- The *catch* block is the code you want to have executed if an error occurs in the try block. This code is not executed unless an error occurs.

- The *finally* block is code executed after the try block (and possibly the catch block) have executed.

Here is a typical error-handling routine:

```
var i = 1, j = 0;
try {
  var myResult = i / j;
} catch (theError) {
  myResult = 0;
} finally {
  // clean up
};
```

This code generates a divide-by-zero error. The catch block sets the value of myResult to 0.

Frequently, there is no finally block. Here is the same code without that block:

```
try {
  var myResult = i / j;
} catch (theError) {
  myResult = 0;
};
```

The catch statement takes a single parameter: it is the error object generated by the try block (if one has occurred). There can only be zero or one error object generated by the try block and its name is immaterial. In most cases, you see error objects named e or err, but the actual name is up to you.

This is a JavaScript object, and it has two properties: name and message. You can use the message to display a message for the user. You can use the name property to determine what has happened. In many cases, certain errors occur that can be ignored, while others must be handled.

The JavaScript alert function can be used to display a message to the user, including the actual text of the error message. In the previously shown code sample, the catch statement could include this call to alert that will display the error message that was generated. As shown here, the actual error message is displayed, along with text indicating what part of the script caused the problem:

```
alert ("Error in the divide example: " + theError.message);
```

In this example, an error is generated by the attempt to divide by zero. You can generate your own errors (the terminology is that an error is *thrown*). To do this, you use the throw statement. The *throw* statement can take a value that is a number, string, or any other value. It can also take a variable. Whatever you throw is accessible to you in the catch block.

If you want to use the most powerful form of error-handling, create your own error object, and then set its message and name properties. If you only want to throw a simple error with a string, you can also do so as in the following example:

```
throw "Unable to connect to API server"
```

You see examples of throwing custom errors in Part III of this book.

Handle JavaScript Environmental Problems

Browsers today let you control the environment with preferences for everything from default font sizes to the behaviors of cookies, caches, plug-ins, and scripts. There are many reasons for turning off scripts or images. One of the most common legitimate reasons is for people using unreliable dial-up connections (a large number, particularly in certain rural areas). Bandwidth needs to be conserved, and if the connections are unreliable, it is important for users to try to get their browsing done as quickly as possible.

There are also security concerns relating to the use of scripts. Unfortunately, scripts provide significant additions to a browser's functionality and, sometimes, those additions have been exploited in various ways. Turning off scripting is rather a blunt tool to use in an attempt to improve security. Most browsers ship with JavaScript functionality turned on, but, sometimes, people have deliberately turned it off. To test if JavaScript is enabled on your browser, one of the simplest ways is to go to the NASA Web site (www.nasa.gov), which uses JavaScript extensively and provides fascinating images from space. If you cannot use the NASA Web site, you may have JavaScript turned off. The site itself provides information on reenabling JavaScript. Two of the standard browsers and their JavaScript controls are shown here.

Figure 5-1 shows the Content tab of Preferences for Safari on Mac OS X. As with all Mac OS X applications, you reach Preferences from the application menu (called Safari in the case of Safari).

Can Most Browsers Today Support JavaScript?

Some browsers do not support JavaScript. This was an issue in the early years of JavaScript, but it is not a serious issue today. The standard method for handling a browser that does not support JavaScript is to enclose the script code within the script element with comment symbols, such as in the following code snippet:

```
script type="text/javascript">
<!--
…script commands
//-->
</script>
```

This is no longer a major concern and, while it does no harm to bracket all your JavaScript code in this way, it is generally safe to ignore the situation and to clean up your code by eliminating those extraneous comment lines.

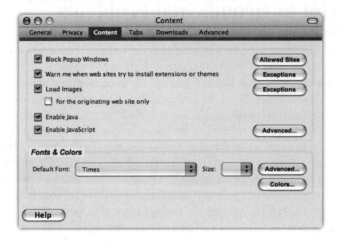

FIGURE 5-1 Safari on Mac OS X Content Preferences

Make certain JavaScript is enabled. If you are on an unreliable dial-up connection, you may want to disable the loading of images, which is also controlled from this tab. The advanced JavaScript preferences let you control precisely what the script can do, as shown in Figure 5-2.

Internet Explorer (IE) has a variety of scripting features. You access them from the Tools menu's Internet Options command. Choose the Security tab and click the Custom level button, as shown in Figure 5-3.

Scroll down to the Scripting settings, and make certain Active scripting is enabled, as Figure 5-4 shows.

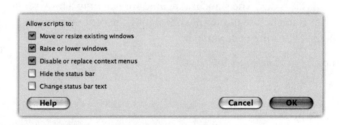

FIGURE 5-2 Advanced Safari JavaScript preferences

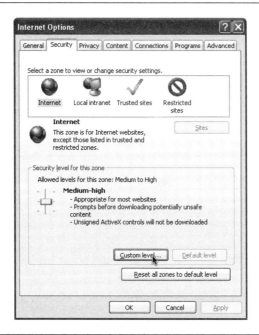

5

FIGURE 5-3   Internet Explorer 7 on Windows Internet content controls

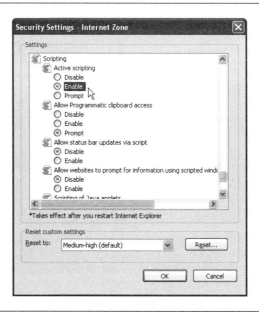

FIGURE 5-4   Advanced scripting

Chapter 6

Use PHP to Perform Server-Side Scripting

How to...

- Understand PHP Structure
- Start a PHP Script by Submitting an HTML Form
- Use PHP Variables and Arrays
- Use PHP Strings
- Control PHP Operations
- Build a Web Page with PHP
- Structure Multiple PHP Files

P HP: hypertext preprocessor (a recursive acronym) is one of the most commonly used programming languages on the Web. PHP is a server-side scripting language run by an application server, such as Apache or Microsoft IIS. PHP can generate HTML, which is then downloaded to a browser to fulfill a user's request. The HTML document that is downloaded can contain anything valid in an HTML document, which means PHP can generate script elements (including JavaScript) that are downloaded. PHP is also used to generate dynamic images and XML and to do general server-side processing.

In this chapter, you see how PHP works in general, and you see how to use its syntax, particularly in ways that differentiate it from other languages and in ways that are useful for mashups. This chapter begins the process of developing the basic mashup shell code that is used later in Chapter 9, as well as in Part III.

PHP is more formal than JavaScript and includes more programming features that may be used if you have programmed in another language. Because PHP runs on the server rather than inside your browser, it has access to all server resources, including databases and communications channels (subject to security constraints, of course). Also, because PHP does not have to cope with the vagaries of browsers (just the vagaries of servers), it can be used for purposes such as providing proxy services to data provided from other domains. As a result, PHP is frequently a critical component of mashups.

> NOTE   *The code discussed in this chapter is more fully developed in Chapter 9. The complete code is available in the Chapter 9 archive. The database code is omitted from this chapter, so you can focus on the PHP code and its structure.*

Understand PHP Structure

You have seen how JavaScript is used to insert scripts into HTML pages. The script is part of the downloaded HTML, and the script along with the HTML is processed by the user's browser. Ultimately, the browser determines what the script can do. You have seen how to turn off JavaScript in a browser. If you do so, the scripts will not run.

Did you know?

Find More Information About PHP

PHP is free software (in the sense defined by the Free Software Foundation http://www .fsf.org/), supported by The PHP Group (http://www.php.net). The current implementation, downloadable from http://www.php.net, is the de facto specification of the language (no separate formal specification exists as for some other languages and for many Internet standards at http://www.w3c.org). The Web site contains documentation, discussions, and further information about PHP, as well as download and installation links. This is the primary source for more information about PHP.

The first section of this chapter describes the PHP structure and how it works with a Web server. In many cases, you will find PHP is already installed and you do not need to do anything else to start using it. However, if you do need to install it, installation instructions for PHP are provided on their Web site. If you have specific problems, look at the FAQs, as well as the messages posted by people encountering and solving problems. If you do not find an answer there, feel free to post your own question.

A server-side script such as PHP has nothing to do with the browser. It runs on the server in response to a request from a user. When the PHP script has finished executing, an HTML page is ready to be downloaded. It may contain scripts, but it does not contain one thing: PHP code. The PHP code interacts with the server and its job is done when the HTML is generated.

TIP

Ten years ago, you needed to check to see which browsers supported JavaScript. Today, you need to do a similar check regarding Web servers and PHP, but that check is usually not a technical one. PHP is one of the most widely used server-side languages on the Web, but not every Internet service provider (ISP) supports it. Even ISPs that do support PHP may not support it for every class of user. A quick look at Web hosting offerings shows the vast majority do support PHP in some version or another, but before you commit to using PHP, make certain it is available to you. The reason this may hit you is it is possible, and even desirable, to test your server-side scripting in any language by using a temporary server (you can even configure your desktop computer to function both as a client and as a server). Having tested your server-side script, you do not want any unpleasant surprises when you move it to your production server. This plan-ahead tip applies both to commercial Web hosts and to corporate hosts inside a firewall. Although much more interoperability exists between servers and operating systems than at some points in the past, some totally Microsoft-based servers may opt for proprietary software rather than free or open source software, such as PHP. Note, too, the differences between versions 4 and 5 of PHP are significant. This book uses PHP 5.

When properly configured, a Web server normally runs a PHP script when a URL ending with .php is requested by a user either by typing it in or by submitting a form. The Web server reads the PHP script and processes it. The result of the PHP script is an HTML document, which is then downloaded to the user. The PHP code is not downloaded.

Use PHP Delimiters

The basic rule of processing PHP is this: all PHP commands are enclosed within delimiters

```
<?php
```

and

```
p>
```

These are not HTML elements or tags. Instead, they are the delimiters of PHP code.

Any text outside these delimiters is passed through as-is to the resulting HTML document. Here is one simple PHP script:

```
echo "<h1>";
echo "Hello World";
echo "</h1>";
```

Because the echo command simply passes the string through to the page being generated, this creates the following HTML code:

```
<h1>Hello World</h1>
```

Here is another PHP script. This one includes the HTML code to generate a page. It has one line of PHP code—a call to the phpinfo function, which generates a text description of the PHP environment. (That line is underlined.) This is a good test document to check that your server's PHP configuration is correct.

```
<!DOCTYPE html PUBLIC "-//W3C//DTD XHTML 1.0 Transitional//EN"
  "http://www.w3.org/TR/xhtml1/DTD/xhtml1-transitional.dtd">
<html xmlns="http://www.w3.org/1999/xhtml">
  <head>
    <title>Untitled Document</title>
    <meta http-equiv="Content-Type" content="text/html;
      charset=iso-8859-1" />
  </head>

  <body>
<?php
  phpinfo();
?>

  </body>
</html>
```

With the exception of the PHP code between the delimiters, this is an ordinary HTML page, and that HTML code is passed through by the PHP processor. Within the delimiters, the PHP script commands are executed.

A PHP script may contain multiple sets of PHP delimiters (although it makes no sense to nest them). Code within the delimiters is processed and can be emitted with the echo command as HTML, but, sometimes, a relatively large amount of static HTML needs to be generated. For those purposes, it makes sense to terminate the PHP script commands, type in the HTML, and then return, if necessary, to PHP to handle variable data.

As is often the case with scripting languages that have evolved over time, variations on the syntax exist that often save keystrokes. This is true regarding the starting and ending tags for PHP. The most commonly used syntax is the combination of `<?php` and `?>`, shown previously. Also available is the standard HTML script element,

```
<script language="php">
...some code
</script>
```

In some environments, you may also be able to use the combination of `<?` and `?>` or `<%` and `%>`. Generally, using one of the two most commonly used combinations is safer. (Some people find using `<? php` and `?>` is helpful because this makes the PHP code stand out more distinctly from scripts such as JavaScript. In addition, some graphical editors, such as Dreamweaver, colorize and highlight the `<? php` and `?>` tags automatically.

Use Comments

PHP supports single-line comments as well as longer ones, just as programming languages such as C and its derivatives do. A single-line comment is introduced by `//` or `#`. All text on the line that follows the `//` or `#` is ignored.

For longer comments, you can use the combination of `/*` and `*/` to delimit a comment that can stretch over several lines.

Because text outside the PHP delimiters is passed on as ordinary HTML code, anomalies will occur if you intersperse comments with that HTML code. Be sure to keep all your comments within the `<? php` and `?>` tags.

Terminate PHP Statements

PHP statements are terminated with a semicolon. As noted previously, this is a common statement delimiter in many languages and, while it is optional in JavaScript, it is required in PHP. By using the optional semicolon in JavaScript, you have one less thing to remember when you switch between the two scripting languages.

Start a PHP Script by Submitting an HTML Form

A common way of invoking a PHP script is by submitting a form. Often mashups begin with a page that lets users specify the data they want to work with (a ZIP code, perhaps). For this example, the HTML page, as shown in Figure 6-1, is used to start the process.

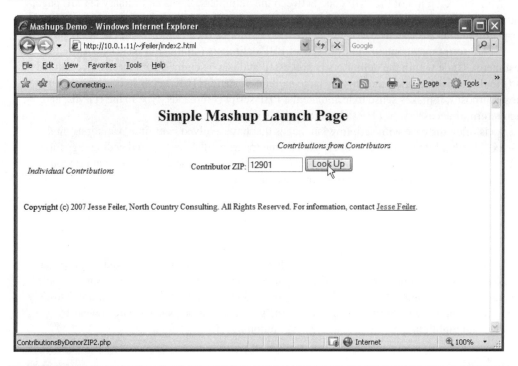

Submit an HTML form to start the PHP script

This form is used to select a ZIP code that is used to look up U.S. Federal Election Commission contribution data from a database. These data are used several times in this book, in part because it is public information that is not copyrighted. The concept is not just pedagogical: it is interesting to see where money comes from and where it goes in a geographic sense. (This also is a particularly good way of demonstrating the Google Maps API.) In the example used here, the contributions donated from a specific ZIP code are displayed, so you can see where they are going. If you work with the example data, you can see a fairly clear pattern to these data: money from a given ZIP code generally goes to the state capital and to the Washington, D.C., area. If the database were to include nonfederal races, you would also probably see contributions going to local races. Given this unsurprising pattern, what is surprising is contributions that go to some other location—such as another state's capital.

Figure 6-2 shows the results of a PHP script that does this task. You see the code in the section "The HTML Source Code to Be Built" later in this chapter.

The code for the page shown in Figure 6-1 is basic HTML and it is shown here. As noted previously, some of the spacing in the file was adjusted for presentation on printed pages. The code is exactly as you would expect to see it on any HTML page, but one line should stand out.

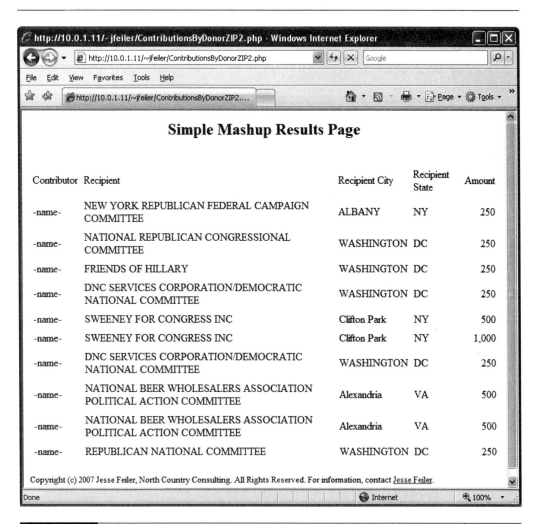

FIGURE 6-2 The result of the submitted form as processed by a PHP script

In the form element, the action attribute specifies the PHP script to be invoked when the form is submitted. (That line is underlined in the code listing.)

```
<html xmlns="http://www.w3.org/1999/xhtml">

  <head>
    <title>Mashups Demo</title>
```

```
    <meta http-equiv="Content-Type" content="text/html;
      charset=iso-8859-1" />
  </head>

  <body>
    <h2 align="center"><font size="+2">
      Simple Mashup Launch Page
    </font></h2>
    <table width="100%" border="0" cellspacing="3" cellpadding="3">
      <tr>
        <td><font size="-1"> </font></td>
        <td><div align="center">
          <font size="-1"><em>
            Contributions from Contributors</em>
          </font></div>
        </td>
      </tr>
      <tr>
        <td><font size="-1"><em>Individual Contributions</em></font></td>
        <td>
          <form name="form1" id="form1" method="post"
          action="ContributionsByDonorZIP2.php">
          <p><font size="-1">Contributor ZIP:
            <input name="zip" type="text" id="zip" size="10"/>
            <input type="submit" name="Submit" value="Look Up" />
            </font>
          </p>
          </form>
        </td>
      </tr>
    </table>

  <p>
    <font size="2">
      Copyright (c) 2007 Jesse Feiler, North Country Consulting.
      All Rights Reserved. For information, contact
      <a href="mailto:jfeiler@northcountryconsulting.com">
        Jesse Feiler
      </a>.
    </font>
  </p>
  </body>
</html>
```

This is how you start the PHP script running that creates the page shown in Figure 6-2. That script is described in more detail in the section "The PHP Code to Build the HTML Source Code" later in this chapter. Before then, you have some specific PHP language constructs to examine.

Use PHP Variables and Arrays

PHP variables are like those in other languages. *PHP variables* can contain letters, numbers, and underscore characters; the first character must be a letter or an underscore. As is the case in JavaScript, variable names are case-sensitive. Unlike many other languages, however, variables are prefixed with a $.

Variables are typed based on your first use of them. This means, as in JavaScript, you can generally ignore the type PHP is ascribing to the variable.

Like other programming languages, PHP enables you to create arrays. Elements of arrays are numbered by default starting at 0, and are accessed with common array syntax:

```
$myArray [0] = "first value";
$myArray [1] = "second value";
```

These are called *numeric arrays*. PHP also supports *associative arrays,* which are arrays in which the values are associated with keys rather than numbers, as in the following examples:

```
$myArray ["first value"] = 34;
$myArray ["second value"] = 28;
```

This concept will be important in receiving data from an HTML form.

Use PHP Strings

You can handle strings in PHP in a variety of ways. Because you so often use PHP to generate an HTML page, you can quickly be in a situation where you need to generate a PHP string, which itself contains an HTML string. The delimiters for each string need to be distinct, so they do not interfere with one another. For example, to generate this line of HTML

```
<font size="2">
```

you can use the PHP echo function. That function can be used to send a string or the string content of a PHP variable to the document being generated. To generate that line of HTML, you need PHP code like this:

```
echo ('<font size="2">');
```

Differentiating Between Single and Double Quotes

By using the single quotes to delimit the entire string, the double quotes within it are treated as string characters, not delimiters of the string. If you were to use double quotes throughout, the opening double quote would begin a string that would be terminated by the double quote just before the 2, and the balance of the line would by syntactically incorrect.

Variables used within double-quoted strings are expanded in PHP. As a result, if you have the following code

```
$myCity ='Plattsburgh';
```

then this code evaluates to Plattsburgh

```
"$myCity"
```

while this code evaluates to $myCity

```
'$myCity'
```

The evaluation of variables in strings in this way is sometimes referred to as *here is* coding.

Using Heredoc

As is the case with UNIX shells, Ruby, and Perl, you can use the *heredoc* construct to create strings with white space and line feeds without fussing about quotation marks or escape characters for the special characters. A heredoc section begins with an identifier of your choice, preceded by <<<. The text that follows is used as a string that respects line feeds and white space. PHP variables are expanded appropriately. The heredoc section terminates with the identifier *at the beginning of its own line,* followed immediately by a semi-colon. Here is a heredoc section:

```
$myVariable = "test variable";
$str = <<<hd
<p align="center">
This is a paragraph with a variable ($myVariable).
</p>
hd;
echo $str;
```

When the PHP document is evaluated, it generates this HTML code:

```
<p align="center">
This is a paragraph with a variable (test variable).
</p>
```

You could also write this to directly output the heredoc string as follows:

```
$myVariable = "a test variable";
echo <<<hd
<p align="center">
```

```
This is a paragraph with a variable ($myVariable).
</p>
hd;
```

This is an efficient way of entering large chunks of HTML, SQL, or JavaScript code.

CAUTION *The syntax for heredoc is strict. The initial <<< cannot begin in the first character position on a line, and the closing identifier must begin in the first character position on its line. Furthermore, the lines of a heredoc construct must be terminated with a newline character (sometimes referred to as a* line feed *or* LF *character). If you are using a Macintosh computer, you must save your PHP document as a UNIX document or as a document with LF line breaks. In Dreamweaver, you set this in Preferences in the Dreamweaver menu, in the section called Code Format. The specific setting is Line Break Type, and the choice you want is LF (UNIX). In BBEdit, you use the Options button in the Save or Save As dialog, and then choose UNIX for Line Breaks.*

Building Concatenated Strings

You can use PHP variables in both heredoc constructs and double-quoted strings. This lets you easily construct code such as this segment from a database query:

```
WHERE candidate_ID = '40'
```

If you have a variable called $candidateID, you can do that in a double-quoted string as follows:

```
"WHERE candidate_ID = '$candidateID'"
```

In the heredoc structure, you would write

```
  <<<SQL
"WHERE candidate_ID = '$candidateID'"
SQL;
```

You can also build a concatenated string that employs the variable. Here is how you could write that code:

```
$theQuery = "WHERE candidate_ID = '";
$theQuery .= $candidateID; // set candidate ID
$theQuery .= "'";
```

This format—particularly with the comment—makes it clear where the variable information is inserted into the string. It is more verbose, but can be more maintainable. Which format you use is up to you.

NOTE *If you are using concatenated strings, remember the first line is a replacement operation using an = sign, but the subsequent lines are concatenation operations in which the string is concatenated to the end of the existing string.*

Control PHP Operations

Any programming language that supports arrays needs to support looping control structures that let you iterate through arrays. PHP is no exception. PHP supports common control statements, such as if/then, while, do/while, for, and foreach. They have the same general meanings as in other programming languages, although the specific syntax may vary from one language to another.

The while statements continue to operate until a condition becomes false. In the case of while statements, the condition is reevaluated each time through the loop (as it must be to avoid an infinite loop). The condition may be set during the loop itself or in the while statement itself. The for statements iterate either a specific number of times or once for each element in an array. As is true in most languages, you can construct a while statement that mimics the behavior of a for statement.

Build a Web Page with PHP

The example of a simple HTML form that causes a PHP script to run was shown previously in this chapter. The form and the output from the PHP script were shown previously in Figures 6-1 and 6-2. Here is the basic script to be run.

The HTML Source Code to Be Built

If you look at the source of the page shown in Figure 6-2, you see the code shown here.

```
<html>
  <head>
    <title></title>
    <meta http-equiv="Content-Type" content="text/html;
      charset=iso-8859-1" />
  </head>

  <body>
    <h1 align="center"><font size="+2">
      Simple Mashup Results Page</font></h1>
    <br>

    <table border="0" width="100%" cellspacing="3"
      cellpadding="3" align="center">
      <tr>
        <td>Contributor</td>
        <td>Recipient</td>
        <td>Recipient City</td>
        <td>Recipient State</td>
        <td>Amount</td>
      </tr>
```

```
<tr>
  <td>-name-</td>
  <td>NEW YORK REPUBLICAN FEDERAL CAMPAIGN COMMITTEE</td>
  <td>ALBANY</td>
  <td>NY</td>
  <td align="right">250</td>
</tr>
<tr>
  <td>-name-</td>
  <td>NATIONAL REPUBLICAN CONGRESSIONAL COMMITTEE</td>
  <td>WASHINGTON</td>
  <td>DC</td>
  <td align="right">250</td>
</tr>
<tr>
  <td>-name-</td>
  <td>FRIENDS OF HILLARY</td>
  <td>WASHINGTON</td>
  <td>DC</td>
  <td align="right">250</td>
</tr>
… similar lines of code omitted
</table>
<br>
<p><font size="2">Copyright (c) 2007 Jesse Feiler,
  North Country Consulting. All Rights Reserved.
  For information, contact
  <a href="mailto:jfeiler@northcountryconsulting.com">
    Jesse Feiler
  </a>.</font>
</p>
</body>
</html>
```

The PHP Code to Build the HTML Source Code

Here is the PHP script to build the code shown previously and in Figure 6-2. Note, in addition to the usual reformatting, this script was modified slightly. In the next section of this chapter, you see how to restructure it to simplify it. The PHP code that is in several sections is delimited by the standard <?php and ?> delimiters.

NOTE   *This code serves as the basis for several examples in the book, and you can find discussions of it in several places as different aspects are discussed. Do not be daunted if some of the details are not yet clear to you. You have several other chances to walk through the code.*

One important PHP function is used repeatedly in this code, as well as in similar code you write for your mashups. The *echo* function takes a single parameter, which is a string to be outputted into the HTML document being built.

In the first section of PHP code, a variable—$pageTitle—is created and initialized:

```
<?php
  $page_Title = "Contributions by Donor ZIP";
?>
```

After this section of PHP code, the file continues with standard HTML code. This is a PHP file (with a .php suffix), so it is processed by the Web server as PHP code, and this HTML code is passed through to the output file. The first line is PHP boilerplate code needed to be emitted as the first line of the output file. This section of code is standard for most PHP scripts. There are two varieties of this code. The simplest is

```
<html>
  <head>
```

The more complex set of code is shown here:

```
<?xml version="1.0" encoding="iso-8859-1"?>
<!DOCTYPE html PUBLIC "-//W3C//DTD XHTML 1.0 Transitional//EN"
  "http://www.w3.org/TR/xhtml1/DTD/xhtml1-transitional.dtd">
<html xmlns="http://www.w3.org/1999/xhtml">
  <head>
```

The difference is the second set of code introduces an XHTML document, while the first introduces an HTML document. If you want to use the stricter XHTML syntax, use the second version. Refer to Chapter 10 for more information about XHTML.

Now, there is another little snippet of PHP code. It sets the page title to the $pageTitle variable declared right at the beginning of the file by using the echo function. The code to be emitted is

```
<title>Contributions by Donor ZIP</title>
```

When the file is restructured in the next section, you can see why this is helpful.

```
    <title><?php echo $page_title; ?></title>
    <meta http-equiv="Content-Type" content="text/html;
      charset=iso-8859-1" />
  </head>

  <body>
    <h1 align="center"><font size="+2">
      Simple Mashup Results Page</font>
    </h1>
    <br>
```

Now, the PHP code needs to query the database. The actual mechanism is described in Chapter 9, but, for now, it is important to see how the information from the form is passed into the PHP script.

The input field for the ZIP code was specified in the HTML code for the form as follows:

```
<input name="zip" type="text" id="zip" size="10"/>
```

The built-in variable $_REQUEST in PHP provides you with an associative array of the variables sent into a GET or POST request (or to a cookie). To retrieve the data from the submitted form, use $_REQUEST with the key of the ID of the input field. In this code, the variable $zip is set to the contents of the form's zip field. Once that is done, you can retrieve data from the database based on this value.

```
$zip = $_REQUEST['zip'];
```

6

At this point, the database is accessed as described in Chapters 7 and 9. You connect to the database with code such as these two lines. Note, the underlined text consists of placeholders.

```
$dbc = @mysql_connect (localhost, yourUserID, yourPassword);
@mysql_select_db (databaseName);
```

After the database call, a variable is set to the result of the query, as shown in the next line of code. After this line of code has executed, $result contains the database query result. All that remains is to format it.

```
$result = mysql_query ($query);
```

The echo function is used to emit HTML code. Note, this function takes a single string that continues across several lines. Blank spaces do not matter, so you can format the HTML code for readability.

```
echo '<table border="0" width="100%" cellspacing="3"
  cellpadding="3" align="center">
  <tr>
    <td>Contributor</td>
    <td>Recipient</td>
    <td>Recipient City</td><td>Recipient State</td>
    <td>Amount</td>
  </tr>';
```

The table's first row was emitted. Now, another database line of code is used to retrieve a single row within a while loop and format it. Compare this simple loop to the actual code used to display the table—line after line of data. The PHP script generates all those lines of code from this one loop, using the elements of the $row array retrieved in the database call.

```
// Display all the values.
while ($row = mysql_fetch_array ($result, MYSQL_NUM)) {
  // Display each record.
```

```
echo "
  <tr>
    <td>-name-</td>
    <td>$row[1]</td>
    <td>$row[2]</td>
    <td>$row[3]</td>
    <td align=\"right\">$row[4]</td
  </tr>\n";
} // End of while loop.
```

Now there is some cleaning up to do. The table element is ended, the database is closed, and the page footer is emitted.

```
echo '</table>'; // End the table.
mysql_close(); // Close the database connection.
<br>
<p><font size="2">Copyright (c) 2007 Jesse Feiler,
  North Country Consulting.  All Rights Reserved.
  For information, contact
  <a href="mailto:jfeiler@northcountryconsulting.com">
    Jesse Feiler
  </a>.</font>
</p>
</body>
</html>
```

This is the PHP code that generated the results shown previously in Figure 6-2.

Structure Multiple PHP Files

In discussing the $pageTitle variable, it was noted noted this file would be restructured. In fact, this file will become three files. Because the page header and page footer will be standard, that code is placed in separate files to be included. A common practice is to create an Includes directory next to the PHP scripts. Here is the first included script, Includes/PageTop.html. (Note, these are HTML files, not PHP files.)

```
<?xml version="1.0" encoding="iso-8859-1"?>
<!DOCTYPE html PUBLIC "-//W3C//DTD XHTML 1.0 Transitional//EN"
  "http://www.w3.org/TR/xhtml1/DTD/xhtml1-transitional.dtd">
<html xmlns="http://www.w3.org/1999/xhtml">
  <head>
    <title><?php echo $page_Title; ?></title>
```

```
  <meta http-equiv="Content-Type" content="text/html;
    charset=iso-8859-1" />
</head>

<body>
  <h1 align="center"><font size="+2">
    <?php echo $page_Title; ?>
  </font></h1>
<br>
```

And here is Includes/PageBottom.html:

```
  <br>
  <p><font size="2">
    Copyright (c) 2007 Jesse Feiler, North Country Consulting.
    All Rights Reserved. For information, contact
    <a href="mailto:jfeiler@northcountryconsulting.com">
    Jesse Feiler</a>.</font>
  </p>
</body>
</html>
```

This means the beginning of the actual PHP file can be written as follows:

```
<?php
$page_Title = "Contributions by Donor ZIP x";
include ('Includes/PageTop.html');
```

The bottom can be written like this:

```
include ('Includes/PageBottom.html');
?>
```

These files are used repeatedly in this book, so the code need not be repeated.

Chapter 7

Use MySQL with PHP to Retrieve Mashup Data

How to...

- Understand SQL and Databases
- Create SQL Queries
- Use the FEC Database
- Use MySQL
- Use PHP to Get to an SQL Database
- Create and Load a Test Database

In the previous chapter, you saw how to use PHP to generate HTML code and how to use data returned from a database call to generate a dynamic table of results. The database calls were omitted from that chapter so you could see the structure of the PHP code. In this chapter, the database calls are provided and explained.

Mashups commonly use data and, often, they use large amounts of data. Those data can be retrieved from a database under your control (perhaps even on the server where the PHP script is running) or they can be retrieved from a database to which you have access, but that you do not control. In the next chapters, you see how to receive data via RSS and Atom, and how to retrieve data yourself from nondatabase sources.

For now, the emphasis is on databases and, specifically, on SQL, which is the basic language of databases today. Even databases that do not support SQL directly generally provide an interface to SQL with technologies such as Open Database Connectivity (ODBC) or Java Database Connectivity (JDBC), which are referred to generically as xDBC.

 As noted previously, the code samples in this book were reformatted for readability. That comment particularly applies to the MySQL syntax shown in this chapter.

```
set col1 = substring(@var1, 2, 2)
```

This snippet of code will be processed correctly by MySQL, while the code below (note the space after "substring") will generate a syntax error. In general, you should be careful about extra spaces in your MySQL syntax.

```
set col1 = substring (@var1, 2, 2)
```

Understand SQL and Databases

Databases let you store, retrieve, and manage data without worrying about the physical storage or the operations involved in reading and writing. Today, SQL is the basic tool for manipulating relational data. Originally named "Structure Query Language," it is now referred to simply as SQL. Some people use the initials, while others pronounce it as "sequel."

How to ... Find More Information About SQL

The classic references on SQL and relational databases are the books by C. J. Date. Online tutorials and references about SQL are available from a number of sites, including a tutorial at http://www.w3schools.com, and documentation from specific database vendors, such as MySQL (http://www.mysql.org), Oracle (http://www.oracle.com), IBM (DB2) (http://www.ibm.com), and Microsoft (SQL Server) (http://www.microsoft.com). From each of those sites, you can search on SQL to find where the current documentation is located. The standard itself is published by ANSI and ISO, and is available for purchase from those organizations.

When it comes to mashups, most of the time you are a consumer of data, so what you need to know about SQL and databases is largely how to retrieve data. (For development and testing, you do sometimes need to create a database. The last section of this chapter provides a recipe for creating a database from the downloadable data referred to throughout the chapter.)

SQL itself is quite simple. You only need to understand a few concepts.

A *column* **represents one data field or element—name, address, and so forth.**

A *row* **represents one set of values for the fields or elements of one individual or observation.**

A *table* **consists of rows and columns.**   A table can have any number of rows and columns (including none of either). That is why everything in SQL—including nothing—is a table.

A *database* **is a collection of tables.**

Rows **can be retrieved based on keys.**   In designing a database table, you can use one or more columns as *keys*. A key is a column used to identify rows. When a key is unique, it contains values that are not repeated in more than one row of the table, such as an employee ID number. When a key is not unique, it may occur in one or more rows of the table. The city in which someone lives is generally not a unique key because more than one person whose data exist in the table may live in the same city.

NOTE   *Rows in one table can be related to rows in another table (or the same table) using the values of a key. For example, if one table contains employee salary information and another table contains employee personal information, those two tables can be related based on a unique employee ID. The unique employee ID appears in a column in each table. When you retrieve the data, you match those two IDs and all the data for one employee can be retrieved from the two tables.*

There is much more to SQL and database theory, but this is enough for you to manage the basics of mashup data retrieval.

Create SQL Queries

SQL lets you retrieve data by using *queries*. A query starts with the keyword SELECT, and it may include a variety of clauses. A SELECT statement always returns a table (although it may be empty).

Here are some of the most basic SELECT uses.

```
SELECT * from mytable;
```

This selects all the rows and columns, and then returns them.

```
SELECT * FROM mytable WHERE age < 21;
```

This retrieves all the rows where the age column is less than 21.

```
SELECT name, address FROM mytable WHERE age < 21;
```

This retrieves only two columns (name and address) from the table, but the WHERE condition is still enforced.

To *join* two tables (that is, to retrieve data from two tables at the same time), you generally need to use a relationship. The employee example cited previously can be implemented in this way.

```
SELECT personaldata, salarydata from personaltable, salarytable
   WHERE personaldataID = salarydataID;
```

This can work provided the columns personaldataID and salarydataID are set up to have the same values in the two tables for the same individual. This syntax is correct, but a problem can quickly arise. As shown here, the assumption is the column names in the two tables are always different. If they were not, sorting out the duplicate names would be confusing. To manage this, you can associate an identifier with each table, rewriting the code as follows:

```
SELECT personaldata, salarydata from p.personaltable, s.salarytable
   WHERE p.personaldataID = s.salarydataID;
```

The *qualifiers p* (for personaltable) and *s* (for salarytable) make the column names unique. In fact, although this may appear as an extension to the basic syntax, the SQL rule is this: qualifiers are required unless the names of the columns makes them unnecessary. Qualifiers often are one character in length, but they can be longer. By using qualifiers, you can rewrite the statement to use identical column names in the WHERE clause. This can be a good idea because it helps people to understand that the columns in the two tables with the same name contain the same data.

```
SELECT personaldata, salarydata FROM p.personaltable, s.salarytable
  WHERE s.employeeID = p.employeeID;
```

The keys need not be separate from the data retrieved. For example, the previous SELECT statement can be rewritten to select personaldata, salarydata, and employeeID by writing it as follows. Because the employeeID value is the same in both tables (that is the point of the WHERE clause), you can retrieve whichever table's value you want.

```
SELECT personaldata, salarydata, p.employeeID FROM
  p.personaltable, s.salarytable WHERE s.employeeID = p.employeeID;
```

You frequently use a number of additional clauses in SELECT statements. A common one is ORDER BY, which lets you sort data. Also of use in mashups is the FORMAT clause, which can format data retrieved from the database. This can be easier than formatting it in PHP or another scripting language.

To sort the table of returned data in the first example, you can use ORDER BY salarydata (or any other field), as shown here:

```
SELECT personaldata, salarydata FROM p.personaltable, s.salarytable
  WHERE s.employeeID = p.employeeID ORDER BY salarydata;
```

To format the salary data in whole dollars, you could use the *FORMAT* function. The FORMAT function takes two parameters: the value to be formatted and the number of decimal places.

```
SELECT personaldata, FORMAT (salarydata, 0)
  FROM p.personaltable, s.salarytable
  WHERE s.employeeID = p.employeeID;
```

If you want to display the salary with dollars and cents, you would use FORMAT (salarydata, 2).

Instead of retrieving the data, you can use the COUNT function to find out how many records could be retrieved. COUNT is used in a SELECT statement in the following manner:

```
SELECT COUNT (employeeID) FROM salarytable WHERE salary > 30000;
```

This function normally is processed quite quickly, so you can easily see if you will be retrieving 5 records or 500,000. If the number of records that would be retrieved is too great, you can either stop the processing or prompt the user to modify the request. Other summary functions, such as SUM, AVG, MAX, and MIN, are also available. Databases are optimized for performance, and many of these operations can be carried out without reading the entire database. In modern relational databases, a variety of indexes are created automatically or on request. Where possible, queries are performed on the indexes rather than on the raw data.

Particularly when you are testing, you may want to arbitrarily limit the amount of data retrieved. You can do that with the LIMIT clause. In the following code, you can never retrieve more than ten records:

```
SELECT personaldata, FORMAT (salarydata, 0)
  FROM p.personaltable, s.salarytable
  WHERE s.employeeID = p.employeeID
  LIMIT 10;
```

When the database is set up, each column is specified as to the data type it contains—text, number, date, and so forth. This allows the database engine to optimize storage and searching.

Columns are sometimes called fields, and rows are sometimes called records.

This is the most basic overview of SQL, but for many mashups, this syntax is sufficient for your needs.

Use the FEC Database

The *FEC* database used in this chapter, as well as in Chapters 12 and 13, contains three tables. The FEC database is a typical example of a relational database, and it is used to illustrate how tables are created and related to one another. Their feilds are shown in Table 7-1.

- *Candidates* contains one record for each candidate. Each record has a unique value for the candidate_ID. Also, each candidate's record has a value for a committee_ID, which is the identifier for that candidate's committee.

- *Committees* contains one record for each committee. Committees are linked to candidates, which they support via the candidate_ID field in committees and candidates.

- *Individuals* contains one record for each contribution. Individual contributions are linked to committees, and then to candidates. The *filer* field in individuals is the committee_ID value of the appropriate committee.

> **NOTE** *A database normally models some type of reality. In this case, the laws and regulations of the FEC determine that a single committee exists for each candidate for the purpose of reporting. If it were possible to have multiple committees for a candidate, an intermediate table, called a* join table, *would be used.*

To find the information on who contributed to which committees from a given ZIP code (12901), this is the SELECT statement you can use. This performs a join based on the committees. committee_ID field and the individuals.filer field, selects the ZIP code, and then sorts the data by contributor name. Note, the FORMAT function is applied to the amount of the contribution, so no digits are to the right of the decimal point.

Candidates	Committees	Individuals
candidate_ID	committee_ID	filer
name	lname	amendment
party_1	treasurer	report_type
party_3	street_1	primary_general
seat_status	street_2	transaction_type
candidate_status	city	contributor
street_1	state	city
street_2	ZIP	state
city	designation	ZIP
state	type	occupation
ZIP	party	transaction_date
committee_ID	filing_frequency	amount
year	interest_group	
district	connected_name	
	candidate_ID	

TABLE 7-1   The table fields

```
SELECT
  individuals.contributor,
  committees.name,
  committees.city,
  committees.state,
  FORMAT(individuals.amount, 0)
  FROM individuals, committees
  WHERE (individuals.zip = '12901')
    AND (committees.committee_ID = individuals.filer)
  ORDER BY individuals.contributor;
```

You learn how to use this code from PHP in the section "Use PHP to Get to an SQL Database."

NOTE   *Each database table generally comes with documentation. When you download the FEC data, note the short documentation files next to the data files. The documentation is always important for a database. Only by reading the documentation would you discover that committees.committee_ID and individuals.filer are the related keys.*

7

Use MySQL

MySQL is a widely used database that supports much of SQL. MySQL interacts well with PHP using the mysqli module.

On both Windows and Mac OS X, MySQL uses a command line interface. On Windows, you can select it from Programs in the Start menu.

On Mac OS X, launch Terminal and start MySQL by changing the directory to the /usr/local/ mysql directory, and then launching bin/mysql, as shown in Figure 7-1.

The syntax for launching MySQL on Mac OS X is

```
bin/mysql -u <yourusername> -p
```

The -p command tells MySQL to ask for a password. If you installed MySQL on Windows, the installation process guides you through the steps of creating a new user. By default, the user is root and the password is blank.

The commands are all terminated by a semicolon. Spaces do not matter, so you can spread the commands over several lines. Remember, on both Mac OS X and Windows, you are working with character-based interfaces, so you cannot go back several lines to correct a typo.

> **TIP**
>
> *On the MySQL Web site, you can find a number of GUI interfaces available in the Downloads section.*

The general sequence of MySQL commands begins with USE <database>;. (Remember the semicolon.) After that, enter your SQL commands that access that database.

> **TIP**
>
> *A good idea is to always test your SQL statements interactively before coding them in PHP.*

FIGURE 7-1   Launch MySQL on Mac OS X

How to ... **Get MySQL**

Log on to http://www.mysql.com to download MySQL. Several versions are available, but you almost always want the MySQL Community Server—Generally Available Release. Look for the Download button on the home page and follow the links. (One way of determining if you are downloading the right product is to see if you can download it free. For learning, testing, and small development projects, that is all you need.)

Separate installers are available for various operating systems. Use the appropriate installer and, if you are installing MySQL for the first time, do not customize it until you are familiar with its use.

7

Use PHP to Get to an SQL Database

You now have almost all the pieces of the puzzle, so you can write the PHP code to query the database and display the results. You saw the basics of the code in the previous chapter, but the database sections were omitted. They are described here.

There are four database sections of code, which is true of nearly every programmatic access of a database.

- Connect to the database. You need to log in to the database manager and select the database to use. This is comparable to executing MySQL and entering the USE statement.
- Create the query and send it to the database.
- Retrieve the results and display them.
- Disconnect from the database.

Connect to the Database

Connecting to the database is boilerplate code, as shown here. If you are using an existing database, your database administrator has the information you need to replace in this code. If you are creating your own database, you can see how to do so (and how to set these values) in Chapter 13.

```php
<?php
$DB_Account = 'jfeiler';  // use your own account-name here
$DB_Password = 'password'; // use your own password here
$DB_Host = 'localhost'; // use the name of your MySQL host here
```

```
$DB_Name = 'fec'; // use the name of your database here
$dbc = @mysqli_connect ($DB_Host, $DB_Account, $DB_Password)
  or die ('Could not connect to MYSQL:'.mysql_error());
@mysqli_select_db ($DB_Name)
  or die ('Could not select the database:'.mysql_error());
?>
```

For readability and maintainability, variables are used for the user name, password, host, and database name. When database security is set up, you may want to create a user name and password used solely for access from programs and scripts. This is so the privileges associated with that user name can be separated from privileges assigned to an interactive user.

The local host is assumed as the location of the database, however, you can supply an IP address instead and that is where the connection will be made.

It the connection cannot be made or the database cannot be selected, the PHP script dies with the appropriate message. Note the concatenation operator (.) used to display the specific error string returned by the MySQL calls.

Because this is standard code and also because it contains password information, a good idea is to place it in an include file, so the main PHP script does not contain confidential information. If you do this, the beginning of the PHP script will include this line of code:

```
include ('Includes/SQLLogin.php'); // this contains the boilerplate
  code shown at the beginning of this section
```

Create and Process the Query

The next step is to create the query. You need to retrieve the selected ZIP code from the form submitted. That is done by setting the local variable $zip. Next, a query string is created. As you can see, it is spaced out for readability. This is exactly the string used to test in MySQL, except the ZIP code is not hard-coded. Instead, the ZIP code is concatenated with the $zip variable.

```
// Query the database.
$zip = $_REQUEST['zip'];
$query = "SELECT
    individuals.contributor,
    committees.name,
    committees.city,
    committees.state,
    FORMAT(individuals.amount, 0)
  FROM individuals, committees
  WHERE (individuals.zip = '"
    .$zip.
    "') AND (committees.committee_ID = individuals.filer)
  ORDER BY individuals.contributor
```

```
        LIMIT 10";
if ! ($result = mysqli_query ($query))
  die (' SQL query returned an error:'.mysqli_error());
```

Because this code is to be used for testing, the LIMIT clause is added at the end of the query. The variable $result receives the result of the query. This is not the data. Instead, it is the result of the call that will be either TRUE or FALSE.

Fetch the Data

If the result of the query is good, you then need to fetch the data and display them using HTML. The first section of code here creates the HTML table to be used to display the data:

```
echo '<table border="0" width="100%" cellspacing="3"
  cellpadding="3" align="center">
    <tr>
      <td>Contributor</td>
      <td>Recipient</td>
      <td>Recipient City</td>
      <td>Recipient State</td>
      <td>Amount</td>
    </tr>';
```

Now you display the data. The key here is the WHILE statement and its call of mysqli_fetch_array. This returns each row in turn, placing the row into the $row variable. You can then access the individual elements to place them in the HTML code. If you want, you can modify the data. For example, although the contributor name is retrieved (in $row[0]), it is not displayed. Instead, the string -name- is used to hide those data. Note, also, the amount is aligned to the right in the last column (the amount was formatted in the SQL query).

> **NOTE** *In reality, there is no reason to retrieve data that you do not want to display as is the case with the name field in this example. However, some data might be partially masked, such as the common situation in which the last few numbers of a credit card are displayed with the previous numbers represented as asterisks. In this case, although the data are in fact public, they are not displayed in the screenshots. If you use the sample code, you can change this line of code to display the real names in your mashup.*

```
// Display all the values.
while ($row = mysqli_fetch_array ($result, MYSQL_NUM)) {
  // Display each record.
  echo "<tr>
    <td>-name-</td>
    <td>$row[1]</td>
    <td>$row[2]</td>
```

```
    <td>$row[3]</td>
    <td align=\"right\">$row[4]</td>
    </tr>\n";
} // End of while loop.

echo '</table>'; // End the table.
```

Disconnect from the Database

Finally, you disconnect from the database. This is a single line of code, but, for readability, and in case you need to do additional processing, it is placed in its own include file.

```
<?php
mysqli_close(); // Close the database connection.
?>
```

This means the end of the PHP file includes this line of code, with Includes/SQLClose.php containing the call to mysqli.close().

```
include ('Includes/SQLClose.php'); // Close the database connection.
```

Create and Load a Test Database

This section describes how to create a database in MySQL and populate it with tables and data. In Chapters 11 and 13, you see how to download specific data from the Federal Election Commission and the Census Bureau to populate database tables.

Create a Test Database

The first step in creating a database is just that—create it. In MySQL enter the following command (you can name the database something more meaningful than test if you want):

```
create database test;
```

Once you create a database, you can USE it:

```
use database test;
```

Once you have a database, you can create one or more tables within it. Each table you create must have at least one column, so the minimal syntax is

```
create table testtable (name varchar (5));
```

This code creates a table called testtable; it has one column, which is called name. That column is set to be a variable-length character field of up to five characters. By using varchar instead of a fixed field length (which would be char), you can avoid storing blank characters.

Then, add whatever columns you want. Because MySQL is character-based, you cannot go back to fix a typo on a previous line you entered into it. For that reason, it may ultimately be faster to add each column individually, rather than typing several lines of code, which may fail. Here is the basic syntax to add a column:

```
alter table testtable add column address varchar (5);
```

TIP *If you download the FEC data, you can construct tables that match the downloaded data exactly. If you are using those data, remember, they are not always cleaned. Because of this, you may be better off not declaring date columns as type date but, instead, as character fields. In that way, if you have invalid date data, you will not generate errors. This tip applies to any data you use: field types may often be goals, not reality in downloaded data.*

To see what you created, you can always check to see what the table looks like:

```
describe testtable;
```

This produces the output shown in Figure 7-2.

MySQL supports standard data types. For a description of the supported types, see http://dev .mysql.com/doc/refman/4.1/en/data-types.html.

Load the Test Database

If you create tables for the downloaded data, filling them with the data themselves is easy. MySQL supports fast importing with the *LOAD DATA* INFILE command.

NOTE *The full syntax for LOAD DATA, as well as feedback from users, is located at http://dev .mysql.com/doc/refman/5.1/en/load-data.html for MySQL version 5.1 in English. If you go to http://www.mysql.org, and then click on Documentation, you can search for LOAD DATA INFILE to find all articles in all languages for all versions of MySQL.*

The LOAD DATA INFILE command lets you quickly load a table from a flat file. The basic syntax for the LOAD DATA command specifies the file, the table to load, and the way in which the input data are to be split apart. The order of the clauses in the LOAD DATA INFILE command matters, although beyond the basic syntax shown next, all the clauses are optional.

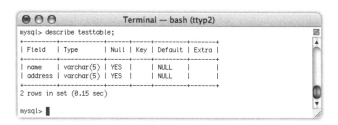

FIGURE 7-2 The result of a describe command

Basic LOAD DATA INFILE Syntax

For example, here is one of the simplest LOAD DATA commands:

```
load data infile local myData.txt
  into table myTable;
```

The *local* keyword tells the command to search for the file locally (that is, on the computer where you are running MySQL, rather than where the database is running). If you want to load a file from the server where the database is running, just omit the keyword. Note, in reality, you need a fully qualified file name (that is, one with the full path specified).

The *into table* clause means exactly what it says.

The defaults, which are assumed here, are as follows: the lines of data are terminated with newline characters, and the fields are terminated with tab characters. Further, the assumption is the input data contain values for the columns of the table in the order in which they are described in the database (you can check on this with the describe table command).

Changing Field and Record Delimiters

If fields are terminated by a character other than a tab, you can specify what that character is. Likewise, you can specify the terminator of each record. In the following code, the fields are terminated by a vertical line (the | character), and the records are terminated by a newline character:

```
load data infile local myData.txt
  into table myTable
  fields terminated by '|'
  lines terminated by '\n';
```

To load data where the fields are terminated by a tab character (\t) and the records are terminated by a return, you would use

```
fields terminated by '\t'
lines terminated by '\r'
```

Note, the line and field terminators are often single characters such as the tab, a comma, or a return character. However, the actual specification shows they are strings.

Ignoring Records

The *ignore* clause uses the line termination characters to determine what to ignore (if anything) at the beginning of the file. This is useful if the first few records of the file contain headings or other descriptive information. As long as each line is terminated with the same character used for the subsequent data records, you can jump over those non-data records.

The following code skips over the first two records of the input file:

```
load data infile local myData.txt
  into table myTable
```

```
fields terminated by '|'
lines terminated by '\n'
ignore 2 lines;
```

If your data load does not work at all or only loads one record, check the line terminator character. Without further investigation, you can simply switch it from newline to return, or vice versa, which often solves the problem.

Loading Specific Columns

The load data command loads data into the records of the table in the same order the data appear in the input record. If you want to reorder the data or skip over some columns, however, you can do so by using a *column/variable list*.

A column/variable list is enclosed in parentheses and specifies the columns to be loaded. The data in the input file are processed based on the field and record delimiters that are specified. Then, the first data field is placed in the first column in the column/variable list, the second in the second, and so forth.

For example, the following code places the first field of the file in column 5, the second field in column 1, and the third field in column 12. The balance (if any) of the fields is ignored.

```
load data infile local myData.txt
  into table myTable
  fields terminated by '|'
  lines terminated by '\n'
  (column5, column1, column12);
```

Loading Data into Variables to Skip Columns

You can also load data into variables during the load process. Variables are specified beginning with @. They can be included in the column/variable list. If you want to load the first field into column 5, the second into column 1, and the third into a variable, you could change the last line of the code just shown to this:

```
(column5, column1, @myVariable)
```

One reason to do this is to use variables to skip over data. If you want to load the first field into column 5 and the third (not second) field into column 2, you need a way to skip over the second field in the input file. You can do so with this code:

```
(column5, @myVariable, column2)
```

You can skip over several fields from the input file by loading them into multiple variables—or even the same one:

```
(column5, @myVariable, column1, @myVariable, column12)
```

The variables used in this way are not stored anywhere.

Setting Data During the Load Process

One of the important features of the LOAD DATA INFILE command lets you set a column to the result of a *calculation*. Calculations can involve columns, constants, and variables. For example, to set a column named myValue to half the input value read into column 3, you could use

```
SET myValue = column3 / 2
```

If you use a variable in the column/variable list, you can include it in a calculation, such as the following:

```
SET column3 = @myValue / 2
```

Reading Fixed-Width Data

You often find data with no delimiters. The documentation tells you the first field is characters 1–12, for example, and the second field is characters 13–20. You can handle this situation by reading the continuous data into a variable, and then splitting it apart. The following code does this:

```
load data infile local myData.txt(
  into table myTable
  lines terminated by '\n'
  (@unDelimitedText)
  SET column=substring(@unDelimitedText, 1, 12),
    column2=substring(@unDelimitedText, 13, 8);
```

You can combine various features of LOAD DATA INFILE, such as in this command, which is used in Chapter 11, to load some census data into a table. Note the realistic file path name, as well as the field and line delimiters. You can see seven fields are read from the input file (there are more fields in the file, but the remaining ones are skipped). The first and third fields are stored in variables that are not used. The second field is stored in the variable $geocode and is then split apart. The fourth, fifth, sixth, and seventh variables are read into columns without any adjustment.

```
load data infile local
  '/Users/jfeiler/Desktop/dc_dec_2000_sf1_u_data1.txt'
  into table population
  fields terminated by '|'
  lines terminated by '\n'
  ignore 2 lines
  (@var1, @geocode, @var2, County_Name,
    TotalPopulation, TotalMen, TotalWomen)
  set State_FIPS_Code=left(@geocode, 2),
    County_FIPS_Code=right(@geocode, 3);
```

Delete Data from the Test Database

Loading data can be fast and efficient, but as is always the case in transferring data from one file or format to another, you may need several tries to get things right. Three commands can help you at this point.

Review the Data

You can select all the data in a table with a simple SELECT command. If you use the LIMIT keyword, you can check the first few records, as in the following syntax:

```
SELECT * from myTable LIMIT 10;
```

The LIMIT keyword can be followed by two numbers. If this is the case, the first number is the first row to display, and the second number is the number of rows. (Note, rows are numbered from zero.) Thus, if you enter this code, you can view ten records, starting with record number 10,000 (which is the 10,001[th] record starting from zero):

```
SELECT * from myTable LIMIT 10000, 10;
```

A good idea is to check the first few records and the last few records. Just as some extraneous records might be at the beginning of a file that you can skip over with IGNORE, you may also find some extraneous records at the end.

Delete Data from the Table

If you want to try again after a load that did not work quite right, deleting records from the table is simple. To delete all of them, use this syntax:

```
DELETE from myTable;
```

Drop the Table

You can drop the table from the database, which removes it totally. If you merely need to adjust columns, you can use the ALTER TABLE command:

```
DROP table myTable;
```

Drop the Database

Finally, you can drop the entire database, all its tables, and all its data. You should obviously be careful about doing this, but if you have been testing, there are times when you want to start over.

```
DROP database myDatabase;
```

Chapter 8

Use RSS and Atom to Receive Data Automatically

How to . . .

■ Understand Syndication, RSS, and Atom

■ Parse a Feed with PHP

■ Create a Search Feed

In Chapter 4, you saw the basics of XML, which is the basis of almost all news feeds. And, you saw how news readers can take the data apart and enable users to interactively sort and resort it by date or subject.

This chapter returns to XML and news feeds to examine how they can be used to drive mashups. Mashups almost always work with large amounts of data, even though only a small subset may be used for a particular mashup to map a location or merge two data items from two sources with one another. In the previous chapters, you saw how to use PHP and databases to enable the user to select data to be retrieved.

At the other extreme of the architecture is a mashup based on a news feed. In such cases, users do not select the data at all. Instead, a news feed delivers data to the mashup, and the mashup takes whatever is delivered and works with it. Some news feeds are traditional news feeds generated by newspapers or broadcasters, as well as by bloggers, social networking sites, and organizations large and small that want to send out their information. Other news feeds are designed for mashups. The latest blogs and Flickr's latest photos are of interest to point-and-click users, but they are valuable resources for mashup authors.

This chapter shows you how to examine a news feed with PHP and to extract its data, so you can then use it in your mashup. Chapters 16 and 17 show you how to apply the architecture and techniques in this chapter to a Flickr news feed, but, remember, although that example uses a Flickr news feed, the architecture and technology can work with any news feed.

You can also create feeds that represent dynamic searches on services such as Yahoo! and Google. You see how to create these searches yourself. You can then use the techniques for parsing static feeds to parse the results of your searches.

How to ...   Find More Information About RSS and Atom

For more information on RSS, go to http://cyber.law.harvard.edu/rss/rss.html. The specification for the Atom format is available at http://www.atomenabled.org/developers/syndication/atom-format-spec.php.

Understand Syndication, RSS, and Atom

Like mashups, *syndication* brings together a variety of basically simple Web technologies to create something new and more powerful than the individual components. Syndication allows publishers (be they journalists or bloggers) to generate XML documents called *feeds* describing the content of their Web site. Typically, these XML feeds list the latest items on the Web site, but they need not do so. Small badges on Web sites indicate they support syndication feeds to which you can subscribe.

Because feeds are automatically generated from blogs and other publishing tools, they are low-maintenance ways of exporting information. In the last few years, users have been encouraged to tag or otherwise categorize blogs, photos, and other items. That identifying information finds its way into feeds.

Two competing formats exists for feed syndication today: RSS and Atom. Referring to them as "competing" is likely to cause one of those philosophical wars that only computer people seem able to sustain. Both formats accomplish the same thing: creating syndication feeds, but they do so in slightly different ways. Both are dialects of XML. As a result, in today's world, both feeds are available, often for automatic feed generation based on the user's choice.

8

RSS

RSS, which is an acronym for Really Simple Syndication (and originally for RDF Site Summary, where RDF stands for Resource Description Framework), is the older format and by far the simpler of the two. It is basically frozen at version 2.0.1, and is described at http://blogs.law.harvard.edu/tech/rss. RSS is managed by Berkman Center for Internet & Society at Harvard Law School.

A typical RSS feed is shown as formatted in the Safari news reader on Mac OS X in Figure 8-1. Figure 8-2 shows the beginning of the XML code that makes up the feed.

The XML code is shown in a version of Firefox that does not support the formatted display of news feeds so you can see the code itself. Firefox presents the XML with hyphens, indentation, and linefeeds, none of which are part of the raw XML. The beginning of the actual XML file shown in Figure 8-2 has none of those features, as shown here.

```
<?xml version="1.0" encoding="UTF-8"?>
<rss version="2.0">
<channel>
<title>NYT > Theater</title>
<link>http://www.nytimes.com/pages/theater/
   index.html?partner=rssnyt</link>
<description></description>
<language>en-us</language>
<copyright>Copyright 2007 The New York Times Company</copyright>
<lastBuildDate>Tue, 20 Feb 2007 13:05:01 EST</lastBuildDate>
<image>
<title>NYT > Theater</title>
```

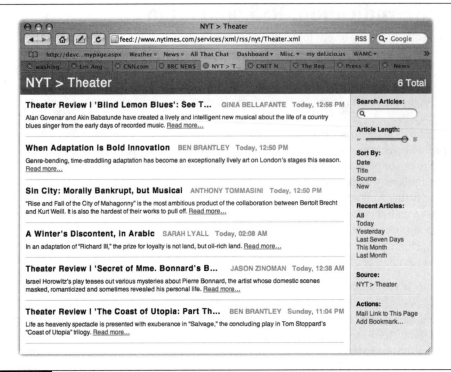

FIGURE 8-1   *New York Times* RSS feed in Safari

```
<url>http://graphics.nytimes.com/images/section/
  NytSectionHeader.gif</url>
<link>http://www.nytimes.com/pages/theater/index.html</link>
</image>
...
```

The first line of the file (as in all such listings in this book) is not shown in the Firefox display. It is always

```
<?xml version="1.0" encoding="UTF-8"?>
```

An *RSS* feed is a structured XML document with certain required elements.

■ The entire feed is contained in an rss element, which must have a version attribute.

■ Within the rss elements, there must be one and only one channel element. Within the channel element in Figure 8-2 you see a title, a link, and other general elements that apply to it. Then, you see a sequence of items within the channel. Each of the items has

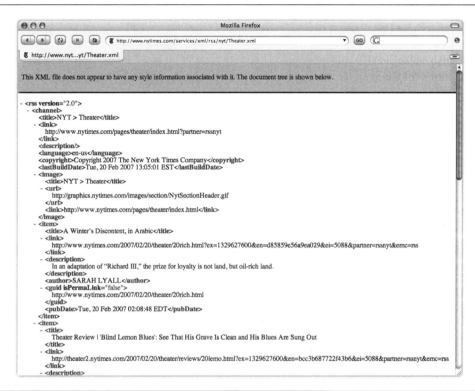

FIGURE 8-2   XML code for the *New York Times* RSS feed

its own link, title, and so forth. You will see how to parse them out in the section "Inside the Feed's XML Document."

■ In addition to the channel element, any number of item elements may occur. Each item element is a story, blog entry, or other component of the feed or channel.

Atom

The Atom format is not frozen the way RSS is. It is more powerful or complicated (depending on which side of the theological war you are on), and it is still evolving. The specification for the Atom format is available at http://www.atomenabled.org/developers/syndication/atom-format-spec.php. In Figure 8-3, you see an Atom feed in Safari.

This feed is generated automatically by the Blogger software. In Figure 8-4, you can see the beginning of the Atom XML document displayed in Figure 8-3.

The main elements of the Atom feed are the feed element and the entry elements.

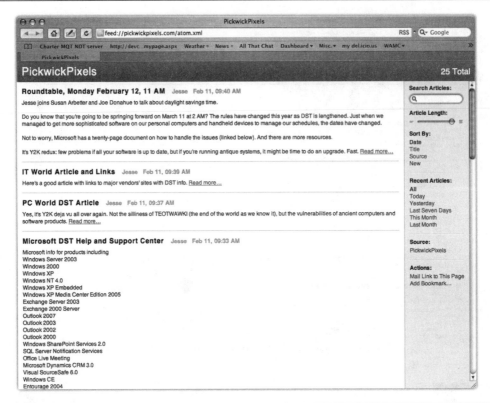

FIGURE 8-3 Blogger blog Atom feed in Safari

The feed element is comparable to the rss element in RSS. There is no channel element. Instead, the elements that would be in an RSS channel element are placed within the feed element itself. Atom has no item elements. They are, instead, called *entry elements*.

Categorize and Label a Feed

One of the things that makes feeds so useful is they can be created when the content is created. Rather than go back and mark up articles and text, the semantic elements can be created automatically, and then formatted appropriately by blogging or publication software. The addition of categories and labels adds value to the feed, and it represents an almost trivial amount of effort when the information is published. Figure 8-5 shows how a label can be attached to a Blogger posting. At the bottom of the posting, you select a label or type in a new one. (Labels are most effective when they are single words without spaces.)

As you can see in Figure 8-6, the labels for a posting are shown on the blog page. Clicking on the label automatically retrieves other posts with the same label.

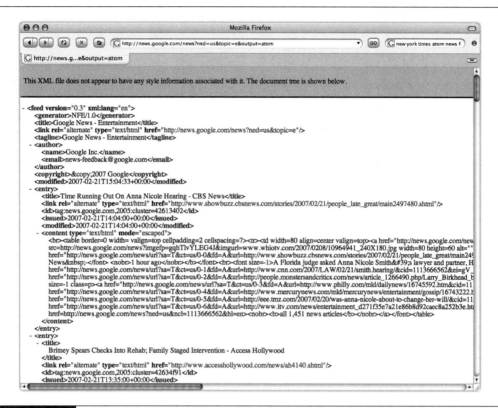

FIGURE 8-4   XML code for the Blogger Atom feed

A news feed reader, such as the one in Internet Explorer 7, can sort feed elements by categories (which is what the labels are), as shown in Figure 8-7. In addition, some blogging software such as Blogger can incorporate the label/category into the URL. In the Blogger style, add /-/<labelname> to the end of the URL. Thus, for a blog published at pickwickpixels.com, you can select postings with the label roundtable by entering

```
http://www.pickwickpixels.com/-/roundtable
```

Parse a Feed with PHP

In the previous chapter, you saw how to write a PHP script to execute a database query, and then parse the results. When you are dealing with a news feed, the "query" is implicit in the URL of the feed, so you have one less step. Also, because the data are returned as an XML document, your parsing and displaying of the data relies not on extracting rows from an SQL results table, but on parsing the XML. This section shows you how to do this.

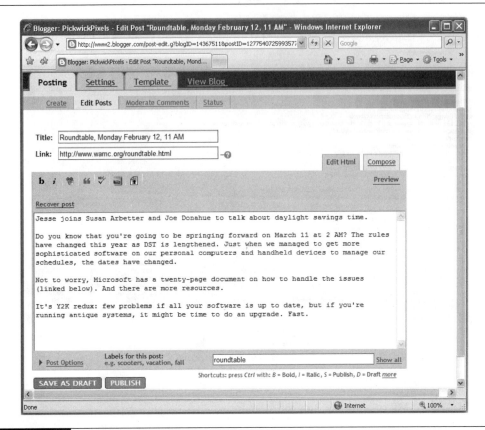

FIGURE 8-5   Add a label to a Blogger posting

> **NOTE**   *This section covers the basics for both RSS and Atom.*

Two files are included on the book's Web site that implement this example:

- index3.html is the starting page. It contains a form submitted to run the PHP script.
- parsefeed3.php is the script launched from the submitted form.

Inside the Feed's XML Document

That parsing of the XML document is built into the DOM module of PHP 5 and later.

> **NOTE**   *Before PHP 5, the DOM XML module was used. The examples in this book all assume PHP 5 and DOM, not DOM XML.*

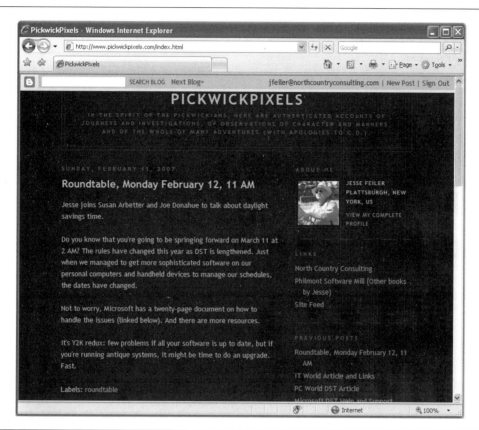

FIGURE 8-6   Labels show up on blogs

You can find the full documentation at http://www.php.net, but the basics are quite simple.

■ Get the XML Document

■ Convert it to a DOM Document in PHP

■ Generate Lists of Elements for Entries or Items

■ Process Each Element

Get the XML Document

First, you retrieve the XML document, usually by using a URL. The *curl library* of PHP is used to issue the call to get the contents of a URL and place the contents in a string.

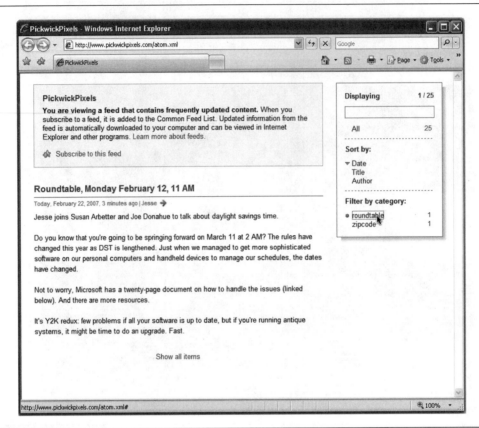

Categories/labels in Internet Explorer's news feed window

NOTE

The curl library is not always compiled into PHP if it is already installed on your computer. Check to see if the code works properly. If it does not, refer to the PHP documentation for instructions about enabling curl (http://us2.php.net/manual/en/ref .curl.php). Note, as in many PHP features, what was optional in an earlier release and required custom installation often is standard in a later release.

Here is the code to load the XML document:

```
$theURL =
  "http://www.nytimes.com/services/xml/rss/nyt/Theater.xml";

$c = curl_init($theURL);
curl_setopt ($c, CURLOPT_RETURNTRANSFER, 1);
$xml = curl_exec($c);
curl_close($c);
```

You can use this code exactly as is in your script. The only change you need to make is the particular URL you want to use. What the code does is to:

- create a curl handle ($c)
- initialize it with the URL
- set the option CURLOPT_RETURNTRANSFER to 1, so the string is returned
- execute the connection and transfer
- store the result in $xml
- close the connection.

You may hard-code a URL value such as this. You also may let users select from a list or type in a URL in the form submitted to start the process. In that case, use the same method shown in the previous chapter to pick up the value from the form. Assume the URL is in a text field called theFormURL. If this is the case, here is the code to set $theURL:

```
$theURL = $_REQUEST[theFormURL];
```

Convert It to a DOM Document in PHP

As noted in Chapter 4, an XML document consists of elements that can contain other elements. An element may have a value and it also may have attributes.

Here is the code to convert $xml to a DOM document:

```
$doc = new DOMDocument();
$doc->loadXML($xml);
```

This code is used without changes in your script.

Generate Lists of Elements for Entries or Items

In PHP, you usually manipulate the DOM elements by referring to their names and, sometimes, by their index number. In general, you start from the root element of the document, setting a variable that you can call $root to the root of the document:

```
$root = $doc->documentElement;
```

Next, you use a function called getElementsByTagName to retrieve all the elements with a given name. In an RSS feed, you usually want to retrieve all the item elements, so you use this code:

```
$theItems = $root->getElementsByTagName("item");
```

In the RSS feed, everything is contained within the rss element, and, within that, all items are contained within the channel element. By searching from the root, you automatically search within the rss and channel elements to get the items.

Did you know?

The PHP DOM Module Uses Objects for Its Implementation

You can use the code shown in this section without knowing the details of how it is implemented. But, if you are going to make changes, knowing exactly what you are dealing with can be particularly useful.

The DOM module in PHP is implemented using object-oriented programming (OOP) techniques. The functions are methods of classes, and the results are generally objects. *documentElement* is a property of the DOMDocument object ($doc), which you created and loaded with $xml. documentElement is a DOMElement object, so that is what is stored in $root.

DOMElement objects, like DOMDocuments, are descendants of the abstract class, DOMNode. The *DOMNode object* implements much of the hierarchical architecture of XML. Each DOMNode object has a parentNode (which can be NULL), as well as a DOMNodeList of childNodes (which also can be NULL). To access the data within a DOMNode (which includes DOMElement and DOMDocument objects), you use the nodeValue property.

getElementsByTagName is a method of DOMElement (and, thus, is accessible from $root). It returns an object that is a DOMNodeList. This is important when you begin to work with the returned elements. You do not get an array back from the getElementsByTagName method as you do in JavaScript.

To get an element from a DOMNodeList, you use the item() method of DOMNodeList. The items are numbered starting at 0, so you pass in the value of the particular item you want to the item method. If you want to determine how many items exist, you can access the length property of a DOMNodeList object.

If you want to iterate through all of the items in a DOMNodeList, you can use the PHP *foreach* statement. Normally used for arrays, foreach loops through each variable in an object. It behaves exactly as you would expect it to, short-circuiting some of the iteration code that, otherwise, you would have to build into a list or collection object.

In an Atom feed, you want the elements named entry, so this is the code you use:

```
$theEntries = $root->getElementsByTagName("entry");
```

The getElementsByTagName function starts from a given node in the XML document—in this case, this is the root element. It only searches within that element (and its child elements). You can see shortly why that matters.

Process Each Element

After you retrieve the entries or items, you can use foreach to loop through them and pick out the information you want. Here is the code to do that for an RSS feed:

```
foreach ($theItems as $anItem) {
  $theTitle = $anItem->getElementsByTagName('title')
    ->item(0)->firstChild->nodeValue;
  //do something with the data
  echo "anItem title:".$theTitle." <br>";
} // End of foreach loop.
```

And here is the Atom code. Both RSS and Atom use title elements in the same way.

```
foreach ($theEntries as $anEntry) {
  $theTitle = $anEntry ->getElementsByTagName('title')
    ->item(0)->firstChild->nodeValue;
  //do something with the data
  echo "anEntry title:".$theTitle." <br>";
} // End of foreach loop.
```

You are calling getElementsByTagName again, but, in this case, you are calling it on each item (or Atom entry) from the list. That limits its operation to the particular item from the feed. The code that sets $theTitle makes two assumptions:

- One and only one title is within a feed item. This is why item(0) from the DOMNodeList returned from getElementsByTagName works. If you want to handle a feed with items that do not have titles, you should check the length property of $anEntry or $anItem.

- It is assumed that within the single item/element returned in the DOMNodeList is a single child node that has a value, and that value is the title.

The code works as is, but if you modify it, you may need to take these assumptions into account.

This is the section of the script where you might choose to use other elements and attributes. In the Blogger label examples shown in Figure 8-5, 8-6, and 8-7, the label is implemented using the category element. Here is the relevant XML code:

```
<category scheme='http://www.blogger.com/atom/ns#'
  term="roundtable"></category>
```

You could retrieve all the labels by calling getElementsByTagName on a specific entry and looking for category tag names. You can parse the category elements as you want. The only difference in a case like this is, instead of looking for the nodeValue of an element, you need to pick up an attribute of the element—a *term* in the case of a Blogger label.

8

To pick up an attribute from a DOMElement, you use the getAttribute method. Here is how you would pick up the term attribute value:

```
$anEntry->item(0)->firstChild->getAttribute ('term');
```

If you are uncertain an attribute exists, you can use *hasAttribute* with the attribute name as a parameter to check that it exists before you try to retrieve its value:

```
if $anEntry->item(0)->firstChild->hasAttribute ('term') {
  $anEntry->item(0)->firstChild->getAttribute ('term');
}
```

Implement the Form to Launch the Script

The starting script contains the basic form. Here is the code. The key line is the action attribute of the form element, which is shown in italics.

```
<html xmlns="http://www.w3.org/1999/xhtml">
  <head>
    <title>Mashups Demo</title>
    <meta http-equiv="Content-Type" content="text/html;
      charset=iso-8859-1" />
  </head>

  <body>
    <h2 align="center"><font size="+2">
      Parse Feed Launch Page
    </font></h2>

    <form name="form1" id="form1" method="post"
      action="parsefeed3.php">
      <p><font size="-1"><input type="submit"
        name="Submit" value="Launch" />
      </font></p>
    </form>

    <p><font size="2">Copyright (c) 2007 Jesse Feiler,
      North Country Consulting. All Rights Reserved.
      For information, contact
      <a href="mailto:jfeiler@northcountryconsulting.com">
        Jesse Feiler</a>
    .</font></p>
  </body>
</html>
```

Implement the PHP Script to Parse the Feed

Putting it all together with the include files introduced previously, here is the script to parse the feed in the RSS version. (The Atom changes were shown previously.)

```php
<?php
  $page_Title = "Parse Feed";
  include ('Includes/PageTop.html');

  $theURL = "http://www.nytimes.com/services/xml/rss/nyt/
    Theater.xml";

  $c = curl_init($theURL);
  curl_setopt ($c, CURLOPT_RETURNTRANSFER, 1);
  $xml = curl_exec($c);
  curl_close($c);

  $doc = new DOMDocument();
  $doc->loadXML($xml);

  $root = $doc->documentElement;

  $theItems = $root->getElementsByTagName('item');

  foreach ($theItems as $anItem) {
    $theTitle = $anItem->getElementsByTagName('title')
      ->item(0)->firstChild->nodeValue;
    echo "anItem title:".$theTitle." <br>";
  } // End of foreach loop.

  include ('Includes/PageBottom.html');
?>
```

Create a Search Feed

Although many feeds change as their underlying Web sites change, they are relatively static in the sense that they represent given Web sites and data—a specific blog, for example, or a specific newspaper. Both Google and Yahoo! now let you create feeds on demand that represent the results of searches.

To create such dynamic search feeds, you would set $theURL used in the call to curl_init with a URL constructed as shown here.

In each case, replace the italicized text with your search query. Be careful of spaces and special characters, which can make the URL invalid.

8

Google atom search feed:

```
http://news.google.com/news?q=greyhounds&output=atom
```

Google RSS search feed:

```
http://news.google.com/news?q=greyhounds&output=atom
```

Yahoo! RSS search feed:

```
http://api.search.yahoo.com/WebSearchService/rss/
  webSearch.xml?appid=yahoosearchwebrss&query=greyhounds
```

Chapter 9

Use XMLHttpRequest, XML-RPC, REST, and JSON to Retrieve Data

How to...

- Understand Web Services
- Deal with Cross-Domain Scripting Issues
- Use XMLHttpRequest
- Implement an XML-RPC Retrieval
- Implement a REST Retrieval
- Implement a JSON Retrieval

You have seen how to retrieve data from a database, as well as how to obtain it from an RSS feed. Database retrieval lets you hone in on exactly the information you want. Parsing an RSS feed often gets you to the general area, and you may have to write code to get at what you want (although what you want may simply be the last *N* entries or whatever the feed itself is presenting).

Web services combine both worlds. You can use them to retrieve specific data from a data provider, which is almost always returned as an XML document. You do not need to know anything about the databases that may or may not be involved in serving up the data you receive. The Web service runs on a server and provides its data on demand to the client.

In this chapter, you see how some of the major protocols and data retrieval methods work. They can be used for purposes other than data retrieval, but in the context of mashups, data retrieval is normally what you do.

XMLHttpRequest and *script tags*, both of which are described in this chapter, are data retrieval methods. XML-RPC, REST, and JSON are protocols. You can mix and match them— for example, use XMLHttpRequest to send (and then receive) XML-RPC, REST, or JSON data.

NOTE *Other protocols are available to implement Web services. In particular, SOAP has been used for highly structured applications. In the mashup world, REST appears to be the protocol of choice, with some significant interest in JSON. Because REST can handle mashup needs and is simpler to implement than SOAP in many cases, SOAP is omitted from this chapter.*

How to ... Find More Information About XMLHttpRequest, XML-RPC, REST, and JSON

You can find information about XMLHttpRequest on the World Wide Web Consortium site at http://www.w3.org/TR/XMLHttpRequest. For XML-RPC, the primary resource is http://www.xmlrpc.com. There is a Yahoo! REST discussion group at http://tech.groups.yahoo.com/group/rest-discuss, and you can find more information about JSON at http://www.json.org/.

Understand Web Services

Since the beginning of the computer age, people have been struggling to connect computers, data, and programs to one another. The Internet and open standards have, in many cases, replaced closed and proprietary protocols. Mashups are just the latest chapter in this saga of interconnectedness.

Web services grew out of the architecture of the Web. Web servers originally just served up static pages. Over time, scripting and other programming tools were added to those servers, and dynamic pages were able to be created. Taken a step further, Web servers did more than just serve up pages. They were able to use the Web protocols to send data back and forth, to and from databases and other applications. The term "application server" came into use, and the whole set of technologies and architectures became known as *Web services*.

The two key protocols were *HTTP*, the transport mechanism, and *XML*, the lingua franca of data formatting. On top of these, almost anything could be built.

But obstacles arose when it came to implementing Web services. The complexity of the data that needed to be sent back and forth strained the HTTP headers. People felt obliged to standardize the requests and responses. A variety of protocols evolved that enabled people to send a request to a server and receive a response, where both request and response were more complicated than just an HTML page. Among the protocols that have become standard are XML-RPC, SOAP, and REST. Recently, JSON has been added to the list as an important player.

Deal with Cross-Domain Scripting Issues

With the exception of JSON, all these protocols rely on HTTP and XML (even JSON may use both HTTP and XML). You have already seen how to decode XML, so you should understand the basics of receiving responses. (In the following chapters, you can find more examples of decoding XML.)

Constructing the initial request, however, can be a matter of concern. The problem that has arisen is this: you initiate processing on a remote server when you send one of these requests. When the Web was simple, the only processing you were initiating was the transfer of an HTML file. With these protocols and technologies, you can initiate all sorts of transactions and operations.

The most recent versions of the major browsers enforce a ban on cross-domain scripting. This means you can only initiate a connection to the same server from which the page was downloaded. This restriction permits typical Web services applications to work—a continuing request/response set of transactions is between the user's browser and the server that is supplying the responses and generating Web pages.

While this works for the model in which a user interacts with a single server (perhaps a bank's Web server), it does not work for the mashup model in which you download the mashup start page and may continue by launching the mashup that begins by going out to a totally different server (Yahoo! or Google, for example) to retrieve the data to be used in the mashup.

You can handle this situation in several ways. You can set up a proxy on your server that can relay the request to the other server. For more information on this technique, see http://developer.yahoo.com/javascript/howto-proxy.html, which provides information specific to Yahoo!, but which you can modify for any other server you need. An example of this is shown in Chapter 14.

Another way of handling the matter is to modify your Web server (instructions for this are also provided on the Yahoo! page).

Still another way is to use the JSON format, which downloads data as a script element, thus avoiding the cross-domain scripting issue. While this sidesteps the cross-domain issue, it opens other potential security issues.

In short, issues are involved in cross-domain scripting. This is an area that is still evolving, and it is an area that tends to affect the use of the protocols described in this chapter, as well as the core of the new architecture known as Ajax (Asynchronous JavaScript and XML). But there are ways around the limitations. And, most important of all, for the many opportunities offered for productivity improvement within organizations (that is, within a single domain), the issue is moot.

 *"Attacking AJAX Applications" is available at http://www.isecpartners.com/files/iSEC-Attacking_AJAX_Applications.BH2006.pdf. This provides a good overview of the issues involved in cross-domain scripting.*

Use XMLHttpRequest

Much of the fuss is over the JavaScript XMLHttpRequest object, sometimes referred to as *XHR*. Introduced by Microsoft in Outlook Web Access 2000, XHR makes it easy to transfer text data to and from a server from a script within a page. In the traditional model, this has been done with HTTP requests generated from links or through forms where the request goes to the server and a new page is returned to the browser.

With XHR, the interaction between the server and the browser is controlled by a script on the current browser page. This means the page can be updated in part without having to be reloaded. This is how many of the Web 2.0 applications are implemented. You do not see a full page reload when you scroll a Google map because there is none: the only thing reloaded is the small map itself within the page.

XHR is an object you can access from JavaScript and other scripting languages. It can function asynchronously, which means the request for server interaction can be sent off and the script can continue with other processing until a response is received. All this is managed by the browser, so you do not have to worry about timing or threading issues as a general rule.

If you are not used to object-oriented programming (OOP) or to the use of callbacks, some of the concepts involved in XHR may be new to you. Fortunately, the object itself is so simple and what it does is so intuitive, if you are unfamiliar with the concepts, XHR is a good way to learn them.

You only need to think about two structural issues:

■ You create the XMLHttpRequest object and place it in a variable, which you can access throughout any parts of your JavaScript that may need to communicate with it or to access its data.

■ You create a callback function that will be called when the state of the XHR changes. You can then access its state and its data using the variable you set up.

Between the creation of the object and processing the callback, you do not touch the object at all.

NOTE *Full documentation of the XMLHttpRequest object is available from the World Wide Web Consortium site at http://www.w3.org/TR/XMLHttpRequest/.*

Constructing and Sending an XMLHttpRequest

As soon as you know the URL you want to access, you can construct an XMLHttpRequest object in your JavaScript code. The evolution of XHR that began with Microsoft has continued with implementations in other environments. The initial implementation used ActiveX technology in Internet Explorer 5 and 6. With Internet Explorer 7, as well as other browsers, the implementation is different. As a result, you need to test to see how the browser you are running in handles XHR.

Because the initialization calls are different in the two environments, the code needs to be enclosed in an if statement. The basic test is

```
if (window.XMLHttpRequest) {
  theXHR = new XMLHttpRequest();
} else if (window.ActiveXObject) {
  theXHR = new ActiveXObject("Microsoft.XMLHTTP");
```

Thus, here is the basic code to construct an XMLHttpRequest:

```
function createRequest (theURL) {
  if (window.XMLHttpRequest) {
    theXHR = new XMLHttpRequest();
  } else if (window.ActiveXObject) {
    theXHR = new ActiveXObject("Microsoft.XMLHTTP");
  }

  if (theXHR) {
    theXHR.onreadystatechange = doShowData
    theXHR.open ("GET", theURL);
    theXHR.send ();
  } else {
    //create customized error message or otherwise recover
    alert ("error in creating new XMLHttpRequest object");
  }
}
```

What happens here is you create a new object called *theXHR*. If this is successfully created, you then set an attribute and call two methods.

Set onreadystatechange

This attribute is a callback function. When the state of the XHR object changes, this function is called. Architecturally, this is the same as an onload or onclick handler—when a certain type of event occurs, this function is called. You see how to code this function in the next section.

Call open

The *open* method initializes the object and sets all the attributes to known values. It does not connect to a remote server. Four sets of parameters exist for this method. The first two are always required.

- Method. This is one of the following standard HTTP methods: GET, PUT, POST, HEAD, DELETE, and OPTIONS. Most commonly, you use GET or POST. This parameter is required.
- URL. This is the URL you want to access. This is also required.
- The third parameter determines whether the call is or isn't asynchronous. If it is set to true, the call is asynchronous and your script continues running after the call is made (but, remember, the call is not yet made in open—you are just setting it up). Most of the time you use asynchronous processing, and the default value for this parameter is true. You may omit the parameter.
- The fourth set of parameters consists of two: a user name and a password. You may supply both or only a user name—or neither.

Call send

To process the request, you call the *send* method. Send may have a single parameter (or none). The single parameter, if it exists, is either a DOMString or a document. If it is not null, it is the body of the entity to be sent.

Handling an XMLHttpRequest Response

The XMLHttpRequest object has a *readyState* attribute, which you can query at any time. The *onreadystatechange* attribute is the callback function you specify to be called whenever this value changes. The *doShowData* function is the function assigned to the onreadystatechange event. It is called whenever the state changes.

The XMLHttpRequest object has two attributes you care about: the readyState and the status. The readyState attribute can have any of five values:

- 0 = uninitialized
- 1 = open (the open method has been called, but nothing more)
- 2 = sent (the send method has been called, but no response has been received)
- 3 = receiving (the send method has been called and a response is being received)
- 4 = loaded (the send method has been called and a response is now completely received)

In your callback routine, you normally only want to check for readyState=4. Anything else is an internal state change that does not concern you.

The values of *status* are the standard HTTP status codes. The two most important are 404 (Not Found) and 200 (OK).

Your callback routine can often ignore every condition except readyState = 4 and status = 200.

Once you determine you want to process the data, you can use either the responseText attribute or the responseXML attribute to obtain it from the object. The first returns the response as a string, and the second returns it as an XML document object, which you can parse just as you would any other XML document object.

NOTE   *You can track state changes and report on errors, but, in general, in mashups and in many scripts, it is easier simply to handle the positive cases. Test thoroughly to make certain the calls are properly formatted, and then be sparing in your error-checking. Users may not understand or want to know what is happening under the hood.*

Here is the basic callback code:

```
function doShowData () {
  if (theXHR) {
    if ((theXHR.readyState == 4) && (theXHR.status == 200)) {
      document.getElementById ('theData').value = theXHR.responseText;
    }
  }
}
```

9

Putting It Together

Figure 9-1 shows a basic implementation of an XMLHttpRequest that is designed for testing. You can type in a URL at the top of the window. When you click the Run button, the object is created and sent off. The script displays the current value of readyState and status. In Figure 9-1, the Run button was just clicked and the request has been sent. The value of readyState is 2 (sent) and the status is 0.

In Figure 9-2, the request has been processed and the response is loaded. It is displayed in the window. As you can see, the readyState is 4 (loaded) and the status is 200 (OK).

The complete script is shown here. The id attributes for the fields in Figure 9-2 that display the readyState and the status are readyState and statusText; the id for the large field that can display data is theData. Note, after the request is created, the changes to the interface are governed simply by the callback routine.

```
<?xml version="1.0" encoding="iso-8859-1"?>
<!DOCTYPE html PUBLIC "-//W3C//DTD XHTML 1.0 Transitional//EN"
"http://www.w3.org/TR/xhtml1/DTD/xhtml1-transitional.dtd">
<html xmlns="http://www.w3.org/1999/xhtml">
<head>
```

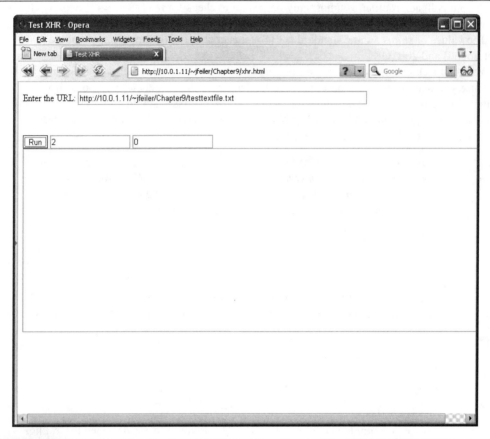

FIGURE 9-1 Create an XMLHttpRequest test script

```
<title>Test XHR</title>
  <meta http-equiv="Content-Type" content="text/html  ;
    charset=iso-8859-1" />
<script type="text/javascript">
 //<![CDATA[

  var theXHR = null;

  function doShowData () {
    if (theXHR) {
      // display results -- for debugging only
```

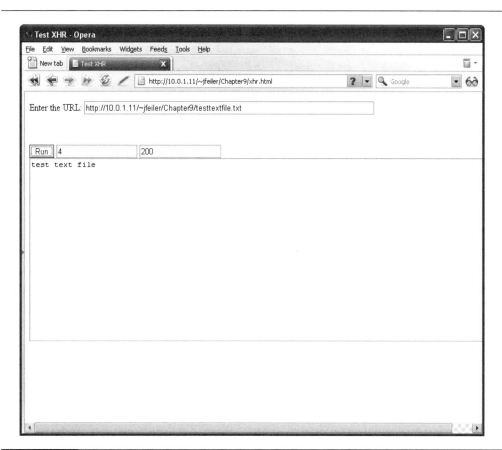

FIGURE 9-2   Completed XMLHttpRequest

```
    document.getElementById ('readyState').value =
      theXHR.readyState;
    document.getElementById ('statusText').value =
      theXHR.status;
  if ((theXHR.readyState == 4) && (theXHR.status == 200)) {
    document.getElementById ('theData').value =
      theXHR.responseText;
    }
  }
}
```

```
function createRequest (theURL) {
  if (window.XMLHttpRequest) {
    theXHR = new XMLHttpRequest();
  } else if (window.ActiveXObject) {
    theXHR = new ActiveXObject("Microsoft.XMLHTTP");
  }

  if (theXHR) {
    theXHR.onreadystatechange = doShowData
    theXHR.open ("GET", theURL);
    theXHR.send ();
  } else {
    //create customized error message or otherwise recover
    alert ("error in creating new XMLHttpRequest object");
  }
}

function doRun () {
  if (theXHR) {
    doShowData ();
  } else {
    theURL = document.getElementById ("theURL").value;
    createRequest (theURL);
  };
}

  //]]>
</script>
</head>

<body>
Enter the URL:
  <input name="theURL" type="text" id="theURL"
    size="80" maxlength="100"
  <button id="theButton" onclick="doRun()">Run</button>
  <input name="readyState" type="text" id="readyState"/>
  <input name="statusText" type="text" id="statusText" />
  <textarea name="theData" id="theData" cols="100"
    rows="20"></textarea>
</body>
</html>
```

With the ability to create and send requests from your JavaScript code, you are now in a position to request information from cooperating resources on the Web. In the balance of this chapter, you see how to use each of the three main protocols. You usually need a key or an ID to access these sites. In the third part of this book, you can see how to handle the security needs of the various services such as Google, eBay, Amazon, and Yahoo!. You also see the specific names and addresses to use in the calls.

> TIP
>
> *You can use a number of libraries to simplify XMLHttpRequest. The libraries handle cross-browser issues and other housekeeping matters for you, but they implement the same functionality shown here. Type **XMLHttpRequest library** into your favorite search engine to find current references.*

Implement an XML-RPC Retrieval

XML-RPC is a specification for making remote procedure calls, which dates to 1998 and is the simplest of the protocols discussed here. There is always a trade-off between simplicity and power, and XML-RPC is no exception to that rule. The simplicity of XML-RPC works and handles many cases. It also serves as a good example for the basic processing, which all these protocols do. So, even if you are using REST (described next), this section provides an overview of the basic architecture.

XML-RPC uses the HTTP POST request to send two sets of information:

- **Method name**   This is the name of the method invoked on the remote server (the *remote procedure* that is *called*).

- **Parameters**   Zero or more parameters to be passed to the remote procedure. They are not named: their positions determine their meaning. The documentation for the method you are calling will provide information about the parameters. This information is packaged in an XML document sent as the payload of the POST request. The structure of this document is simple:

```
<methodCall>
  <methodName>yourMethod</methodName>
  <params>
    <param>
      <!-- application specific data here -->
    </param>
  </params>
</methodCall>
```

Here is the sample XML document for the Flickr echo service. Although the values within the param sub-element of the params element are identified by order, not name, a param may contain a single value that itself can be a struct, as happens in this example. Within the struct there are one or more member elements, each of which has a name element and a value element. Thus, the basic idea of unnamed values is reimplemented at a lower level with name/value pairs.

9

In the sample code that is shown here, each of the member elements has a name element in which you would replace the underlined word with the specific name the method is expecting.

```
<methodCall>
  <methodName>flickr.test.echo</methodName>
  <params>
    <param>
      <value>
        <struct>
          <member>
            <name>name</name>
              <value><string>value</string></value>
          </member>
          <member>
            <name>name2</name>
              <value><string>value2</string></value>
          </member>
        </struct>
      </value>
    </param>
  </params>

</methodCall>
```

The response to an XML-RPC request is an XML document.

In part, because XML-RPC relies on positional parameters, it can be fragile in use. Today, the slightly more complex protocols described next are used more frequently.

NOTE *More information on XML-RPC is available at http://www.xmlrpc.com/.*

Implement a REST Retrieval

Because the parameters in a REST query are named, the syntax is more stable. The principle, however, is the same as for XML-RPC: identify the remote procedure (method) to be called, and pass in the parameters. You normally do this with an XML document, but the entire syntax can be entered into the URL (this is convenient for testing), or it can be used with XMLHttpRequest from your mashup code.

Here is a Yahoo! REST query:

```
http://api.search.yahoo.com/WebSearchService/V1/webSearch?
  appid=Test&
  query=plattsburgh&
  results=20
```

Because the parameters are named, you can place them in any order without worrying about creating a struct element. A REST response for the query shown here is an XML document. It is shown (abridged and formatted) here:

```
<?xml version="1.0" encoding="UTF-8"?>
  <ResultSet
    xmlns:xsi="http://www.w3.org/2001/XMLSchema-instance"
    xmlns="urn:yahoo:srch"
    xsi:schemaLocation="urn:yahoo:srch
    http://api.search.yahoo.com/WebSearchService/V1/
      WebSearchResponse.xsd" type="web"
    totalResultsAvailable="2280000"
    totalResultsReturned="10"
    firstResultPosition="1"
    moreSearch="/WebSearchService/V1/webSearch?
      query=plattsburgh&amp;appid=Test&amp;region=us">
    <Result>
       <Title>SUNY Plattsburgh</Title>
      <Summary>
         SUNY Plattsburgh is a state college...
      </Summary>
    </Result>

    <Result>
      <Title>Experience Plattsburgh, NY</Title>
      <Summary>
        Experience Plattsburgh, New York, the Lake City...
      </Summary>
    </Result>
  </ResultSet>
```

Some services let you request output in a different format from the incoming request. For example, the Flickr request shown here uses REST for the request, but it requests output in xmlrpc format:

```
http://flickr.com/services/rest/?method=flickr.test.echo&
  format=xmlrpc&
  foo=bar&
  api_key=yourKey
```

If you look at the Flickr and Yahoo! REST requests, you can see the basic syntax is the same, but the specific parameter names vary. You need to look at the documentation for each service to see what the URL and parameter names should be.

9

Implement a JSON Retrieval

JavaScript Object Notation (JSON) is a newcomer to the data interchange world. JSON shares the spirit of RSS in that it is declared to be final with its first release: it is not extensible, and what it can do it does from the start.

JSON can represent data in a structured manner just as XML can, but it is far less complex— just as RSS is less complex than ATOM. It uses JavaScript syntax to describe the data that consist of values. The data may also contain names. In the case of name/value pairs, you have an unordered collection in which the elements are identified by name. In the case of unnamed values, you have what is essentially an array in which order or sequence may matter. A JSON *object* is enclosed in brackets, { and }, with the values or name/value pairs separated by commas. The whole is recursive, so you can have arrays inside collections inside arrays, and so forth. JSON uses the JavaScript object notation, so it is parsable JavaScript.

This means JSON is also a way to get around the cross-domain scripting issue. You can declare an HTML script element and download JSON to it. The limitations of executing scripts across domains do not apply if you include a script from another location. The fact that the URL you provide for the location of the remote script to be included happens to run a script on the other server is immaterial. You are not using syntax recognized as running a script, and what you are receiving is not a resultant XML file, but, rather, some JavaScript.

This does not handle the security concern—malevolent JSON code can contain JavaScript beyond the JSON syntax and you can wind up with it in your SCRIPT element. Normally, you do not execute the SCRIPT element, but you evaluate it to extract the data. Still, a theoretical danger exists.

You can specify JSON as an output format for Flickr (and other services). Here is a REST request to the flickr.test.echo method with the output requested as JSON:

```
http://www.flickr.com/services/rest/?
  method=flickr.test.echo&
  format=json&
  api_key=yourKey
```

And here is the JSON output (formatted for readability):

```
jsonFlickrApi(
  {"method":
    {"_content":"flickr.test.echo"},
     "format":{"_content":"json"},
     "api_key":{"_content":"yourKey"},
     "stat":"ok"
    }
  )
```

NOTE   *More information is available at http://www.json.org/.*

Chapter 10

Use XHTML to Structure the Mashup Pages

How to...

- Understand the Need for XHTML
- Use XHTML Structures
- Use XHTML Syntax
- Validate XHTML Code

This part of the book began by looking at the design principles that are part of mashup technologies, starting with XML. It ends by examining *XHTML,* which is the replacement for HTML and is written in XML. XHTML incorporates not only the XML syntax, but also the principles of structured data described in Chapter 3.

NOTE   *Examples in this book so far have typically presented HTML code, not XHTML code (the XML and DOCTYPE lines described in this chapter were omitted). The code in the balance of the book presents XHTML code, unless otherwise noted.*

Understand the Need for XHTML

HTML has been a key component of the Web. Its remarkably simple markup syntax enabled people all over the world to easily build Web pages. Almost from the beginning, HTML authors have been divided into two groups: those who write raw HTML code and those who use graphical HTML editors to generate their code. Originally, there was no choice: you had to write raw HTML code. But, because it was not particularly difficult, people were able to do so—and they did so to create millions of pages. (There is no count today of the number of pages on the Web, but estimates are generally in excess of 20 billion pages.)

How to ... Find More Information about XHTML

The primary source for information about XML and XHTML, as well as many other Web standards, is http://www.w3c.org, the site of the World Wide Web Consortium (W3C). Some common standards are administered elsewhere (RSS, for example), and some technologies have been maintained by other organizations for a variety of reasons. But, http://www.w3c.org is normally your first stop for the last word on Web standards.

HTML's Ease of Use Is a Two-Edged Sword

There were several reasons why it was not particularly difficult to write raw HTML code. The first was that HTML was simple. Concepts such as frames were not part of the original specification (and fierce battles were waged over whether frames were a good idea). The second reason for the ease of writing HTML pages was this: the browsers focused on displaying the information the coder meant to code. A certain amount of forgiveness for syntax ambiguities was built into browsers. Sometimes, this was because the specification itself was ambiguous. In other cases, widespread misinterpretation of the specification (or common careless errors) caused strict browser interpretation of syntax to fail. In such cases, the browser was sometimes blamed (it couldn't have been the HTML code written by your friend), and if the common error or misinterpretation was easy to adjust by reprogramming in the browser, that was sometimes what happened.

In yet other cases, browsers had errors in them. Sometimes, they were outright errors, but in other cases they, too, were the result of varying interpretations of the standards. It was not easy to explain to people why Browser *A* did not display their Web page properly, while Browser *B* did—and that, in fact, Browser A was correct while Browser B and the Web page itself were wrong. In several cases, browsers were modified to handle incorrect or ambiguous syntax that was improperly handled by another browser that managed to display the faulty code. Even today, browsers sometimes are tweaked to handle HTML that is not standards-compliant on pages that are important to large numbers of users.

It is not just that the various permutations of standards, browsers, and creative HTML coding cause headaches and battles for coders, browser authors, and users. Perhaps even more significant is that, increasingly, Web pages are being generated dynamically in response to user queries (which is how mashup pages are generated). Even static Web pages are often generated in part by automated processes ranging from elaborate formatting routines to simple Save as HTML commands in word-processing applications. These pages proliferate quickly and "creative" HTML generated by automatic code generating routines can suddenly cause browsers to apparently misbehave (although the misbehavior is in the code-generating routines).

The XHTML Solution

XHTML is a response to all these concerns. XHTML tightens up HTML and enforces some rules that were stylistic recommendations in HTML and that now are requirements. HTML pages will exist on the Web for a long time to come, and browsers will handle them just as they do today. This means ambiguous and even incorrect behavior of browsers and syntax of Web pages will still work. But, in the future, new pages can be constructed using XHTML in a more controlled environment.

XHTML is the replacement for HTML; it is also based on XML. XML provides the strictness and structure, while HTML provides the existing mark-up concepts. Because XHTML, with its XML heritage, has stricter rules than HTML, it generally is more compatible with a variety of browsers and operating systems than is HTML. More important, validation routines are available to validate the XHTML code. You see how to use them in the section "Validate XHTML."

Why This Matters for Mashups

Most mashups have two basic pages: the start page and the mashup results page. The *start page* may be built dynamically but, frequently, it is hard-coded and static. You can code the start page by hand in HTML (even including some questionable syntax). You can then test it on a variety of browsers and operating systems until you are reasonably certain that most of your potential users can use the page as you intend.

But the *results page* is another matter. The results page is created when the mashup runs, and it normally contains different data each time the mashup runs, so you have no way to test it on various browsers and operating systems. You can write your mashup's code to generate HTML and pray . . . or you can use XHTML.

By using XHTML, you are able to run the mashup and take the source code produced and run it through a validator. Although this is not an iron-clad guarantee of compatibility, the chances are good if the XHTML code you generate from your scripts validates, then it will display properly in many browsers and OSs, no matter what data are shown. (This applies to all XHTML code, not just the code used for mashups.) In the early days of personal computers, the "blue screen of death" cropped up periodically when the operating system gave up the ghost. In the world of Web browsers, a comparable phenomenon could be called the "white page of death"—a blank Web page. Validating your mashup result code can help minimize the chances of this happening.

Not All Browsers Are Standards-Compliant

Using XHTML and abiding by standards can certainly help your pages display properly, but that does not always happen. Not everyone runs the latest browsers or operating systems—finding five-year-old (or even older) software running in everyday use is not unusual.

Furthermore, although the standards process has been instrumental in the development of the Internet, it is not always as speedy as people would like. Sometimes, browsers are not compliant because they have introduced new concepts that have not yet made it through the standards process.

The most commonly used browsers today are the various versions of Internet Explorer and Firefox, with other Mozilla browsers, Opera, and Safari having smaller, but significant, presences. If you test your code—mashup or other HTML—against the most commonly used browsers on the most commonly used operating systems, you are usually in good shape.

What Makes XHTML Code Tricky for Mashup Results Pages?

The mashup results page is normally produced by JavaScript or PHP (or both). This code may be located in several different scripts. As a result, making certain that XHTML is well-formed and valid can be tricky unless you take a variety of precautions in preparing both the code and the scripts. Overall, the strategy is to design the XHTML code with care and to implement your scripts in such a way that what is happening and what code they are intending to generate is completely clear.

The Sample XHTML Code

In this chapter, the start page for the mashup to be created in Chapter 11 is used as an example. Figure 10-1 shows that simple page.

   Here is the code for that page. Throughout the balance of this chapter you will walk through the details of the code.

```
<?xml version="1.0" encoding="iso-8859-1"?>

<!DOCTYPE html PUBLIC "-//W3C//DTD XHTML 1.0 Transitional//EN"
   "http://www.w3.org/TR/xhtml1/DTD/xhtml1-transitional.dtd">

<html xmlns="http://www.w3.org/1999/xhtml">

<head>
   <title>Chapter 11 Start Page</title>
   <meta http-equiv="Content-Type" content="text/html;
```

10

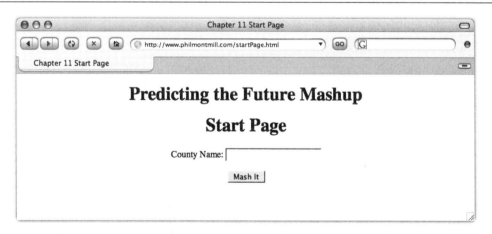

The Chapter 11 start page

```
      charset=iso-8859-1" />
  </head>

<body>
  <h1 align="center">Predicting the Future Mashup</h1>
  <h1 align="center">Start Page</h1>
  <form name="mashupForm1" id="mashupForm1" method="post"
    action="predutFuture.php">

    <p align="center">
      County Name         :
      <input name="countyName2" type="text" id="countyName2"
        maxlength="50" />
    </p>

    <p align="center">
      <input type="submit" name="Submit" value="Mash It" />
    </p>

  </form>
</body>

</html>
```

Use XHTML Structures

XHTML documents have three primary structures:

- An XML declaration (recommended, but not required)
- A DOCTYPE declaration (required)
- A single root element, which is an html element (required)

NOTE
XHTML uses lowercase element and attribute names. When these names are used in text or headings in this book, they are capitalized in accordance with normal editing standards. When these names are used in text or code in their syntactic meanings, they are set in lowercase.

The XML Declaration

The *XML declaration* is recommended as the first line of all XML documents, but it is not required. If you encounter parsing errors with your mashups on this line of code, you can remove it. The XML declaration identifies the version of XML being used in the document, as well as the encoding method. Common encodings are UTF-8, UTF-16, and iso-8559-1. The encoding specified in the XML declaration must match the encoding of the document itself. UTF-8 and UTF-16 encodings are automatically detected from the document itself by the XML processor, so if you use either of those encodings, you do not have to worry about specifying an encoding method. Also, if you use a tool such as Dreamweaver, the defaults are set automatically when you create an XHTML document.

Here is the XML declaration for the start page:

```
<?xml version="1.0" encoding="iso-8859-1"?>
```

The XML declaration may also provide information about whether this is a standalone document and how white-space characters should be handled.

Your XML declaration will almost always be exactly the same as this one. Note the delimiters consist of two-character pairs: `<?` and `?>`.

The Document Type Declaration (DTD)

Following the XML declaration, you must have a document type declaration (DTD). These have three varieties:

- The *transitional* DTD enables you to use HTML formatting:

```
<!DOCTYPE html
   PUBLIC "-//W3C//DTD XHTML 1.0 Transitional//EN"
   "http://www.w3.org/TR/xhtml1/DTD/xhtml1-transitional.dtd">
```

- The *strict* DTD requires you to move your formatting out of the XHTML document and to use cascading style sheets (CSS):

```
<!DOCTYPE html
   PUBLIC "-//W3C//DTD XHTML 1.0 Strict//EN"
   "http://www.w3.org/TR/xhtml1/DTD/xhtml1-strict.dtd">
```

- The *frameset* DTD is used for XHTML pages that include frames:

```
<!DOCTYPE html
   PUBLIC "-//W3C//DTD XHTML 1.0 Frameset//EN"
   "http://www.w3.org/TR/xhtml1/DTD/xhtml1-frameset.dtd">
```

One of these must appear at the beginning of your XHTML document. You do not need to change the text. Most of the examples in this book use transitional XHTML (as do a large number of XHTML pages). Because formatting can be included in the document, just as is done with HTML, the transition from HTML to XHTML transitional is the easiest to make.

10

The HTML Element

A single root element, the *html* element, must reference a namespace for the document. Normally, you use this code without alteration:

```
<html xmlns="http://www.w3.org/1999/xhtml">
```

The last line of the XHTML document closes this element with this code:

```
</html>
```

Use XHTML Syntax

As described in Chapter 4, you saw the simple basics of XML:

- XML documents consist of *elements*
- Elements begin and end with *tags*
- Elements may have *attributes*
- Values of attributes are enclosed in quotes
- Capitalization matters

Because XHTML is an XML application, all these principles apply. In addition, you should be aware of further aspects of XHTML syntax. Many of them relate to the specific purposes of refining, extending, and tightening HTML syntax for XHTML.

XHTML Documents Can (and Should) Contain Comments

The syntax for a comment is shown here:

```
<!-- This is a comment -->
```

Worth noting is that the space between the last word and the end of the comment is required. Although these spaces are optional in many cases, a good idea is usually to leave a space before any syntactic elements that immediately precede the closing > in an element.

Not only can XHTML documents contain comments, they also should do so, unless they are generated automatically and are not designed for people to maintain them.

XHTML Element Syntax

Because XML is case-sensitive, the decision was made that all XHTML elements and attributes would be in lowercase letters. In HTML, *<form>* and *<FORM>* are the same syntactic element. Rather than ask people to remember capitalization rules for each element, the rule is simple: lowercase.

All XML elements must have a starting tag and be properly closed. Typically, the close is a closing tag. Thus, a nonempty paragraph must look like this:

```
<p>
This is some paragraph text.
</p>
```

Some elements are defined as being allowed to be empty. In the start page example used in this chapter, the form submitted has two *input* elements: one is the button and the other is a text field. Although each element has attributes, neither has any content. Thus, the text field syntax can be written as follows:

```
<input name="countyName2" type="text" id="countyName2" maxlength="50" />
```

There is no closing tag. Instead, the single tag is terminated with a / before the >. This syntax terminates the element. Common elements that can be closed in this way are the br (line break), li (list item), img (image), and hr (horizontal rule) elements.

TIP *If you terminate the element with a slash at the end of the start tag as shown here, leave a space before the slash. Some browsers do not properly render the valid XHTML code if the space is missing.*

The last aspect of XHTML element syntax you should be aware of is the use of the name and id attributes. The name attribute will be deprecated in a future release. For the time being, you should use the id attribute in your scripts. A good idea is to provide a name attribute with the same value as the id attribute while the standard and browsers are in flux.

10

XHTML Attribute Syntax

Like elements, attributes are in lowercase letters. Each attribute has a value, and that value must be quoted whether or not it appears to be a string. For example, in the input element that is a text field in the start page, you may think the maxlength attribute is a number, but it is not. Here is the line of code (note the quotation marks around 50):

```
<input name="countyName2" type="text" id="countyName2"
  maxlength="50" />
```

Attributes always have a value. In HTML, you could write the following and it would be legal.

```
<input type="checkbox" checked name="access" value="Restricted" />
```

The checked attributed is said to be *minimized* here. In XHTML, you would need to assign a value to it because all attributes have values. Here is the corresponding XHTML code:

```
<input type="checkbox" checked="checked" name="access" value="Restricted" />
```

Documents Should Be Well-Formed and Valid

Well-formed XML documents have a single root element, which may contain other elements. If it is well-formed, each element is properly terminated, and all attributes are enclosed in quotation marks. Further, if an element contains other elements, they are properly nested.

A *valid XML document* ensures that the specific elements, attributes, and uses of the DTD are correct. Thus, a well-formed XHTML document with a single root element that is not an html element is not valid. Likewise, a well-formed XHTML document that sets a paragraph element's *sound* attribute (which does not exist) is not valid.

The distinction between well-formed and valid documents matters particularly when you are debugging your code, running it through a validator, and looking at the results in a browser. By knowing the distinction, you may be able to hone in on why your XHTML code looks the way it does (rather than the way you want it to look).

Validate XHTML

By tightening the syntax, XHTML can be shown more reliably by browsers. Even more important, XHTML can be parsed more easily by scripts and applications. This includes validators that can be more thorough with XHTML than with HTML. You should get in the habit of validating your XHTML code periodically. You do so by going to http://validator.w3.org. This is the validator of the W3C page, which works with a variety of standards and has links to other validators you can use.

As you can see in Figure 10-2, you can supply the URL of a page you have already uploaded to the Web or you can upload a file directly. You can also type in short sections of code to validate them on the fly.

How to ... Validate Your Mashup Result Page During Development

One strategy for generating valid and well-formed XHTML on your results page is to use an incremental top-down approach, described in the examples of this book. Begin by creating a mockup of the results page using your favorite XHTML/HTML editor. Use dummy data, and design the page as you like. Then, run this XHTML through the validator to make certain your code is valid.

Once it is valid, put the code aside where you can refer to it. As you build the mashup and its scripts, begin by generating the mockup page from your scripts.

Next, begin to replace the dummy data with actual data. At each stage, once you have run the scripts and produced the mocked up page, you can display the source code in your browser, and then copy it to another document (or even paste it into the W3C validator). Thus, you can continue to use the validator even though your code is generating the XHTML.

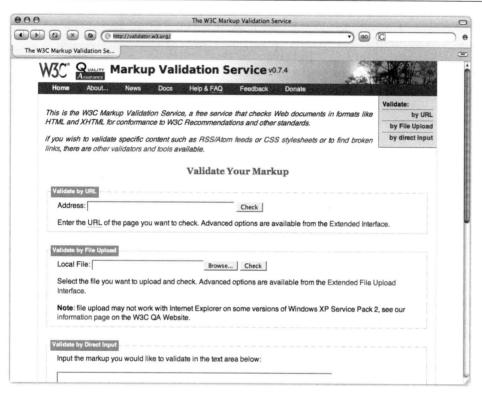

FIGURE 10-2   W3C validator page

As you can see in Figure 10-3, you can select a number of options. Because the validation process is so fast, using the most basic validation without verbose output, showing the source code, and so forth, is often easiest. If your XHTML code validates, that is the end of the matter.

If the code does not validate, as shown in Figure 10-4, you are given some clues as to what is wrong.

You can ask the validator to show you the source code it has read, as shown in Figure 10-5. Depending on what you are using to edit the XHTML, this may be a useful tool. You can be certain the line numbers in the errors are the line numbers in the source code the validator shows you.

In the example shown here, the closing tag for the <p> element that starts on line 17 has been removed. As always in compilers and validators, you should take the specific error message somewhat generally. In this case, the error of the missing closing tag is encountered at the end of the end tag for the form element on line 19. You may need to look one line before or after the error message. However, do not go much further afield than that. Also, if you have a number of errors (particularly involving unclosed elements or mismatched quotes), correct the ones you see at the top of the list and rerun the validator. Gradually, the validation will be clearer.

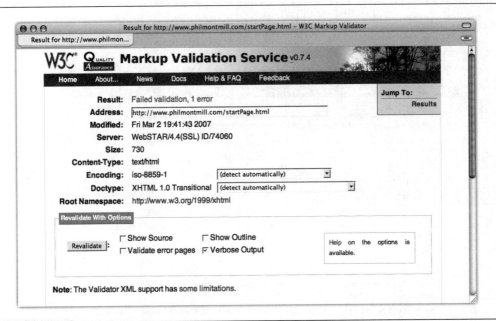

FIGURE 10-3 Validator options

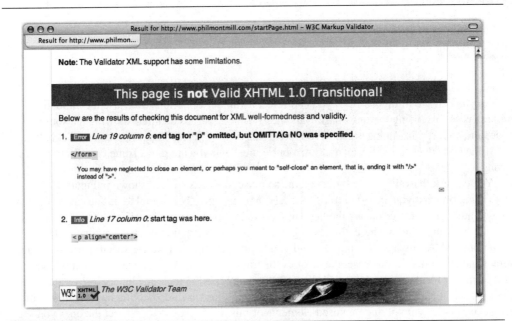

FIGURE 10-4 Validator provides feedback

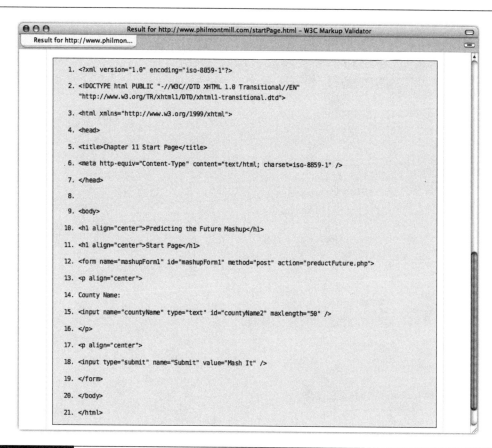

```
1. <?xml version="1.0" encoding="iso-8859-1"?>

2. <!DOCTYPE html PUBLIC "-//W3C//DTD XHTML 1.0 Transitional//EN"
   "http://www.w3.org/TR/xhtml1/DTD/xhtml1-transitional.dtd">

3. <html xmlns="http://www.w3.org/1999/xhtml">

4. <head>

5. <title>Chapter 11 Start Page</title>

6. <meta http-equiv="Content-Type" content="text/html; charset=iso-8859-1" />

7. </head>

8.

9. <body>

10. <h1 align="center">Predicting the Future Mashup</h1>

11. <h1 align="center">Start Page</h1>

12. <form name="mashupForm1" id="mashupForm1" method="post" action="productFuture.php">

13. <p align="center">

14. County Name:

15. <input name="countyName" type="text" id="countyName2" maxlength="50" />

16. </p>

17. <p align="center">

18. <input type="submit" name="Submit" value="Mash It" />

19. </form>

20. </body>

21. </html>
```

FIGURE 10-5   Validator source code listing with line numbers

10

Part III

Build Your Own Mashups

Chapter 11

Implement a Basic Mashup

How to...

- Decide on Your Mashup's Objective
- Identify the Data and the Keys
- Get Access to the Data
- Regroup
- Design the User Interface
- Implement the Mashup
- Implement the Starting Page

In this part of the book, you put the various technologies from Part II together to build your own mashups. Some of the code shown here was discussed previously when the technologies were introduced in Part II, so the basics of the technologies are not repeated here (except for specific APIs for mashups, such as Google Maps).

This chapter outlines the most basic mashup development process—providing an ad hoc combination of data from two sources based on a user's request. Mashups generally provide two or more data sources, sometimes with one of the data sources being a re-presenting of another one (for example, a map displaying a location also shown as text). In this chapter, there is no mapping and no querying of an online service, such as eBay or Amazon. Instead, a local database is used to drive the mashup and to deliver the data the user requests. This mashup involves no calls to external APIs across the network, so duplicating it should be possible in almost any environment, provided you have a Web server, such as Apache, and a MySQL database, as well as PHP installed. (The Web server can be your own computer.)

You also see how to download data and load them into MySQL using different file formats and various loading options.

In the next two chapters, you see how to use the Google mapping APIs to implement another mashup, as well as how to add mapping to this mashup.

The URLs for free downloads of those products are http://www.apache.org, http://www.mysql.org, and http://www.php.net.

Decide on Your Mashup's Objective

This mashup combines population data from the U.S. Census with employment data from the U.S. Department of Labor to show the population and labor force for any given county in the United States.

Identify the Data and the Keys

The data for this mashup reside in a local MySQL database. The two main data files are among the many large sets of data that can be downloaded from U.S. government Web sites and used to help drive mashups. The first data set is data from the Census Bureau about population for each county in the U.S. The second data set is data from the Department of Labor's Bureau of Labor Statistics about the labor force.

The keys that allow matching are numeric codes for each state and for each county within a state. These values are set by the Federal Information Processing Standards (FIPS) and maintained by the National Institute of Standards and Technology (NIST). The FIPS publications can be found at http://www.itl.nist.gov/fipspubs/. Any time you are using federal information or information derived from it, you may need to use these standards to identify the data. In practice, you do not have to worry about the details because all you will care about most of the time is matching data in two locations using a common FIPS code (whatever it is).

The Population Data

The basic source for U.S. population data is the Census Bureau—http://www.census.gov. The Web site provides an excellent resource for data, along with estimates (adjusted data) and projections (into the future). Because such a vast amount of data is on the site, and because the FIPS codes are consistent throughout the government, using census data in your mashups is easy. What is not always so easy is finding the data you want in a downloadable format—the site is particularly geared to interactive users. Here are the steps to follow to get the data file for this mashup. As you can see, you will be able to select many other data sets for other mashups. Begin with the Census Web site, as shown in Figure 11-1.

American FactFinder, at the left of the Census site, is the gateway to the data you need. Once you navigate to American FactFinder, ignore the forms that let you select ZIP codes and the like. Instead, choose Download Center at the left, as shown in Figure 11-2.

Inside the Download Center, select the data set in which you are interested. The most basic census data are in summary file 1, as shown in Figure 11-3. (Click the links at the left to learn more about the census data sets.) The most important item to know is the decennial census provides actual enumeration of the people in the United States by having a relatively short form completed. Smaller samples are then asked to fill in a longer form. That is the meaning of the "100-Percent" and "Sample" annotations.

As you can see from Figure 11-4, you can select many different levels of detail for the data. In this case, the level of detail is the county level, so you choose All Counties (050). Choose the download method for Selected Detail Tables with the radio button at the bottom, and then click Go. (Eschew summary file formats—you want the detailed table, so your mashup can manipulate it, and then you can summarize it yourself, if necessary.)

11

TIP *When matching data, make certain the granularity of the data matches. In this case, the labor force data are collected by county, so it makes sense to match them to county-level census data. Census tracts (which are normally smaller than counties) would be useless, as would state-level data.*

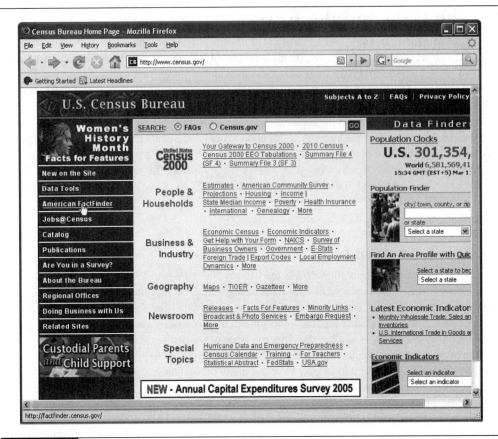

FIGURE 11-1   Start with http://www.census.gov

As you can see in Figure 11-5, you now can choose what data you want. For this mashup, "P12. Sex by Age (Total Population)" is the data needed. It is presented based on the geographic entity you chose in the previous step.

You highlight the table you want, and then click the Add button. You can create any download file you want with any combination of tables (but the data are all aggregated by the geographic entity you chose.) Click Next to continue to the confirmation.

Figure 11-6 shows the confirmation for the download. Double-check you are downloading the geographic entities (*geographies*) you want and the number of entities is more or less what you expect. Then, click Start Download.

The download begins and you see the standard dialog, as shown in Figure 11-7, which lets you decide what to do with the file (this depends on the system preferences you set). The names of these files can be long—in this example, it is dc_dec_200_sf1_u.zip—and they can change

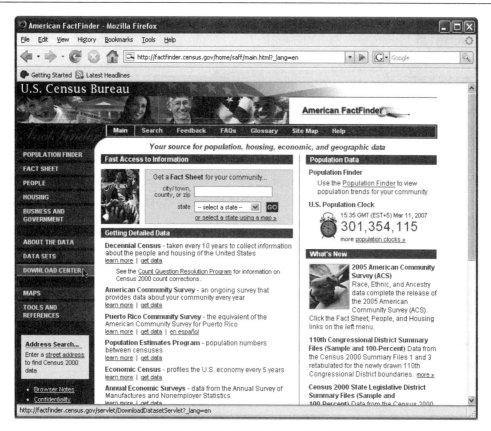

FIGURE 11-2   Go to the Download Center

because you are creating them dynamically based on your choices of data and geographies. Make sure you note where you put the file. If you cannot locate the file, check your browser's downloads window to find it.

Inside the zipped archive, you find three files:

- ■ A read me file gives you additional information about the data set. It normally is brief (readme_dec_2000_sf1.txt in this example)

- ■ Another file provides the FIPS codes (dc_dec_2000_sf1_u_geo.txt in this example—look for geo in the name)

- ■ Finally, the data file provides the data you will be handling (dc_dec_2000_sf1_u_data1.txt in this case).

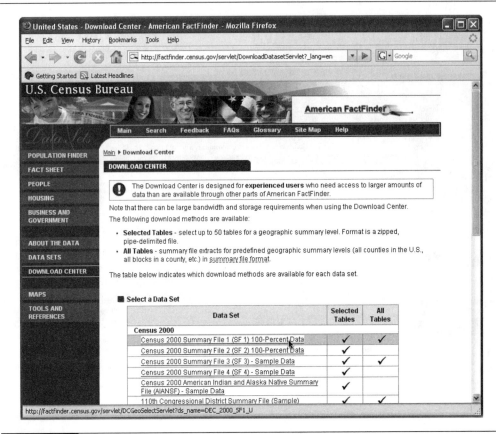

FIGURE 11-3 Select Summary File 1 (SF1)

If you download census data in this way, you will have text data delimited with | between each field. The beginning of the file is shown in Figure 11-8. Look at the beginning of the file before you begin to load the data into a database so that you know what you are dealing with.

The Labor Force Data

The data from the Bureau of Labor Statistics (BLS) are reachable from the main site at http://www.bls.gov. Go to the State and Local Unemployment Rates page at http://www.bls.gov/lau/home.htm, as shown in Figure 11-9.

If you scroll down that page, you can find the county data available for download, as you can see in Figure 11-10.

The data used in this mashup are the first data set, the county data for 2005. You can download them as text, which is basically the same process as you saw for the census data. If you choose to download the zipped archives, you get an Excel spreadsheet with the data. You can open it in

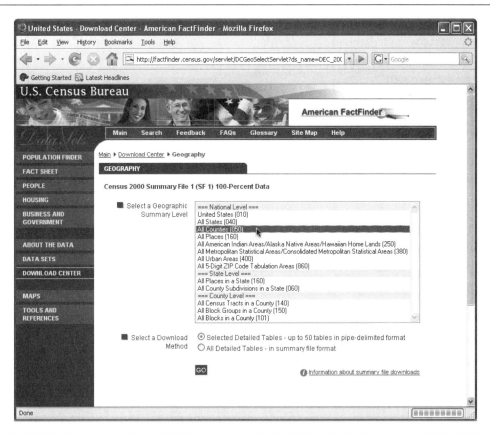

FIGURE 11-4   Select the level of detail

Excel, and then save it as a comma-separated value (CSV) file or a tab-delimited text file (which is what was done in this example). The Excel spreadsheet contains column headings describing the data. Before saving the spreadsheet as a tab-delimited file, delete the heading rows from the spreadsheet.

The beginning of the data file is shown in Figure 11-11, after it was saved as a tab-delimited file.

TIP   *Some applications "help" you when saving comma- or tab-delimited data. In particular, they may insert commas into numeric values. If at all possible, save the data as a text file, not as a spreadsheet where such formatting may come back to haunt you. If you are using a spreadsheet, you might want to change the column cell formatting to numeric with no commas to make the data as plain as possible for their later import into MySQL.*

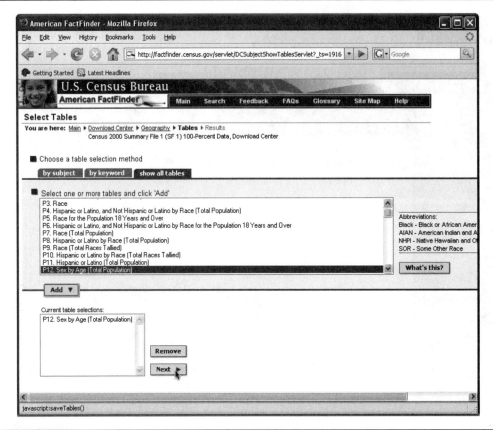

FIGURE 11-5 Select your data

Get Access to the Data

Now that you have selected the data and downloaded them, you need to load them into MySQL. Launch MySQL as described in Chapter 7, and then create a new database to use for your mashups. In this book's code, the database is called *mashups_sql*, but you can name it anything you want. (Using the same database, table, and column names may make it easier to reuse the code.)

There will be two tables: one for the population data and one for the labor force data. You could merge the data at this point, but that would make the mashup somewhat irrelevant. The database structure assumed you will dynamically join the two tables, based on the user's mashup request.

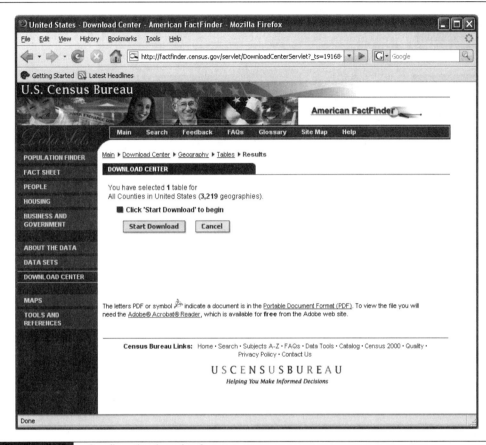

FIGURE 11-8   The downloaded data file

Load Labor Force Data into MySQL

The labor force data are a little easier to load than the population data, so they are the first to be loaded. There are two steps: creating the table and loading the data. These processes were described in Chapter 7. This section provides you with the specific code to use with these data sources.

Create the Table

This table will contain all the fields from the data file. The first step is to create a table with all the fields from the data file. Putting them in the same order makes loading easier.

```
create table labor_force (
  LAUS_Code varchar (25),
  State_FIPS_Code Varchar (2),
  County_FIPS_Code Varchar (3),
  County_Name Varchar (60),
  year varchar (4),
  blankcol varchar (10),
  labor_force mediumint unsigned,
  employed mediumint unsigned,
  unemployed mediumint unsigned,
  rate float);
```

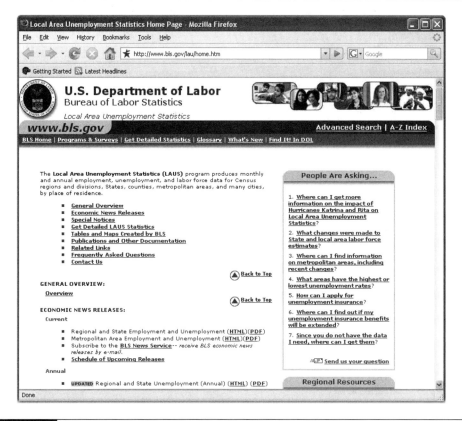

FIGURE 11-9   Go to the state and local unemployment rates page

Load the Data

Because you are loading all the fields in sequence, the load data command merely needs to specify the input file and the field terminator (the tab character). Note, the fully qualified file name includes some spaces that are escaped with a \. Depending on where you downloaded the file, your file name and path may differ. The file name in this example is

```
Users
  jfeiler
    Documents
      Projects
        CurrentProjects
          Mashups
            Labor force by county 2005
              laucnt05.txt
```

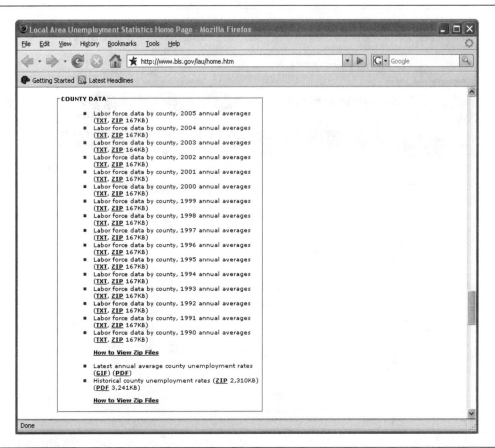

FIGURE 11-10 Select county data

FIGURE 11-11 Save the Excel file as tab-delimited text

Here is the command to use:

```
load data infile local
  /Users/jfeiler/Documents/Projects/CurrentProjects/
    Mashups/Labor\ force\ by\ county\ 2005/laucnty05.txt
  into table labor_force
  fields terminated by '\t';
```

When the data are loaded, look at them in MySQL (remember to use the LIMIT clause), as shown in Figure 11-12. (If your data do not load properly, review the section in Chapter 7 on loading a database. Pay attention to the "lines terminated by" clause, which is frequently the culprit.)

Load Population Data into MySQL

This step consists of creating a table, and then loading the data into it.

Create the Population Table

You need to create a table for the population data from the Census Bureau. More information is in the downloaded file than you need, so your table only needs to have the state and county FIPS codes, and the population. The table created has total population, as well as population by sex. It also has the country name field in it.

Note, when you access the data, you are performing a join on the population and labor force tables. You need to be able to display the county name, so it must be available in one (or both) of those tables or in a separate table joined to them. In this database design, the county name is provided in both tables, so that either can be reused in other contexts. As a result, the data are not normalized, because the combination of state/county/country name is repeated.

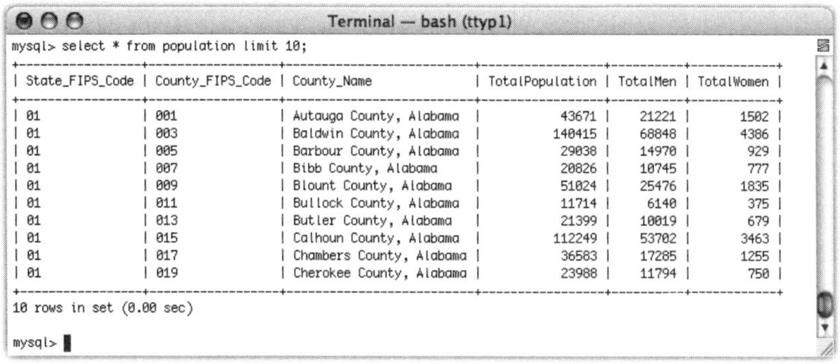

11

```
mysql> select * from population limit 10;
+----------------+-----------------+-------------------------+-----------------+----------+------------+
| State_FIPS_Code | County_FIPS_Code | County_Name            | TotalPopulation | TotalMen | TotalWomen |
+----------------+-----------------+-------------------------+-----------------+----------+------------+
| 01             | 001             | Autauga County, Alabama |           43671 |    21221 |       1502 |
| 01             | 003             | Baldwin County, Alabama |          140415 |    68848 |       4386 |
| 01             | 005             | Barbour County, Alabama |           29038 |    14970 |        929 |
| 01             | 007             | Bibb County, Alabama    |           20826 |    10745 |        777 |
| 01             | 009             | Blount County, Alabama  |           51024 |    25476 |       1835 |
| 01             | 011             | Bullock County, Alabama |           11714 |     6140 |        375 |
| 01             | 013             | Butler County, Alabama  |           21399 |    10019 |        679 |
| 01             | 015             | Calhoun County, Alabama |          112249 |    53702 |       3463 |
| 01             | 017             | Chambers County, Alabama|           36583 |    17285 |       1255 |
| 01             | 019             | Cherokee County, Alabama|           23988 |    11794 |        750 |
+----------------+-----------------+-------------------------+-----------------+----------+------------+
10 rows in set (0.00 sec)

mysql>
```

FIGURE 11-12   Review the loaded data

Here is the MySQL code to create the population table:

```
create table population (
  State_FIPS_Code varchar (2),
  County_FIPS_Code varchar (3),
  County_Name Varchar (60),
  TotalPopulation mediumint (8),
  TotalMen mediumint (8),
  TotalWomen mediumint (8));
```

Load the Population Data

First, refer to Figure 11-8 to look at the actual data. Note, two records are at the beginning of the file that should not be loaded. The first contains field names (such as GEO_ID , GEO_ID2, and P012016). The second contains more readable field names with spaces in them.

When you come to the third record, which is the beginning of the actual data, notice the fields do not map perfectly into the database table. Not only are the age and sex breakdowns omitted, but the first geography identifier (the value 05000US01001 in the first record) is not used, and the second geography identifier (the value 01001 in the first record) contains both the state and county FIPS codes. (You can determine this from reading the documentation and looking in the geo file, which is part of the download package.)

Thus, the load data command not only needs to specify the basics of what table is to be loaded with what data file, but also:

- how the fields are delimited
- how the records are delimited
- that the first two records are to be ignored
- some data munging needs to be done

Chapter 7 describes how to do these manipulations. Here is the actual load data command to use:

```
load data infile local
  '/Users/jfeiler/Desktop/dc_dec_2000_sf1_u_data1.txt'
  into table population
  fields terminated by '|'
  lines terminated by '\n'
  ignore 2 lines
  (@var1, @geocode, @var2, County_Name,
    TotalPopulation, TotalMen, TotalWomen)
  set State_FIPS_Code=left(@geocode, 2),
    County_FIPS_Code=right(@geocode, 3);
```

```
● ● ●                          Terminal — bash (ttyp1)
mysql> select * from labor_force limit 10;
+-----------+-----------------+------------------+---------------------+--------+---------+-------------+----------+------------+------+
| LAUS_Code | State_FIPS_Code | County_FIPS_Code | County_Name         | year   | blankcol | labor_force | employed | unemployed | rate |
+-----------+-----------------+------------------+---------------------+--------+---------+-------------+----------+------------+------+
| CN010010  | 1               | 1                | "Autauga County, AL" | 2005  | NULL    |       23454 |    22680 |        774 | 3.3  |
| PA011000  | 1               | 3                | "Baldwin County, AL" | 2005  | NULL    |       76943 |    74410 |       2533 | 3.3  |
| CN010050  | 1               | 5                | "Barbour County, AL" | 2005  | NULL    |       10872 |    10303 |        569 | 5.2  |
| CN010070  | 1               | 7                | "Bibb County, AL"    | 2005  | NULL    |        8897 |     8539 |        358 | 4    |
| CN010090  | 1               | 9                | "Blount County, AL"  | 2005  | NULL    |       26437 |    25618 |        819 | 3.1  |
| CN010110  | 1               | 11               | "Bullock County, AL" | 2005  | NULL    |        3772 |     3445 |        327 | 8.7  |
| CN010130  | 1               | 13               | "Butler County, AL"  | 2005  | NULL    |        9162 |     8625 |        537 | 5.9  |
| PA010250  | 1               | 15               | "Calhoun County, AL" | 2005  | NULL    |       54019 |    51837 |       2182 | 4    |
| CN010170  | 1               | 17               | "Chambers County, AL" | 2005 | NULL    |       16498 |    15649 |        849 | 5.1  |
| CN010190  | 1               | 19               | "Cherokee County, AL" | 2005 | NULL    |       12127 |    11663 |        464 | 3.8  |
+-----------+-----------------+------------------+---------------------+--------+---------+-------------+----------+------------+------+
10 rows in set (0.02 sec)

mysql>
```

FIGURE 11-13 Look at the loaded data

Once you load the table, you can check it by retrieving data, as shown in Figure 11-13. Note, the LIMIT clause prevents too much output.

Test

Before continuing, check to see if the data are working the way you want them to. You already looked at each table, but use MySQL to type in a query that performs a join, as shown in Figure 11-14. A lot of redundant data are here because the test is to make certain you are picking up the correct values from each table.

Once you are certain your joins work, you can ignore the redundant data, as shown in Figure 11-15.

11

```
● ● ●                          Terminal — bash (ttyp1)
mysql> select population.State_FIPS_Code, population.County_FIPS_Code, labor_force.State_FIPS_Code, population.County_FIPS_Code,
    -> population.County_Name,TotalPopulation,labor_force
    -> from population, labor_force
    -> where population.State_FIPS_Code = labor_force.State_FIPS_Code and
    -> population.County_FIPS_Code =labor_force.County_FIPS_Code limit 10;
+-----------------+------------------+-----------------+------------------+---------------------+-----------------+-------------+
| State_FIPS_Code | County_FIPS_Code | State_FIPS_Code | County_FIPS_Code | County_Name         | TotalPopulation | labor_force |
+-----------------+------------------+-----------------+------------------+---------------------+-----------------+-------------+
|               1 |                1 |               1 |                1 | Autauga County, Alabama  |          43671 |       23454 |
|               1 |                3 |               1 |                3 | Baldwin County, Alabama  |         140415 |       76943 |
|               1 |                5 |               1 |                5 | Barbour County, Alabama  |          29038 |       10872 |
|               1 |                7 |               1 |                7 | Bibb County, Alabama     |          20826 |        8897 |
|               1 |                9 |               1 |                9 | Blount County, Alabama   |          51024 |       26437 |
|               1 |               11 |               1 |               11 | Bullock County, Alabama  |          11714 |        3772 |
|               1 |               13 |               1 |               13 | Butler County, Alabama   |          21399 |        9162 |
|               1 |               15 |               1 |               15 | Calhoun County, Alabama  |         112249 |       54019 |
|               1 |               17 |               1 |               17 | Chambers County, Alabama |          36583 |       16498 |
|               1 |               19 |               1 |               19 | Cherokee County, Alabama |          23988 |       12127 |
+-----------------+------------------+-----------------+------------------+---------------------+-----------------+-------------+
10 rows in set (0.08 sec)
```

FIGURE 11-14 Check that the database functions as you expect it to

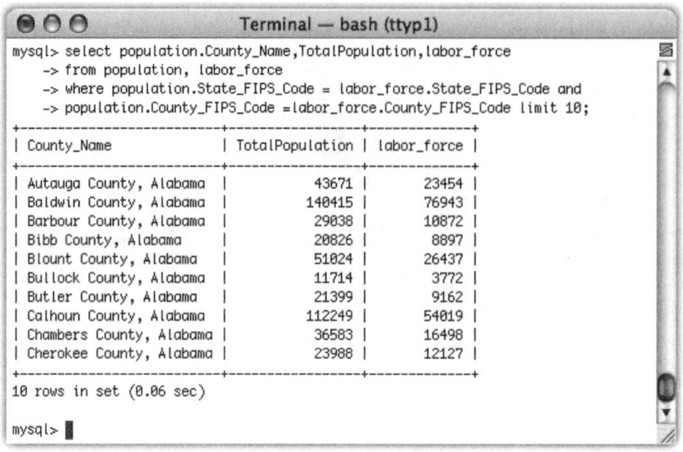

FIGURE 11-15 Retest with only the columns you care about

Regroup

After loading the data and testing the database, you may need to regroup. Perhaps the keys do not match up. Perhaps you have two different levels of granularity in the data. This is the time to confirm that the data side of the mashup works.

Design the User Interface

Most mashups have two main components: a start page and a page that displays the result of the mashup. It makes sense not to design the interface until after you have tested (and regrouped). As you experiment with the data, you may discover you need more or fewer input fields for the user. In this case, it is clear you need the user to specify the county and the state. For the purpose of this mashup, those are specified by numbers. You can use PHP to populate selection lists, so the user can choose states and counties. Or, the start page might have a list of counties and states. Whatever you do, you need to pass the county and state to the mashup.

Implement the Mashup

Even though you have tested, until the mashup runs, you may need to change the interface to add or remove data elements that need to be passed to the mashup. For this reason, it is easier to start by programming the mashup.

Using the principles outlined in Chapter 7, this mashup uses include files for the top and bottom of the page. Here are the include files. First, PageTop.html. Note, it is incomplete and relies on the main script to complete its elements.

```
<?xml version="1.0" encoding="iso-8859-1"?>
  <!DOCTYPE html PUBLIC "-//W3C//DTD XHTML 1.0 Transitional//EN"
    "http://www.w3.org/TR/xhtml1/DTD/xhtml1-transitional.dtd">
  <html xmlns="http://www.w3.org/1999/xhtml">
  <head>
    <title><?php echo $page_title; ?></title>
    <meta http-equiv="Content-Type" content="text/html;
      charset=iso-8859-1" />
  </head>

  <body>
    <h1 align="center">Jesse Feiler's Mashups Book</h1>
    <h1 align="center"><?php echo $page_title;?></h1>
    <br>
```

Next is the MySQLLogin.php script. You need to customize this script for your user name and password. You may also need to customize it for your host and database names.

```
<?php
  $DB_User = 'yourUserName';
  $DB_Password = 'yourPassword';
  $DB_Host = 'localhost';
  $DB_Name = 'mashups_sql';
  $dbc = @mysql_connect ($DB_Host, $DB_User, $DB_Password) or
    die ('Could not connect to MYSQL:'.mysql_error());
  @mysql_select_db ($DB_Name) or
    die ('Could not select the database:'.mysql_error());

  ?>
```

At the bottom of the main script, include MySQLLogout.php:

```
<?php
  mysql_close(); // Close the database connection.
?>
```

And, finally, PageBottom.html closes the page:

```
<br>
  <p>Copyright (c) 2007 Jesse Feiler,
    North Country Consulting. All Rights Reserved.
```

11

```
  </p>
  <p>For information, contact
    <a href="mailto:jfeiler@northcountryconsulting.com">
      Jesse Feiler
    </a>.
  </p>
</body>
</html>
```

Testing the script at this stage makes sense. Here is how you can create the script so dummy text is displayed. If this does not work, in most cases, something is wrong with an include file. Check spacing, punctuation, and so forth. If you do not quickly see the problem, remove code until you get to an absolutely bare-bones page that works. Then begin adding in code until you find the problematic line. This test version of the file performs no database accesses, so you can safely remove the login and logout files, if necessary, for testing.

All this page does is display the word test, as well as the headers and footers. You can test it by putting it in your Sites folder (or wherever your Web server documents are kept), and then typing in its name. Remember to terminate the name with .php.

```php
<?php
  $page_title = "Chapter 11";
  include ('./Includes/PageTop.html');
  include ('./Includes/MySQLLogin.php');

  $resultText = 'test';
  echo $resultText;

  include ('./Includes/MySQLLogout.php');
  include ('./Includes/PageBottom.html');
?>
```

If this works, you can add the database call. For now, you can hard-code the state and county, as shown in the underlined code. The query has been split onto several lines for readability on the page, as well as in the actual code. It can be written more compactly with the "here is" style described in Chapter 6. If the query fails, you can remove some of the AND clauses. You will get more data back without the qualifications of the AND clauses you remove, but you hone in on the syntax errors. Note, also, the query itself is echoed back, so you can see what you are constructing and debug it that way.

```php
<?php
  $page_title = "Chapter 11";
  include ('./Includes/PageTop.html');
  include ('./Includes/MySQLLogin.php');
```

```
// Query the database.

$state = 1;
$county = 1;

$query = "SELECT population.County_Name, TotalPopulation,
  labor_force ";
$query .= " FROM population, labor_force ";
$query .= " WHERE (population.State_FIPS_Code = '".$state."')";
$query .= " AND ";
$query .= " (labor_force.State_FIPS_Code = '".$state."')";
$query .= " AND ";
$query .= " (population.County_FIPS_Code = '".$county."')";
$query .= " AND ";
$query .= " (labor_force.County_FIPS_Code = '".$county."')";
$query .= " LIMIT 10";

echo $query;

$result = mysql_query ($query);

// Get the data.
$row = mysql_fetch_array ($result, MYSQL_NUM);

$CountyName = $row[0];
$Population = $row[1];
$WorkForce = $row[2];

$resultText = $CountyName." population=".$Population.",
  work force=".$WorkForce;
echo $resultText;

include ('./Includes/MySQLLogout.php');
include ('./Includes/PageBottom.html');
?>
```

Once this works, remove the echo of $query, and remove the hard-coding of the state and county. You pick them up from fields in a form, so change those lines as follows:

```
$state = $_REQUEST['state'];
$county = $_REQUEST['county'];
```

Implement the Starting Page

The last step is to implement the starting page. You need a form that calls the php script and has fields for the state and county. Here is that file with the customizations for this particular mashup underlined:

```xml
<?xml version="1.0" encoding="iso-8859-1"?>
  <!DOCTYPE html PUBLIC "-//W3C//DTD XHTML 1.0 Transitional//EN"
    "http://www.w3.org/TR/xhtml1/DTD/xhtml1-transitional.dtd">
  <html xmlns="http://www.w3.org/1999/xhtml">
  <head>
  <title>Chapter 11</title>
  <meta http-equiv="Content-Type" content="text/html;
    charset=iso-8859-1" />
  </head>

  <body>
    <h1 align="center">Jesse Feiler's Mashups Book</h1>
    <h1 align="center">Chapter 11</h1>
    <form name="form1" id="form1" method="post"
      action="GetBLSCensusData.php">
      <p align="center"><font size="-1">Select state for data retrieval:
        <input name="state" type="text" id="state" size="10"/>
        </font>
      </p>
      <p align="center"><font size="-1">Select county for data retrieval:
        <input name="county" type="text" id="county" size="10"/>
        </font>
      </p>
      <p align="center"><font size="-1">
        <input type="submit" name="Submit" value="Look Up" />
        </font>
      </p>
    </form>
    <p><font size="2">Copyright (c) 2007 Jesse Feiler,
      North Country Consulting. All Rights Reserved.
      For information, contact
      <a href="mailto:jfeiler@northcountryconsulting.com">
        Jesse Feiler</a>.
      </font>
    </p>
  </body>
</html>
```

Chapter 12

Use the Google Maps API

How to...

- Get Access to the Google Maps API
- Create the Basic Mapping Page
- Create a Map
- Identify a Location with a GLatLng
- Use a Geocoder
- Create a Marker
- Add Text to a Marker
- Wrap It Up in PHP

The remaining chapters in this book are in pairs: the first of each pair discusses a specific mashup technology, such as Google maps, and the second walks you through the process of creating a mashup using that technology, as well as the technologies described in Part II.

For many people, mashups started with the Google Maps API. Other mapping *APIs* are available today, including Yahoo! Maps Web services, at http://developer.yahoo.com/maps/. (Yahoo! APIs are discussed in Chapters 16 and 17, which explore the Flickr site.) All mapping APIs are basically the same: they take a location and plot it on a map. A marker can be used to pinpoint the location, and you can add text to the marker. The maps can be zoomed and moved around. You can also generally switch between maps, aerial or satellite photos, and composite maps.

Maps are a powerful tool for visualizing information. In addition to the location of a site, a map can easily show clusters of data, which is the case of the political contributions mashup shown in the following chapter. Geographic clusters are not always evident from text data—nearby locations may be in different states or ZIP codes, but the little markers on a map unambiguously show clusters of data.

Get Access to the Google Maps API

The first step to using the Google Maps API is to go to http://www.google.com/apis/maps/ and click the link to sign up for a Google Maps API key, as shown in Figure 12-1.

Previously in this book, you saw how to access sites with public data, so you have not needed keys to download data. In the case of APIs, you generally need a key to enable you to use the API. Terms of service exist to which you must agree for the use of the key. Although most of these APIs are available without payment for many purposes, certain high-volume uses and other cases require payments. The keys are unique to you, your application, or even the URL from which your mashup is launched. If you are using the Google Maps API in several mashups located on different servers, you may need different keys. Because using a key has no charge, this is not a problem.

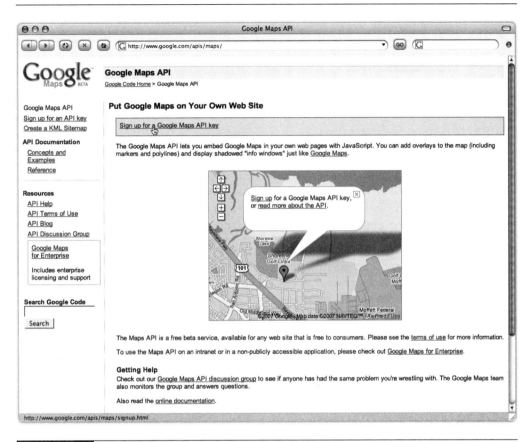

FIGURE 12-1   Sign up for a Google Maps API key

In code samples throughout this book, you can see references to yourKey. This is always a placeholder for the API key you need to register for.

When you click the link to sign up for a Google Maps API, you are prompted to agree to the terms of service and to specify the URL for the Web site on which the key is to be used. After you click the SUBMIT button, you see a confirmation screen with your key on it, as shown in Figure 12-2.

The key is a long string of numbers and characters. Carefully copy-and-paste it into a secure location, so you can find the key when you need it. Also on this page is the URL for which the key is valid, as well as some sample code in a box. Copy the sample code, and then paste it into a blank HTML document.

Immediately save the HTML document and place it in your Web folder, either on a server or on your local computer, and then attempt to open it in a browser, as shown in Figure 12-3.

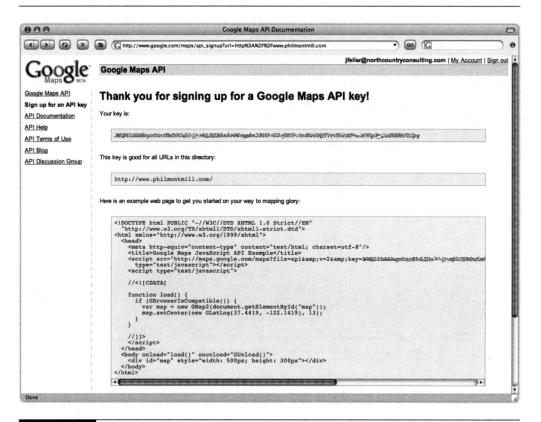

FIGURE 12-2   API key confirmation screen (with API key data erased)

Do not make any changes to the code you paste into the document: it should run exactly as is. If it does not, troubleshoot the problem now: magic does not happen in the world of software. One potential problem is something may be wrong with your publishing environment. If you have not published an HTML page to that server or directory, take an existing page (or create something such as a standard "Hello World" page) and verify that you can publish it. Check that your browser is current and that JavaScript is not turned off in the browser. Then, go to the Google Maps API site (http://www.google.com/apis/maps/) and look in the documentation and discussions to see if you can find any information. Failing that, participate in a discussion and pose your question. You must get past this basic point to proceed.

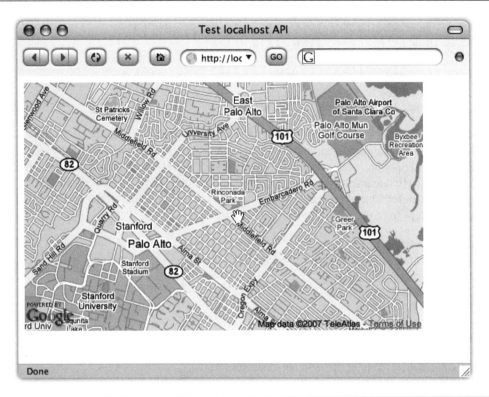

FIGURE 12-3   Try the Google Maps API sample code.

Create the Basic Mapping Page

The code you have just run is the most basic mapping code. In addition to the normal beginning and ending code, three sections appear in every mapping page you create:

- You include the basic Google mapping script
- You write your own script to manipulate your map and data
- You write the HTML that will display the map

Here is the complete sample code with annotations to show you what is happening. The code begins with standard HTML document headers, as shown here. The only two changes made in this code are the addition of a title for the page and the obscuring of the actual key value.

```
<!DOCTYPE html PUBLIC "-//W3C//DTD XHTML 1.0 Strict//EN"
    "http://www.w3.org/TR/xhtml1/DTD/xhtml1-strict.dtd">
<html xmlns="http://www.w3.org/1999/xhtml">
<head>
  <meta http-equiv="content-type" content="text/html;
    charset=utf-8"/>
  <title>Test localhost API</title>
```

Next, you include a *script element,* which is an external script loaded with the src attribute. Note, the src attribute loads the script from the maps.google.com server. It includes the version number and, most important, your unique Google maps key. This script element is used exactly as is for all the HTML documents that use this key (that is, all the HTML documents that will reside in the domain for which you registered the key). This script contains all the code to manipulate the maps from the Google side.

```
<script
    src="http://maps.google.com/maps?file=api&amp;v=2&amp;
      key=yourKey"
    type="text/javascript">
</script>
```

Next, you write a script of your own, which is normally written directly into the page, although you could include it with the src attribute from another location you control. The important point is this is your script, and not Google's script.

```
<script type="text/javascript">

//<![CDATA[

function load() {
  if (GBrowserIsCompatible()) {
    var map = new GMap2(document.getElementById("map"));
    map.setCenter(new GLatLng(37.4419, -122.1419), 13);
  }
}

//]]>
</script>
```

In the example script, a single function tests for browser compatibility, and then creates a map in the element called map, which is accessed with the document.getElementById function. This is the code you will change and expand for your own purposes. In the remainder of this chapter, you find the primary functions and classes you use in your own script.

Following the script is the end of the head element and the body element. In the body element, the onload handler is set to the function declared in your script. The onunload handler is set to a Google function, GUnload, that releases memory. In your mapping scripts, you normally call the GUnload function and, most often, you call your own load function.

Finally, a div element with a named id (map) and a given size is declared. Note, in the load function, document.getElementById is used to access this HTML element. You name graphical elements in the body of your HTML code and access them in this way from your script.

```
</head>

<body onload="load()" onunload="GUnload()">
  <div id="map" style="width: 500px; height: 300px"></div>
</body>

</html>
```

Create a Map

The Google Maps API documentation is located at http://www.google.com/apis/maps/documentation/. Examples and discussions are there, as well as sample code. The heart of the documentation is the API documentation itself, and the most important part of that is the documentation of the GMap2 class. You have already seen the most basic code for creating a map: you call a constructor to create a map. Next, you usually center the map on a particular location. Here is the code from the example that creates the map:

```
var map = new GMap2(document.getElementById("map"));
```

The map you create is normally stored in a variable because you need to access it throughout your script. In the example, the variable is local to the load function. In the examples you see in the next chapter, as well as in your own mashups, the variable into which you place the map is likely to be global to your script, so you can access it repeatedly as you process data. The constructor for a GMap2 object takes, at the least, an HTML container into which the map is placed. Normally, that is a div element, which is identified with an id attribute. Options are described in the Google documentation, but this is sufficient for most cases.

When you create a map, you often add controls to it. The most common controls are *map controls* and *maptype controls*. The map control is the set of controls that lets you move up or down by clicking arrows, as well as zoom in or out by clicking the + or − control. The maptype control lets you choose among map, satellite, or hybrid maps. To add these controls to a map, as soon as it is created, issue these calls:

```
map.addControl (new GSmallMapControl());
map.addControl (new GMapTypeControl());
```

12

You have other choices than these. Instead of GSmallMapControl, you can add GLargeMapControl. Or, you can use a GSmallZoomControl, which has only the zoom buttons or a GScaleControl. The best way to familiarize yourself with these is to experiment. Many people start with and stay with the GSmallMapControl, as shown here.

Identify a Location with a GLatLng

After you create the map in the example, you need to set its center point. The code that sets its center point is shown here:

```
map.setCenter(new GLatLng(37.4419, -122.1419), 13);
```

The setCenter method takes a single parameter, which is a point on the Earth expressed in latitude and longitude. This is a GLatLng object that is constructed inline in this code. The code in the example is equivalent to writing the following two lines of code:

```
var myLatLng = new GLatLng(37.4419, -122.1419)
map.setCenter (myLatLng, 13);
```

The setCenter method requires a GLatLng object as its first parameter. It may optionally have a zoom factor (13, in the example) and a map type. In the next chapter's examples, you see how to set other zoom factors.

Now you have seen the basics: how to create a map, how to create a GLatLng object identifying a location on Earth, and how to center the map.

Use a Geocoder

Latitude and longitude are the generally accepted ways of identifying a point on the Earth's surface. But, in much of the data you want to map, you do not have those values. This is where geocoding comes in. A *geocoder* converts an address to latitude and longitude. If you are going to do that, you need to create a GClientGeocoder object in your script. You need only one such object, and you can reference it as you need to while your script runs. If you need a geocoder, you typically create it when you initialize the map (usually in a load function). Thus, the standard code for a load function may look like this:

```
function load() {
  if (GBrowserIsCompatible()) {
    map = new GMap2(document.getElementById("map"));
    map.setCenter(new GLatLng(37.4419, -122.1419), 13);
    geocoder = new GClientGeocoder();
  }
}
```

Two variables are accessible from anywhere in the script. They should be declared at the beginning of your script as follows:

```
<script type="text/javascript">
  //<![CDATA[
  var map = null;
  var geocoder = null;
```

To use the geocoder, you pass an address into its getLatLng method along with a dummy callback function that is used by getLatLng. Here is the code in line-by-line detail. Note, in the Google examples, callback routines are typically coded inline. For clarity, the callback routine is coded separately in this example.

```
var addressPoint = null;
var address = null;
// add your code to set address to some value
geocoderCallback = function(point) {
  if (!point) {
    alert (address + " not found");
  } else {
    // do something such as set a marker
  }; // if (!point)
}; // end geocoderCallback
if (geocoder) {
  geocoder.getLatLng(address, geocoderCallback);
}
```

The inline version of this code is shown here:

```
if (geocoder) {
  geocoder.getLatLng(address, function(point) {
      if (!point) {
        alert (address + " not found");
      } else {
      // do something such as set a marker
      }; // if (!point)
    } // end inline callback function
  ) // end getLatLng call);
} // if geocoder
```

As you can see, the first thing the callback function does is to check to see if the point exists. When the callback routine calls, it either passes in a value for a point or a null. If it is null, the address sent into getLatLng was not found, and you should take appropriate action.

12

Create a Marker

If you run the geocoder example, you see you can enter an address and click the Go! button, as shown in Figure 12-4. This creates a map, using the code you saw. It also creates a *marker* and an *InfoWindow*.

Once you have a GLatLng point, you can use it to create the marker for that point. This process has two steps. The first is to create the marker, and then to add it as an *overlay* to the map. This is boilerplate code you can use over and over again—as long as you have a map and a GLatLng point. Here is the code from the example:

```
var marker = new GMarker(point);
map.addOverlay(marker);
```

Note, the marker is local to the function, but the map, like the geocoder, is global to the script.

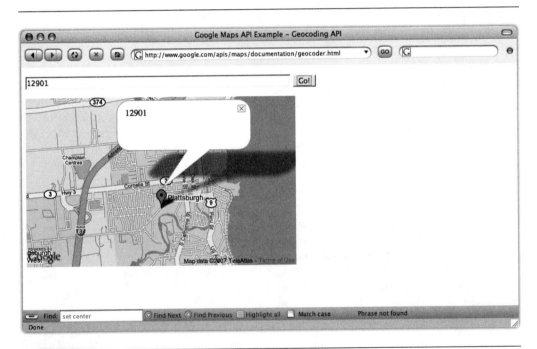

FIGURE 12-4   Use the geocoder example

Add Text to a Marker

The infowindow can be opened by passing some HTML code to the marker's openInfoWindowHtml method. The reason this is a method of the marker is the mapping API knows the location of the marker and it can then appropriately offset the infowindow. The method takes HTML code, but it can be as simple as you want—plain text will do.

If you follow the example and pass in an address in the *address* variable, here is the code to display the infowindow:

```
marker.openInfoWindowHtml(address);
```

Or, you can add a listener to the map that will open the infowindow. If you choose this route, here is the code to use. It is a call to GEvent.addListener to which you pass in the marker you just created and a function to be called when an event (in this case, *click*) occurs. Here, the function is declared inline; it consists of a single line of code—which is the call to openInfoWindowHtml shown previously. The difference is, in this case, the infowindow is only opened when the marker is clicked. Note, this is an inline callback function. This is shorter than the previous callback function and it is usually not customized, so keeping it inline should not make your code obscure.

```
GEvent.addListener (marker, "click", function () {
  marker.openInfoWindowHtml (address);
}
```

Putting It Together in the Callback Function

If you combine all these statements, you now have a functioning callback function. You can further enhance it by including a call to map.setCenter, so the map is centered on the point passed into the callback function by getLatLng and zoomed appropriately (13 is the zoom value used in this example).

Here is the full callback function:

```
geocoderCallback = function(point) {
  if (!point) {
    alert (address + " not found");
  } else {
    var marker = new GMarker (point);
     map.addOverlay(marker);
     map.setCenter(point, 13);
     GEvent.addListener (marker, "click", function () {
       marker.openInfoWindowHtml (addressText)
      } // end inline callback for addListener
    ) // addListener
  }; // if (!point)
}; // end geocoderCallback
```

12

Wrap It Up in PHP

What you have seen so far in this chapter is JavaScript code. Normally, in a mashup, you create that JavaScript code using PHP, incorporating variable data into it. This section shows you how to generate the JavaScript code from PHP. It is based on the geocoder example from Google, but it hard-codes the address you will map. That lets you see the bones of the code. (The code can be downloaded as noted in the Introduction.) The only thing you must change is you must add your own Google Maps key to it. Then, you can place it in your Web folder and access it through your browser as sampleMap.php. Because no variable data are passed in, there is no need to have an HTML document with a form on it.

The code begins with standard headers:

```
<!DOCTYPE html PUBLIC "-//W3C//DTD XHTML 1.0 Strict//EN"
    "http://www.w3.org/TR/xhtml1/DTD/xhtml1-strict.dtd">
<html xmlns="http://www.w3.org/1999/xhtml">
  <head>
    <meta http-equiv="content-type" content="text/html;
      charset=utf-8"/>
    <title>Google Maps JavaScript API Example</title>
```

Next, you have two scripts. The first is the included script from Google. Make certain to substitute your own key in the script element. After that comes scripts you write. At the beginning of your script, declare the geocoder and map variables you will use.

```
<script src="http://maps.google.com/maps?file=api&amp;v=2&amp;
  key=yourKey"
  type="text/javascript"></script>
<script type="text/javascript">
//<![CDATA[

var map = null;
var geocoder = null;
```

Next comes a function to create the map. Here, the architecture differs from the Google example. In the Google example, the load function is used to create the map. In this example, the createMap function is called whenever the map is needed to be created—not just on load. It is a somewhat more generalizable version of the code. This is the code you saw previously to check for browser compatibility, create a map, add map and type controls, center it, and create a new geocoder.

```
function createMap () {
  if (GBrowserIsCompatible()) {
    map = new GMap2(document.getElementById("map"));
```

```
    map.addControl (new GSmallMapControl());
    map.addControl (new GMapTypeControl());

    map.setCenter(new GLatLng(37.4419, -122.1419), 13);

    // Create the geocoder
    geocoder = new GClientGeocoder();
  }
}
```

The *showAddress function* is the function that shows an address. As you will see, the first thing it does is to create a map if one does not exist. Then, if a geocoder exists, the parameter address is used to generate a GLatLng point.

Here is the showAddress function. It contains code you have seen before to call the geocoder with the address parameter, to add a marker, and to open an infowindow. Note, the function has two parameters. This lets you use different text for the address to be geocoded than for the text to be shown in the info window. This is a flexible structure that is used in Chapter 13.

```
function showAddress (address, addressText) {

  geocoderCallback = function(point) {
    if (!point) {
      alert (address + " not found");
    } else {
      var marker = new GMarker (point);
      map.addOverlay(marker);
      map.setCenter(point, 13);
      GEvent.addListener (marker, "click", function () {
        marker.openInfoWindowHtml (addressText)
        } // end inline callback for addListener
      ) //end addListener
    }; // if (!point)
  }; // end geocoderCallback

  if (!map) {
    createMap();
  }

  if (geocoder) {
    geocoder.getLatLng(address, geocoderCallback);
  } // if geocoder
} // end showAddress
```

12

Error Messages

If the map does not exist and cannot be created in the call to createMap, under most circumstances, the geocoder will also not exist (because it is created in createMap). The only way you could have a map without a geocoder is if, somehow, the map were removed after having been created along with the geocode. If you want to be careful, you could make the testing more complex, but this is reasonably thorough. One possible addition would be an error message, but in mashups, the code is often so straightforward, you can avoid them. Just be careful to check internally for conditions such as the nonexistence of a map and make certain you either fail gracefully or do nothing. If your mashup requires extensive error-checking, it is probably too complex.

TIP *Because the code can quickly become complex with nested parentheses and if statements, not only should you be careful with indentation, but you should also use comments to indicate what closing parentheses and brackets are closing.*

Following your scripts, you close your script element and close the head element. In the body element, you assign the GUnload function to the onunload handler. Then, you create a div element with an id, which you can reference from createMap. This is the container for the map:

```
//]]>

</script>
</head>
<body onunload="GUnload()">
  <div id="map" style="width: 500px; height: 300px"></div>
```

Now comes the last piece of code. Create another script element in the body of your HTML document and, within it, place some PHP code. This code sets a variable *$jsCode* to a string that reads

```
myAddress = '32 Macdonough Street, Plattsburgh, NY';
```

What you are doing is constructing a JavaScript statement by concatenating several lines of PHP code. Pay attention to the matching of single and double quotes. In fact, you might want to extract this section of PHP code into its own file, so you can run it and make certain the value of $jsCode that is echoed is what you want. Having set myAddress, you then generate a call to showAddress. The same text is passed in to both address and addressText, but that need not always be the case. You then terminate the PHP script, terminate the SCRIPT element, and close the HTML document.

Once you have downloaded or typed in this code, you should be able to run it simply by inserting your own key.

```
<script type="text/javascript">
//<![CDATA[
<?php
  $jsCode = 'myAddress = ';
  $jsCode .= "'32 Macdonough Street, Plattsburgh, NY'"    ;
  $jsCode .= ";";
  echo $jsCode;

  echo "showAddress(myAddress, myAddress);";
  echo "\n";
?>
//]]>
</script>
</body>
</html>
```

Chapter 13

Build Mashups with the Google Maps API

How to...

■ Add a Map to the Chapter 11 Mashup

■ Create a Campaign Contributions Mashup

You saw in the previous chapter how to use the basics of the Google Maps API. In this chapter, you see how to build two mashups. The first is an extension of the basic mashup from Chapter 11 that extracted county data from two database tables. You add a map identifying the county to that mashup.

In the second mashup, you use the campaign contribution data described in Chapter 7 to build a mashup showing the destination of campaign contributions by ZIP code. This differs from the first mashup in that the first one simply displays a map with one marker on it, while this one uses a multitude of markers to identify the multiple ZIP codes to which money has been sent.

The steps in building these mashups are the same as those described in Chapter 11. For the first mashup, only three of the steps need to be redone to add the map. The second mashup requires all the steps to be implemented because there is no mashup to start from.

> **NOTE** *If you download the files, index.html is for the first mashup and index2.html is for the second one. Each calls its own PHP file.*

Identify the Data and the Keys

The data you used in Chapter 11 are insufficient to use in a mapping mashup. The reason is this: although a geocoder can convert many aspects of an address to a GLatLng point, it cannot convert a county name, which is the only text you have to identify the data.

Once again, the Census Bureau comes to the rescue. It has a collection of Gazetteer files you can download from http://www.census.gov/geo/www/gazetteer/places2k.html. Figure 13-1 shows that page.

If you scroll down the page, you can see the sort of data contained in these files, as shown in Figure 13-2.

The same Federal Information Processing Standard (FIPS) state and county codes are used to identify counties. This means you can match these data to the data in the files used in Chapter 11. Along with some summary data from the 2000 census, you can find the latitude and longitude of the county. Other files on this page provide the same information for other geographic entities, so between the geocoder in the Google Maps API and this information, you should be able to map nearly anything in the United States. Once you have the latitude and longitude, you can create a GLatLng object and use it to map data.

> **NOTE** *Mapping addresses with a geocoder can give misleadingly precise location information, when using an address or description that covers a wide area.*

The description of the data uses the old punched-card terminology of columns for character positions. Unlike the data you manipulated in Chapter 11, there are no delimiters: everything is based on location. You see how to split the data apart without delimiters in the next section.

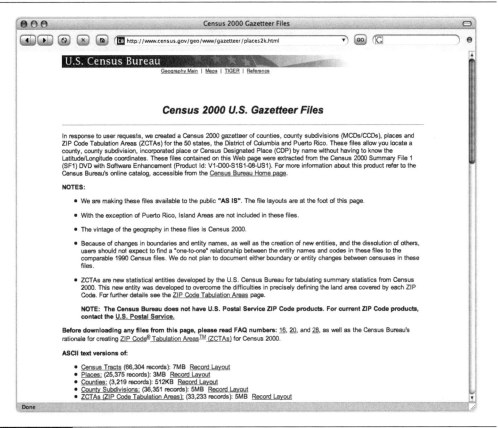

FIGURE 13-1   The Census Gazetteer page

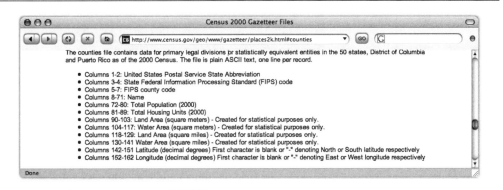

FIGURE 13-2   Look at the county data

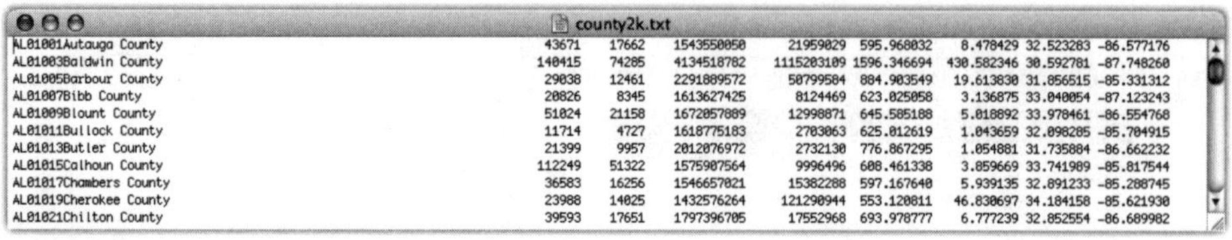

county2k.txt

AL01001Autauga County	43671	17662	1543550050	21959029	595.968032	8.478429	32.523283	-86.577176
AL01003Baldwin County	140415	74285	4134518782	1115203109	1596.346694	430.582346	30.592781	-87.748260
AL01005Barbour County	29038	12461	2291889572	50799584	884.903549	19.613830	31.856515	-85.331312
AL01007Bibb County	20826	8345	1613627425	8124469	623.025058	3.136875	33.040054	-87.123243
AL01009Blount County	51024	21158	1672057889	12998871	645.585188	5.018892	33.978461	-86.554768
AL01011Bullock County	11714	4727	1618775183	2703063	625.012619	1.043659	32.098285	-85.704915
AL01013Butler County	21399	9957	2012076972	2732130	776.867295	1.054881	31.735884	-86.662232
AL01015Calhoun County	112249	51322	1575907564	9996496	608.461338	3.859669	33.741989	-85.817544
AL01017Chambers County	36583	16256	1546657021	15382288	597.167640	5.939135	32.891233	-85.288745
AL01019Cherokee County	23988	14025	1432576264	121290944	553.120811	46.830697	34.184158	-85.621930
AL01021Chilton County	39593	17651	1797396705	17552968	693.978777	6.777239	32.852554	-86.689982

FIGURE 13-3 Raw county Gazetteer data

Download the county data from the link on the page. As always, it makes sense to look at the raw data. The first few records are shown in Figure 13-3.

Get Access to the Data

Just as you did in Chapter 11, the next step is to create a table in your database for the Gazetteer table. Use the same type of syntax you used in Chapter 11 to create the table. The syntax to create the table is shown here:

```
create table gazetteer (
  State_Code varchar (2),
  County_Code varchar (3),
  State_USPS varchar (2),
  County_Name varchar (63),
  Latitude varchar (10),
  Longitude varchar (11)
);
```

You do not need all the data from the downloaded file. All the fields are character fields; you calculate their lengths from the description of the data file, shown previously in Figure 13-2. The essential fields are the state and county FIPS codes, the two-character USPS state abbreviation, the county name, and the latitude and longitude.

NOTE *In the previous files, the state and county were concatenated into a single field. Because you will be using the FIPS codes in all cases, this does not matter. In fact, you could omit the state USPS abbreviation and county name entirely from this table. The reason for keeping them in is you might want to use this table with data that contain the FIPS codes, but not the descriptive information.*

The completed table is shown in Figure 13-4.

Now you need to load the data. The same principle used in Chapter 7 to split apart the two-digit FIPS state code from the three-digit FIPS county code is used to split up the whole text record.

The strategy is to load each record—with no field delimiters—into a temporary variable, *@var1*. You then use the substring function to split that variable apart into the fields you need.

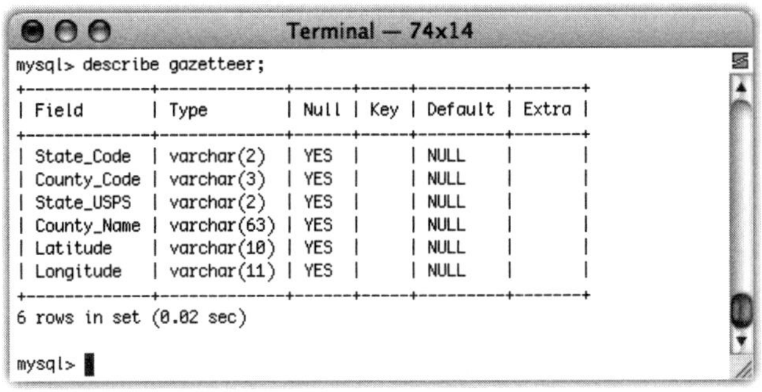

FIGURE 13-4   The Gazetteer table in MySQL

The starting positions and lengths of the fields are determined by the file description, shown in Figure 13-2, which is your bible for converting data in all cases. Here is the load code:

```
load data infile
  '/Users/jfeiler/Documents/Projects/CurrentProjects/
  Mashups/Book/Chapter13/county2k.txt'
into table gazetteer
lines terminated by '\n'
(@var1)
set
  State_Code=substring(@var1, 3, 2),
  County_Code=substring(@var1, 5, 3),
  State_USPS=substring(@var1, 1, 2),
  County_Name=substring(@var1, 8, 63),
  Latitude=substring(@var1, 142, 10),
  Longitude=substring(@var1, 152, 12);
```

Once the table is loaded, you can look at the first ten records, as shown in Figure 13-5. You should compare them with the text file you downloaded to make certain the field boundaries are correct and the data match.

Implement the Mashup

This mashup is implemented as a combination of the mashup in Chapter 11 and the Google mapping code in Chapter 12. Four modifications are to be made in the Chapter 11 code to incorporate the new code. Also, a little restructuring must be done that will serve you well in the remaining mashups in this book.

- You need to add the mapping script code to include both the Google mapping API script (with your key) and your own script.
- You need to modify your HTML to create a div that contains the map.

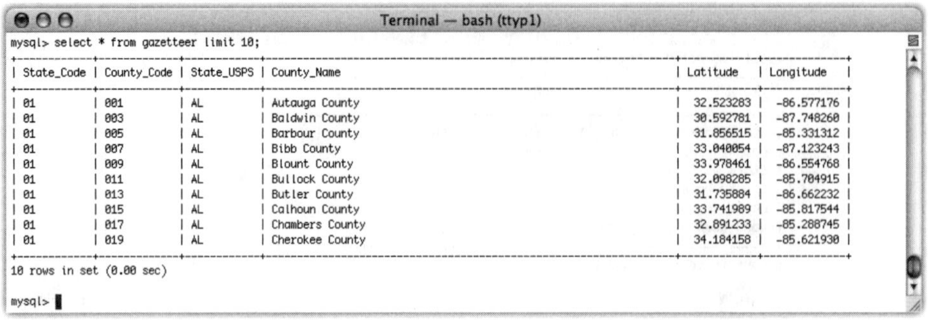

```
● ● ●                          Terminal — bash (ttyp1)
mysql> select * from gazetteer limit 10;
+------------+-------------+------------+----------------+-----------+------------+
| State_Code | County_Code | State_USPS | County_Name    | Latitude  | Longitude  |
+------------+-------------+------------+----------------+-----------+------------+
| 01         | 001         | AL         | Autauga County | 32.523283 | -86.577176 |
| 01         | 003         | AL         | Baldwin County | 30.592781 | -87.748260 |
| 01         | 005         | AL         | Barbour County | 31.856515 | -85.331312 |
| 01         | 007         | AL         | Bibb County    | 33.040054 | -87.123243 |
| 01         | 009         | AL         | Blount County  | 33.978461 | -86.554768 |
| 01         | 011         | AL         | Bullock County | 32.098285 | -85.704915 |
| 01         | 013         | AL         | Butler County  | 31.735884 | -86.662232 |
| 01         | 015         | AL         | Calhoun County | 33.741989 | -85.817544 |
| 01         | 017         | AL         | Chambers County| 32.891233 | -85.288745 |
| 01         | 019         | AL         | Cherokee County| 34.184158 | -85.621938 |
+------------+-------------+------------+----------------+-----------+------------+
10 rows in set (0.00 sec)

mysql>
```

FIGURE 13-5   The loaded Gazetteer data

- You need to add the SELECT statement to retrieve the latitude and longitude.
- You need to add the code to draw the map based on the latitude and longitude.

Add the Mapping Scripts

The mashup in Chapter 11 used PHP to perform the database accesses and to generate the JavaScript code. This mashup needs a lot of JavaScript code (basically the code from the last chapter) so, for readability, the mashup is slightly restructured. The PageTop include file is split into two. The first is the beginning of the head element, and the second is the end of the head element and the beginning of the body. Between the two, you can insert JavaScript code outside of PHP. Also, the new PageTop include file contains the Google mapping script and the key. Here is what PageTop.html now looks like:

```
<?xml version="1.0" encoding="iso-8859-1"?>
<!DOCTYPE html PUBLIC "-//W3C//DTD XHTML 1.0 Transitional//EN"
  "http://www.w3.org/TR/xhtml1/DTD/xhtml1-transitional.dtd">
<html xmlns="http://www.w3.org/1999/xhtml">
  <head>
    <title><?php echo $page_title; ?></title>
    <meta http-equiv="Content-Type" content="text/html;
      charset=iso-8859-1" />
    <script src="http://maps.google.com/maps?file=api&amp;v=2&amp;
      key= yourKey"
      type="text/javascript">
    </script>
```

Here is what the new PageTop2.html file looks like:

```
</head>

<body>
  <h1 align="center">Jesse Feiler's Mashups Book</h1>
  <h1 align="center"><?php echo $page_title;?></h1>
  <br />
```

The included script is now in PageTop.html. All you need to do is add the script you wrote in the head element of the page in the previous chapter. Here is the file as it should appear now. (The bodies of the functions in the script were removed to show the structure.) One other change was made to MySQLLogin. The $DB_NAME variable was removed, so you can select the database you want. The user name and password are hard-coded as before.

```
<?php
  $page_title = "Chapter 13";
  include ('./Includes/PageTop.html');
?>

  <script type="text/javascript">
    //<![CDATA[
    var map = null;
    var geocoder = null;

    function createMap () {
      // function code body removed
    }

    function showAddress (address, addressText) {
      // function code bode removed
    }

    //]]>

  </script>

<?php
  include ('./Includes/PageTop2.html');
  $DB_NAME = 'mashups_sql';
  include ('./Includes/MySQLLogin.php');
```

The file now continues as it did in Chapter 11.

```
// Query the database.

$state = $_REQUEST['state'];
$county = $_REQUEST['county'];
$query = "SELECT population.County_Name, TotalPopulation, labor_force ";
$query .= " FROM population, labor_force ";
$query .= " WHERE (population.State_FIPS_Code = '".$state."')";
$query .= " AND ";
$query .= " (labor_force.State_FIPS_Code = '".$state."')";
$query .= " AND ";
$query .= " (population.County_FIPS_Code = '".$county."')";
$query .= " AND ";
$query .= " (labor_force.County_FIPS_Code = '".$county."')";
$query .= " LIMIT 10";

$result = mysql_query ($query);

// Get the data.
$row = mysql_fetch_array ($result, MYSQL_NUM);

$CountyName = $row[0];
$Population = $row[1];
$WorkForce = $row[2];

$resultText = $CountyName." population=".$Population.",
   work    force=".$WorkForce;
echo $resultText;
?>
```

Modify the HTML to Add the DIV

Now that the scripts are in and the file is restructured, adding the div is simple. It follows immediately on the preceding code:

```
<div id="map" style="width: 500px; height: 300px"></div>
```

At this point, you can test the code using the example from the previous chapter. Instead of mapping the actual county that was selected, you can use the hard-coded address to create the map. After the div element, create a script element and, within it, enter the PHP code to create the JavaScript to call showAddress. Here is that code (it is the same as in the previous chapter):

```
<script type="text/javascript">
  //<![CDATA[
```

```php
<?php

  $jsCode = 'myAddress = ';
  $jsCode .= "'32 Macdonough Street, Plattsburgh, NY'"     ;
  $jsCode .= ";";
  echo $jsCode;

  echo "showAddress(myAddress, myAddress);"; // this is a comment
  echo "\n";
?>
```

```
  </script>
```

You can close the file with these lines:

```php
<?php
  include ('./Includes/MySQLLogout.php');
  include ('./Includes/PageBottom.html');
?>
```

You now have a file that combines the mapping API with the MySQL data retrieval. Test to see that it works, remembering the map uses the hard-coded address. If you are using the downloaded file, remember to insert your own Google key.

Add the SELECT statement

The next step is to add the SELECT statement to retrieve the latitude and longitude from the Gazetteer table. Like all database syntax, testing it outside the mashup is best. Using MySQL, enter this statement:

```sql
select County_Name, Latitude, Longitude
  from gazetteer
  where County_Code=5 and State_Code=1;
```

The results are shown in Figure 13-6. Compare the data with the raw data file shown previously in Figure 13-3, and you can see the numbers match. Now, it is just a matter of adding the statement to the mashup.

Just beneath the existing database call, add the new call. This is the end of the existing database call:

```php
// Get the data.
$row = mysql_fetch_array ($result, MYSQL_NUM);
```

13

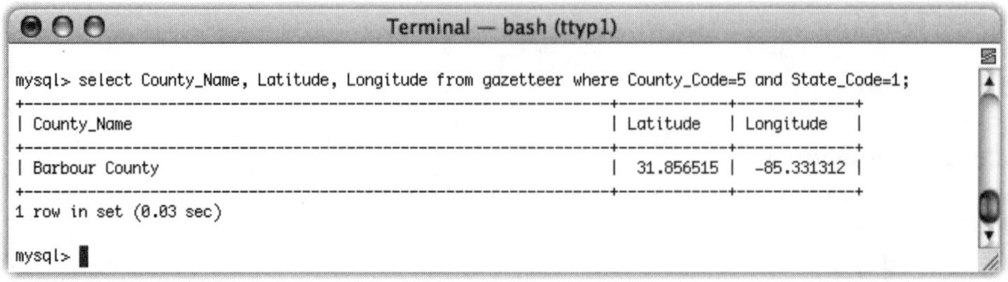

FIGURE 13-6 Test the SQL syntax outside the mashup

```
$CountyName = $row[0];
$Population = $row[1];
$WorkForce = $row[2];

$resultText = $CountyName." population=".$Population.",
  work force=".$WorkForce;
echo $resultText;
```

The code you add is in exactly the same format as the previous database call. You can even reuse the variables because the previous call is completed and $resultText was echoed to the JavaScript code being built. As you can see, this terminates this section of PHP code.

```
$query = "SELECT Latitude, Longitude ";
$query .= " FROM gazetteer ";
$query .= " WHERE County_Code=5 AND State_Code=1";

$result = mysql_query ($query);

// Get the data.
$row = mysql_fetch_array ($result, MYSQL_NUM);

$latlng = array ($row [0], $row [1]);

echo " latitude=".$latlng[0]." longitude=".$latlng[1];
?>
```

The last two lines of code are slightly different than in the first database call. Instead of storing latitude and longitude in two variables, they are stored in an array, *$latlng*, which is created here. The indices happen to be the same as the indices in $row, but that is only a coincidence. The reason for storing the latitude and longitude values in an array is they are intimately related to one another. In an array, they can move around together. Note, also, a space is at the beginning of the echo string. This is so the two echo strings do not run into one another. If you run the mashup now, you should see the result shown in Figure 13-7.

FIGURE 13-7   Run the mashup

Draw the Map

Now that all the data were retrieved successfully, it is simply a matter of passing them into the Google mapping API. A function, called showAddress, already exists that calls a geocoder to map an address. Rather than create another function that does similar things with latitude and longitude, showAddress can be modified to handle both the case of geocoding from an address and the case of using latitude and longitude.

The strategy is twofold. First, two more parameters are added to the function: latitude and longitude. The logic is that if the address parameter is given, it is used. Otherwise, latitude and longitude are used. If you want to make this more robust, you can add tests to make certain that if the address is not provided, both latitude and longitude must be provided.

Because more logic is in showAddress, the code that creates the marker is pulled out into its own function. That function, setMarkerAndText, uses the global map to set a marker at a specific point and to set its text. This is code that was in showAddress. Here is the new function:

```
function setMarkerAndText (mapPoint, text) {
  var marker = new GMarker (mapPoint);
  map.addOverlay(marker);
```

13

```
map.setCenter(mapPoint, 7);
GEvent.addListener (marker,
  "click",
  function () {
    marker.openInfoWindowHtml (text);
  } //function
); // addListener
}
```

The new showAddress function calls this as needed. Here is showAddress with its two new parameters. The body of code that uses the geocoder is now enclosed in an if statement that tests to see if the address parameter has been passed in. If so, it functions exactly as before, except the new setMarkerAndText function is called instead of executing that code inline.

If the address parameter is null, setMarkerAndText is called with a new GLatLng point that is constructed from latitude and longitude.

```
function showAddress (latitude, longitude, address, addressText) {

  if (!map) {
    createMap();
  }

  if (address != undefined) {
    if (geocoder) {
      geocoder.getLatLng(
        address,
        function(point) {
          if (!point) {
            alert (address + " not found");
          } else {
            setMarkerAndText (point, addressText);
          } // point returned
        } //function
      ) //getLatLng
    };// if geocoder
  } else {
    setMarkerAndText (new GLatLng (latitude, longitude), addressText);
  };
} //showAddress
```

All that remains is to call the new function. It handles the case of geocoding an address, as well as using latitude and longitude. Because the call to Gazetteer has provided the latitude and longitude, null is passed in as the address. Furthermore, because the marker's infowindow is automatically created from text, instead of displaying the retrieved data with an echo statement, that data can be displayed in the infowindow just by passing it in.

Here is the balance of the mashup code. It begins with the div and continues by creating a JavaScript variable with the text to be displayed, and then a call to the revised showAddress. (Note, the latlng array that was so carefully put together is now split up again. If it had been manipulated more often, the advantages of encapsulating the data would be clearer.)

```
<div id="map" style="width: 500px; height: 300px"></div>

<script type="text/javascript">
  //<![CDATA[

<?php

  $jsCode = 'theText = ';
  $jsCode .= "'".$resultText."'";
  $jsCode .= ";";
  echo $jsCode;
  echo "\n";

  echo "showAddress(".$latlng[0].", ".$latlng[1].", null, theText);";
  echo "\n";
?>
  //]]>
</script>

<?php
include ('./Includes/MySQLLogout.php');
include ('./Includes/PageBottom.html');
?>
```

13

Now, you need to make two little final changes. First, remove the statement that echoes $resultText to the HTML document after the data are retrieved. Second, split up the text, so it does not appear all in one line (the infowindow can be stressed by this). Because the parameter to the openInfoWindowHtml is HTML, you can add some breaks to the text, as shown here:

```
$resultText = $CountyName."
  <br>
  Population=".$Population."
  <br>
  Work Force=".$WorkForce;
```

Now, if you run the mashup and click on the marker, you can see the result shown in Figure 13-8.

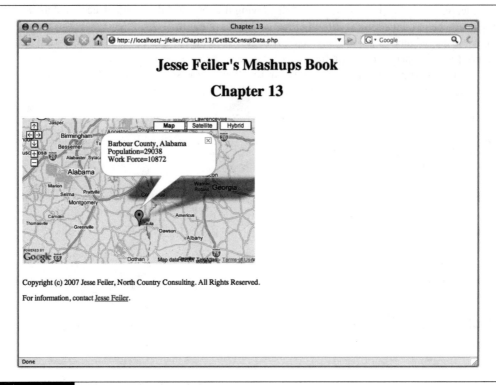

FIGURE 13-8   The completed mashup

Create a Campaign Contributions Mashups

The restructuring of the basic mashup provides you with a powerful set of tools to map data. You can see this in action as the campaign contributions mashup is constructed with little effort when you build on those tools. What also makes it fairly easy is the data were already discussed in Chapter 7, so you should be familiar with the structure of the data. This is not uncommon: mashups can frequently emerge from an individual's in-depth knowledge of specific data, combined with the imagination of presenting that information in an understandable manner.

Figure 13-9 shows the completed mashup. For a given ZIP code, markers show where donations were sent and infowindows display the total amounts sent to a specific ZIP code.

Decide on Your Mashup's Objective

The freely downloadable data from the FEC provides information about individuals and their campaign contributions. Both individual donors and the committees that are their recipients are identified by ZIP code. This means you can not only look at individuals, but also at ZIP codes. When you look at ZIP codes, you are right in the middle of a data set that lends itself to mapping.

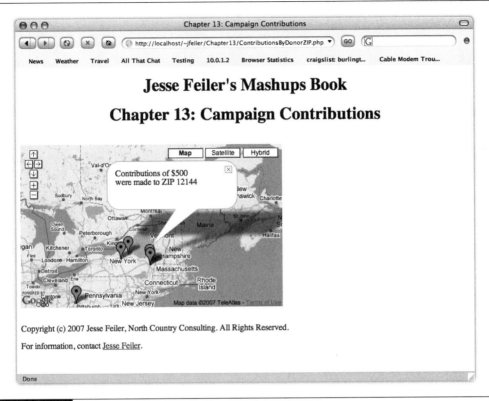

FIGURE 13-9   The campaign contributions mashup

This mashup lets you identify the recipients of contributions sent from a specific ZIP code. It maps the ZIP codes of the recipients, as well as sending the ZIP code.

The data can be used in a variety of other ways. For example, it is trivial to reverse the process and specify a ZIP code to which contributions are sent, and then map from where those contributions were sent.

Identify the Data and the Keys

The data consist of the three tables described in Chapter 7: individual contributions, committees, and candidates. For the purpose of this mashup, you only need data from individual contributions and committees.

Individual Contributions

These are the fields you need from the file:

- contributor
- amount

- city
- state
- ZIP
- filer

Committees

These are the fields you need from the file:

- name
- city
- state
- ZIP
- committee_ID

Get Access to the Data

Sample data for this book are available through the author's Web site, http://www
.northcountryconsulting.com. Just follow the link to Mashups Downloads and you can find
compressed archives of data for various chapters. This chapter uses data from the U.S. Federal
Election Commission. These data are particularly useful for experimenting with mashups because
they not only are public and not copyrighted, but also because they are quite voluminous. When
you are testing your mashup and experimenting with the data, being able to look at thousands of
records is important. The mashup maps the locations of campaign contributions both by donor and
by recipient. Without a large body of varied data, you do not have interesting maps to look at.

And that is where a problem arises. The data for the 2005/6 election cycle are now complete
on the Federal Election Commission (FEC) Web site. The basic files take up just under 300 MB
of data. Even with compression, the archive takes up over 50 MB of data. For that reason, the
files available on the book's Web site are early files from the 2007/8 election cycle. Together,
these files take up 2.6 MB and about 0.5 MB when compressed. They can easily be downloaded
and experimented with, but to get the full flavor of the data, the recommendation is you either
download the whole 2005/6 set of files or you download the 2007/8 files from the FEC when
you are ready to start working. Those files grow rapidly over the course of the election cycle, and
then the next cycle begins with small files.

To download data from the FEC Web site, connect to http://www.fec.gov, as shown in
Figure 13-10.

Remember, Web sites occasionally are rearranged, so you may have to navigate somewhat
differently to get to the data. From the navigation menu at the left, mouse over "Campaign
Finance Reports and Data," and then choose Download Data Files Using FTP. (Do not worry:
you can download the files with your browser.)

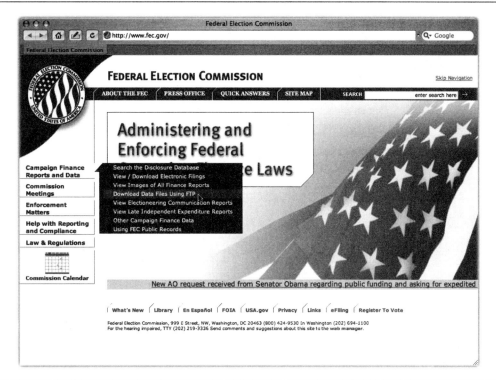

FIGURE 13-10   Connect to fec.gov

On the download page, shown in Figure 13-11, you want to choose Detailed Files. In this, and in the previous step, you want to avoid the interactive aspects of the site, which provide powerful browsing capabilities. They are wonderful, but you want the raw data, so you can add your own browsing capabilities.

When you click Detailed Files, the next page shows you the available election cycles, as shown in Figure 13-12. The current cycle's data is a smaller corpus of data than the previous cycles' data. (The later in the cycle, the more voluminous the data.)

For each cycle, there are download links, as shown in Figure 13-13.

The current and two previous cycles of data are updated on a regular basis—usually once a week on Sunday. For this mashup, you need only the first three files: Committee Master File, Candidate Master File, and Contributions by Individuals.

If you are following along with the data, you can download the large file (Contributions by Individuals), and then download the Adds, Changes, and Deletes that should be applied to it. For the purpose of the mashup, it is easier to simply download Contributions by Individuals over a broadband connection and ignore Adds, Changes, and Deletes.

13

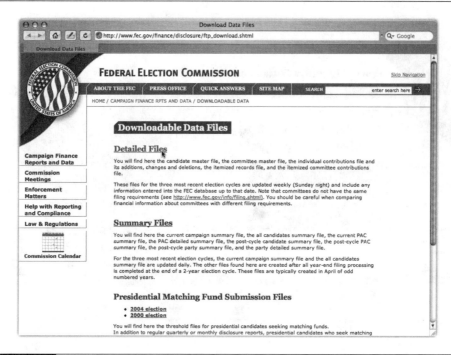

FIGURE 13-11   Go to the download page

Creating tables and loading data should be a familiar process by now. First, look at the data description downloaded with the data files. Table 13-1 shows the data description for individual contributions.

Load Individual Contributions Data

Next, create the table in an existing or new database with the following code. The names of the columns should more or less match the names of the variables in the data description, but they need not be so lengthy. The description of the data description fields can be used for each column. The number is the width of the column, and you can use varchar for strings (s) and mediumint (for values in the range of data provided here) for numbers (n).

```
create table individuals (
  filer varchar (9),
  contributor varchar (34),
  city varchar (18),
  state varchar (2),
  zip varchar (5),
  amount mediumint (9)
);
```

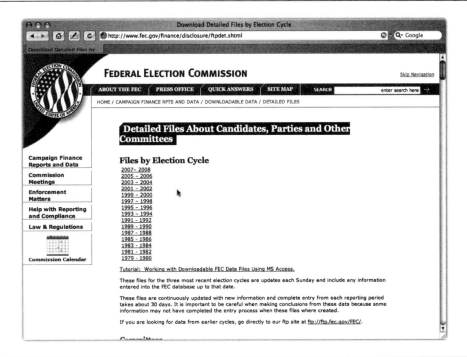

FIGURE 13-12   Choose the election cycle

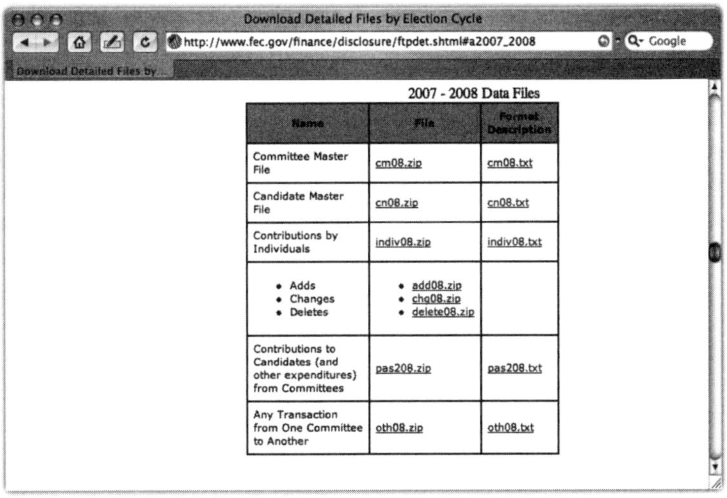

FIGURE 13-13   Download the files you need

Variable	Columns	Description
Filer Identification Number	1–9	9s
Contributor/Lender/Transfer Name	29–62	34s
City/Town	63–80	18s
State	81–82	2s
ZIP Code	83–87	5s
Amount	131–137	7n

TABLE 13-1   Individual Contributions Data Description

Because the data file is not delimited, use the same strategy for splitting apart each record, as shown previously in this chapter. Here is the load statement. Use the starting column in the data description for the starting position, and use the width of the field shown in the description column.

```
load data infile
  '/Users/jfeiler/Documents/Projects/CurrentProjects/
    Mashups/Book/Chapter13/itcont-3.dta'
  into table individuals
  lines terminated by '\n'
  (@var1)
  set
    filer=substring(@var1, 1, 9),
    contributor=substring(@var1, 29, 34),
    city=substring(@var1, 63, 18),
    state=substring(@var1, 81, 2),
    zip=substring(@var1, 83, 5),
    amount=substring(@var1, 131, 7);
```

Load Committee Data

In the same way, use the data description shown in Table 13-2 to create a table using this code:

```
create table committees (
  committee_ID varchar (9),
  name varchar (9),
  city varchar (18),
  state varchar (2),
  zip varchar (5);
```

Variable	Columns	Description
Committee Identification	1–9	9s
Committee Name	10–99	9s
City or Town	206–223	18s
State	224–225	2s
ZIP Code	226–230	5s

TABLE 13-2   Committee Data Description

This statement loads the data from foiacm.dta:

```
load data infile
  '/Users/jfeiler/Documents/Projects/CurrentProjects/
    Mashups/Book/Chapter13/foiacm.dta'
  into table committees
  lines terminated by '\n'
  (@var1)
  set
    committee_ID=substring(@var1, 1, 9),
    name=substring(@var1, 10, 9),
    city=substring(@var1, 206, 18),
    state=substring(@var1, 224, 2),
    zip=substring(@var1, 226, 5);
```

Regroup

You have already seen the types of SELECT statements that can be used to retrieve and join these data in Chapter 7, so you can continue to design the interface.

Design the User Interface

The interface consists of a map with a marker for each contribution. The infowindow for each marker shows the recipient and the amount.

13

Implement the Mashup

The basic PHP code for implementing the data retrieval was already shown. Here it is again, so it can serve as a starting point for the mapping code. This code displays the results of the query in an HTML table. You can see the *$zip* variable is hard-coded for now because the start page is not yet implemented. You may want to run this code to see that it works.

```php
<?php
include ('./Includes/PageTop2.html');
$DB_Name = 'fec';
include ('./Includes/MySQLLogin.php');

// Query the database.
//$zip = $_REQUEST['zip'];
$zip = "12901";

$query = "SELECT
    individuals.contributor,
    committees.name,
    committees.city,
    committees.state,
    FORMAT(individuals.amount, 0)
  FROM individuals, committees
  WHERE (individuals.zip = '"
    .$zip.
    "') AND (committees.committee_ID = individuals.filer)
  ORDER BY individuals.contributor
  LIMIT 10";

$result = mysql_query ($query);

echo '<table border="0" width="100%" cellspacing="3"
  cellpadding="3" align="center">
  <tr>
    <td>Contributor</td>
    <td>Recipient</td>
    <td>Recipient City</td>
    <td>Recipient State</td>
    <td>Amount</td>
  </tr>';

// Display all the values.
while ($row = mysql_fetch_array ($result, MYSQL_NUM)) {
```

```php
  // Display each record.
  echo "  <tr>
    <td>-name-</td>
    <td>$row[1]</td>
    <td>$row[2]</td>
    <td>$row[3]</td>
    <td align=\"right\">$row[4]</td>
    </tr>\n";
} // End of while loop.

echo '</table>'; // End the table.
```

To do the mapping, you need to add a div element and to replace the HTML table output with calls to showAddress. Remember, these need to be placed in the body of the document, which means they must be placed after the include PageTop2.html file. Thus, here is the file, starting from the end of the JavaScript code in the head element that contains the mapping functions:

```php
<?php
include ('./Includes/PageTop2.html');
$DB_Name = 'fec';
include ('./Includes/MySQLLogin.php');
?>

<div id="map" style="width: 500px; height: 300px"></div>

<script type="text/javascript">
    //<![CDATA[

<?php
// Query the database.
$zip = $_REQUEST['zip'];
```

The SELECT statement differs from the previous one in two ways. First, the SELECT statement uses the GROUP function to add up all the contributions for each ZIP code. More important, the SELECT statement omits the ORDER BY clause. Sorting a database is expensive, but this makes sense if you are presenting the information as text in a table. When a SELECT statement is mapped, it does not matter what the sequence of the data is—the markers are where they are.

```php
$query = "SELECT ";
$query .= " individuals.zip, ";
$query .= " committees.zip, ";
```

13

```
$query .= " committees.city,   ";
$query .= " committees.state,   ";
$query .= " SUM(individuals.amount) ";
$query .= " FROM individuals, committees   ";
$query .= " WHERE (individuals.zip = '";
$query .= $zip;
$query .= "') AND (committees.committee_ID = individuals.filer)   ";
$query .= " GROUP BY committees.zip";

$result = mysql_query ($query);
```

Here is the while loop. Instead of generating HTML code, it is generating JavaScript code. The code that is generated looks like this:

```
myText = "Contributions of $1500<br>were made to ZIP 12065";
showAddress(0, 1, '12065', myText);
```

Note, the <br> tag is included in the infowindow to split the text into two lines. This is a sample of the code to be generated. The code you write in your PHP file is here:

```
while ($row = mysql_fetch_array ($result, MYSQL_NUM)) {
  $jsCode = 'myText = "';
  $jsCode .= 'Contributions of $'. $row[4] .
    '<br>were made to ZIP ' . $row[1];
  $jsCode .= '";';
  echo $jsCode;
  echo "\n";

  echo "showAddress(0, 1, '".$row[1]."', myText);";
  echo "\n";
}
```

You complete the script with the usual ending code:

```
?>
 //]]>
     </script>

<?php
include ('./Includes/MySQLLogout.php');
include ('./Includes/PageBottom.html');
?>
```

Implement the Starting Page

All you need on the starting page is a form that submits a ZIP code and calls the PHP script. You can provide additional information on the starting page, including links to information about the data, advertisements, or whatever you want.

Here is the form code you need. Note the ZIP code field and the name of the PHP script to run.

```
<form name="form1" id="form1" method="post"
  action="ContributionsByDonorZIP.php">
  Contributor ZIP:
    <input name="zip" type="text" id="zip" size="10"/>
  <input type="submit" name="Submit" value="Look Up" />
</form>
```

Chapter 14

Use the Amazon Web Services and Google Search APIs

How to...

- ■ Get Access to the Amazon API
- ■ Search Amazon for an Item
- ■ Build an Amazon Link
- ■ Build an Amazon Shopping Cart
- ■ Use the Google Search API

This chapter and the next one deal with the Amazon Web Services API. You see how to use the basic calls of the API to search the Amazon database and how to implement a shopping cart in two different ways.

The previous examples have all run off data retrieved from databases. They use databases you can create yourself from publicly available downloaded data. You can use the same techniques and architectures to access data from other databases to which you have access. Starting with this chapter, the emphasis is on data you access without direct SQL calls and to which you may need formal access clearance.

NOTE   *Amazon API URLs contain the date of the version of the API to which they apply. As a result, it is impossible to provide direct links to pages with further documentation on the Amazon Web Services site in this chapter. The basic pages are shown, as well as the navigation links that can get you to more detailed information for the current version—whatever that is. In addition, links to detailed information are provided here, but they may be outdated as the site is updated. If they are outdated, navigate through the pages with the current links on them. The navigation paths are provided along with the URLs.*

Get Access to the Amazon API

Using the Google mapping API, you need to get a key to provide access to the API. You supply your own data to be mapped, and you use the key to access a Google script at runtime using the script element and the src attribute.

With Amazon, you need access to Amazon's Web Services API—code that is architecturally comparable to the Google mapping (and other) APIs, as well as to the data Amazon stores. You also may need to implement shopping carts and the capability to track (and profit from) sales referred through your site. All this is simple, but it requires you to create three separate accounts and to manage several different keys and tags. The three accounts are an Amazon account, an Amazon Web Services (AWS) account, and an Amazon Associate account. (The Amazon account is not specifically required to use the API, but if you want to do much testing, you need it.)

Setting Up an Amazon Account

The Amazon account is the basic account you may already have. It consists of your e-mail address and a password, along with other information you provide. If you have ordered from Amazon, you have created such an account. Even if you have not placed an order, you may have accepted the offer to create an account.

Once you have an Amazon account, create your Associate and AWS accounts. Start by going to www.amazon.com and looking for the Amazon Services section shown in Figure 14-1. Often, this is at the left side of the home page. (As is always the case with companies such as Amazon, services and offerings are frequently being added or changed, so the Amazon Services box may look different.)

Setting Up an Amazon Associate Account

Click the Associates link in the Make Money section of Amazon Services. You can log in if you are a member already or join the Associates program now. The *Amazon Associates program* was founded in 1996 as one of the first online affiliate marketing programs. It is the program by which links to specific Amazon listings can generate a referral fee to the referrer. This is done by including an associate account ID in an Amazon request. For example, the following code goes to a page for a book on Amazon, and it also indicates that the associate account, philmontsoftware, should be credited with the page view and the sale:

```
http://www.amazon.com/exec/obidos/ISBN=0672328569/
   philmontsoftware
```

Amazon Services

Make Money
Advantage
Associates
Corporate Accounts
Paid Placements
Sell Your Stuff

For the Community
Amazon Connect
Amazon Fishbowl
Amazon Podcasts
E-Mail Subscriptions
Giving at Amazon

For Developers
Amazon Web Services

For Advertisers
Advertise With Us

Partner Services
Broadband Services
Financial Services
Travel Services

FIGURE 14-1   Locate Amazon Services on the home page

14

An alternative format that does the same thing is shown here:

```
http://www.amazon.com/gp/product/0672328569/
  ?tag = philmontsoftware
```

When you log into the Associates area, as shown in Figure 14-2, you can examine the activity for your account. You also have access to support resources, such as discussions and a blog. The Performance Tips section helps Amazon associates improve their sales, and the tips there— although primarily directed to Web site developers—are equally relevant to mashup designers who link to Amazon and generate sales for their Associates account.

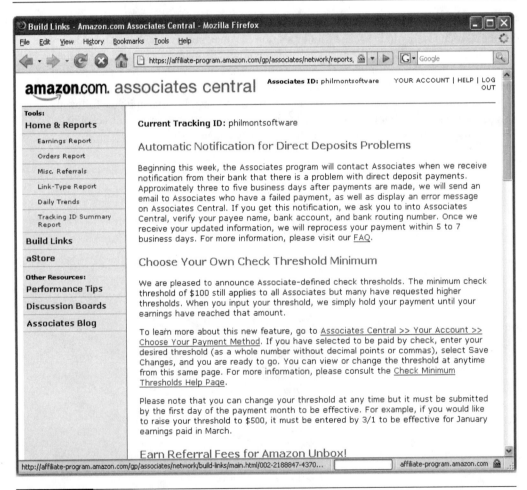

FIGURE 14-2   Amazon Associates home

Setting Up an Amazon Web Services Account

In the For Developers section of Amazon Services, you can find Amazon Web Services. Click it to go to the home page, which is shown in Figure 14-3. You can also reach this page with

```
http://www.amazon.com/gp/browse.html?node=3435361
```

In the upper-right of the page is the button you click to sign up. You can also navigate through the many links on this page—even without an account—to find out more about Amazon Web Services. Once you have signed up, you will see that the Your Web Services Account button is accompanied by Welcome text as shown in Figure 14-4.

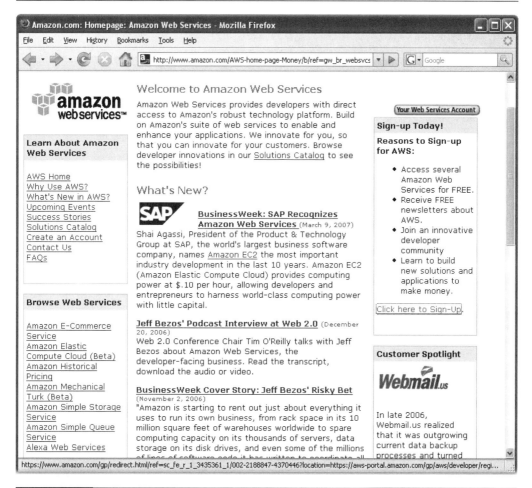

FIGURE 14-3   Go to the Amazon Web Services page

14

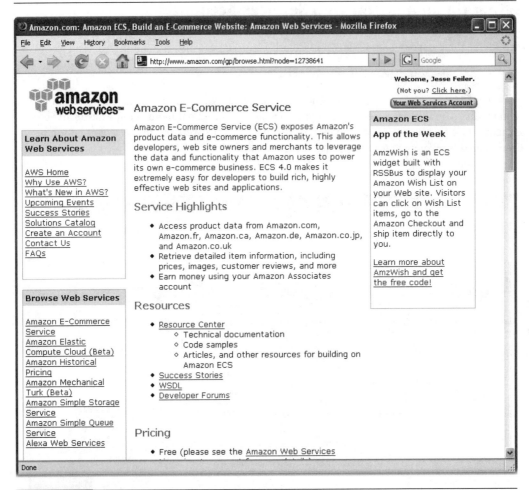

FIGURE 14-4 Use your Amazon Web Services account

When you sign up for an AWS account, you receive two keys: an *access key* ID and a *secret access key* ID. If you forget them, you can always click the Your Web Services Account button to see them again.

The access key is functionally similar to the Google mapping API key: it provides access to services, including searching Amazon's database and creating a shopping cart.

The secret key is part of a two-step authentication step you need to use to access some of the AWS functionality—currently the functionality that is not free. The secret access key is used to generate a signature used in sending requests to AWS. Because the secret access key ID itself is not sent to AWS, it can remain secret. AWS can use the information generated when you signed up to decode the signature on the request.

What "Free" Means

Amazon Web services that are free include searches and shopping carts. The fact that a customer eventually pays for the items in a shopping cart at checkout means those items are paid for, but the shopping cart service is free—a way for Amazon (and you) to generate sales.

Services that, in and of themselves, provide value, such as Amazon Historical Pricing, which lets you look up average, minimum, maximum, and medium prices for items sold over the last three years through Amazon, are not free.

Search Amazon for an Item

Searching Amazon for one or more items is a simple matter using the basic architecture described in Chapters 8 and 9.

From the Welcome to Amazon Web Services page shown previously in Figure 14-2, click Amazon E-Commerce Service in the Browse Web Services section at the lower-left of the screen. Continue clicking Resource Center on the next page and Technical Documentation on the Resources page. You see the API documents for the recent versions of AWS ECS, with the most recent first. Click this one, and then click the HTML or PDF version you want to look at. If you click the API reference shown in Figure 14-5, you find the API operations, shown in Figure 14-6. You can also get to it at http://developer.amazonwebservices.com/connect/kbcategory.jspa?categoryID=19.

If you know the date of the most recent API revision (and the site structure does not change), you can go directly to the page, as you saw in Figure 14-4, by replacing the date as appropriate in this URL: http://docs.amazonwebservices.com/AWSEcommerceService/2007-02-22/.

All the operations are relatively similar. The biggest distinction is in the search routines and the lookup routines—searches do just that, while *lookups* get specific data identified by an identifier. The identifier can be an International Standard Book Number (ISBN) or a Universal Product Code (UPC), both of which are common identifiers for objects—not just at Amazon, but throughout the world of books (ISBN) and other products (UPC).

In addition, Amazon generates its own identifiers. The most common is the Amazon Standard Item Number (ASIN). Other identifiers locate sellers, items on wish lists, and the like.

The operations listed in Figure 14-6 can all be initiated with REST requests. They accept six classes of parameters. *XSL parameters* are used when you add XSLT style sheets to the XML output; *operation formatting parameters* handle the escape character mechanism; and *debugging parameters* let you pass the syntax through for debugging, but not for actual operation. Three other sets of parameters are used more often:

14

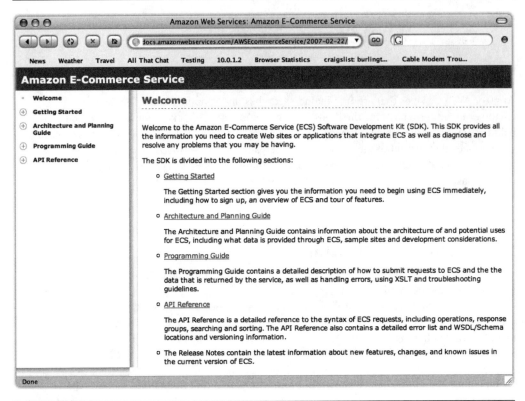

FIGURE 14-5 Locate the API reference link on the Welcome page

- *Required parameters* are required in every request.
- *General parameters* are optional in every request.
- *Specific parameters* are defined for each operation.

Required Parameters

You must use your Amazon Access Key ID in each request; its parameter name is AWSAccessKeyId. In the past, Amazon distributed keys called SubscriptionIds, but these are no longer distributed. If you have one, you can use it instead of the Access Key ID; you cannot use both.

You also must specify an Operation. The operation types are shown in Figure 14-6 and are fully described if you click the links on that page.

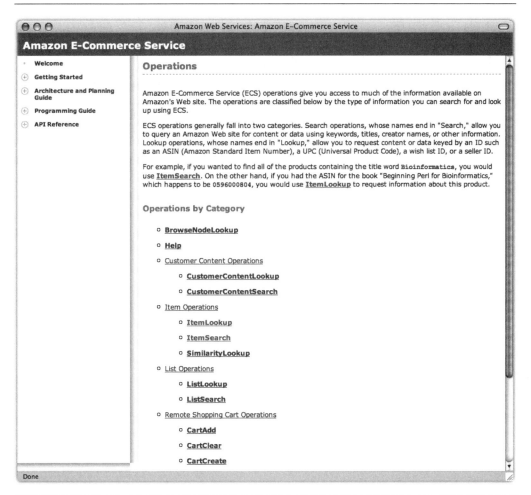

FIGURE 14-6   Click on API reference

14

General Parameters

General parameters are optional. You can find links to them on any Operation page (go to ItemSearch, for example, and a link to general parameters is there). The two most commonly used are *AssociateTag* and *ResponseGroup*.

The AssociateTag identifies your Associate account that is credited with the click and subsequent sale.

The ResponseGroup specifies the data to be returned from a request. In the example given in this chapter and the next, the *medium, small response group* is used. The medium, small response group provides exactly what its name describes: a limited amount of information on each item returned. This is a good response group to start with in your experiments.

Specific Parameters for ItemSearch

Each operation has its own parameters that may be required or optional. For ItemSearch, other than the required Operation parameter, the required parameter is *SearchIndex*, which specifies what Amazon store you want to search—books, movies, electronics, and so forth. Other ItemSearch parameters let you sort results, specify complex queries, and limit a price range. You can also use parameters such as Author, Title, Keywords, and the like to create the query.

Put It Together: An Amazon Search REST Query

If you put the parameters together for an ItemSearch REST query, here is an example of what you might have. The REST query is placed in a PHP variable called *$theURL,* which assumes a variable or is defined for your access key ID and for your associate tag. You could code them like this. (By placing them in defines, you can hide them in an include file.)

```
define ("amazonAccessKeyID", yourKey);
define ("amazonAssociateTag", yourTag);
```

With those two defines, this is what the query looks like:

```
$theURL =
"http://webservices.amazon.com/onca/xml?
  Service=AWSECommerceService&
  AWSAccessKeyId=amazonAccessKeyID &
  AssociateTag=amazonAssociateTag &
  Operation=ItemSearch&
  Keywords=".$theKeywords."&
  SearchIndex=Books&
  ResponseGroup=Request,Small&
  Version=2007-02-22";
```

This REST request is used in the following chapter.

Build an Amazon Link

When you get data back from a search or a lookup, you generally want to build a link to the returned data, so people can click on it and order it. The Amazon Associates page, shown previously in Figure 14-2, has a Build Links tool that you can use to build various types of links. A good idea is to use that tool to experiment with the links you will use in your mashup. Select an ASIN, UPC, or ISBN to use as a test and hard-code the link. Then, copy the code and use the structure to dynamically create your link for the mashup. (Go to an appropriate product page on Amazon. You find the ASIN, UPC, or ISBN somewhere on that page, so you can use it for your testing.)

When you first click Build Links, you see the page shown in Figure 14-7. At the left, select the type of link that is approximately what you want—you can customize it later.

On the next page, enter the ISBN, ASIN, or UPC for the test product. You do not want a search that will return multiple items (such as an author search), so use a specific number, as shown in Figure 14-8.

You can see the product, but the link is not yet built. You still have a chance to customize it after you click Get HTML. In Figure 14-9, you can see the ways in which you can customize

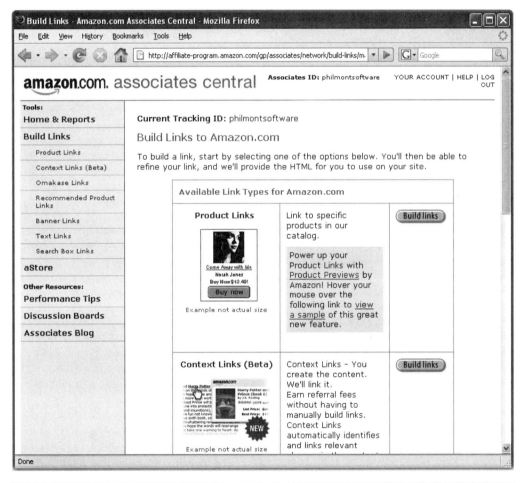

FIGURE 14-7   Select a link type

14

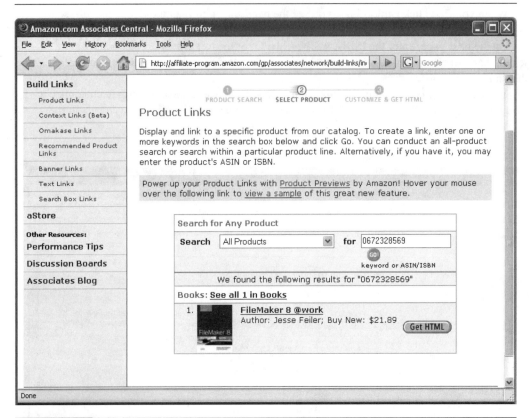

FIGURE 14-8   Enter the link product ID

the link. This page is live, so as you change the options, the sample link at the right changes and the HTML at the bottom changes. When you are happy, copy the HTML and paste it somewhere safe, so you can use it in your mashup later. (In the next chapter, what you do is replace the specific ASIN, ISBN, or UPC in the link with the dynamic value returned in a search or lookup.)

Build an Amazon Shopping Cart

The Amazon API lets you build a shopping cart that you can control. You also can create a perfectly good and powerful mashup using an Amazon shopping cart. In fact, the differences are subtle for many people. In Figure 14-10, you can see what a shopping cart looks like that you create. Notice the text, "We have teamed with Amazon.com...." When you create a shopping cart and add items to

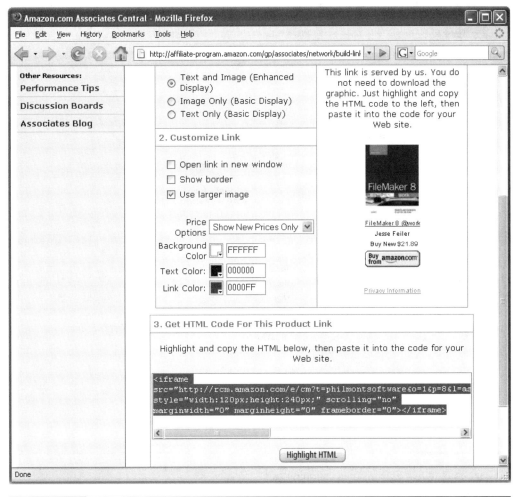

FIGURE 14-9   Finish building the link and the HTML

it in your mashup, this is the page people see when they display the shopping cart. This page uses their Amazon customer information, and it contains the items they have ordered through you.

If you do not create your own shopping cart, users can click on the links you created, and then add items to their regular Amazon shopping cart. That page is shown in Figure 14-11.

The page looks remarkably similar, but when you use an Amazon shopping cart, the user controls additions or deletions to it. As long as your Amazon Associate tag is in the link, you are credited for purchases. The example in the next chapter uses an Amazon shopping cart.

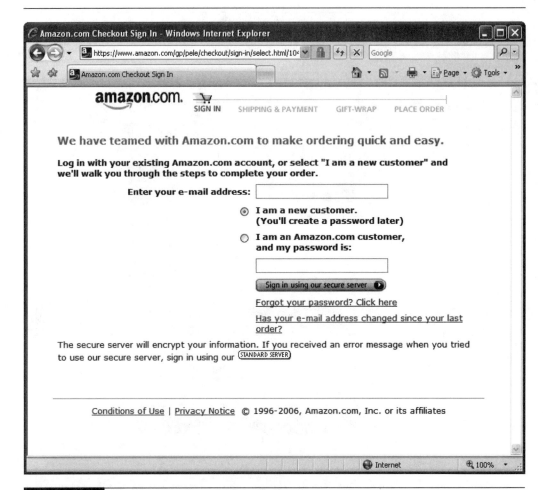

FIGURE 14-10   Creating your own shopping cart

Use the Google Search API

Google, Yahoo!, and other companies provide a variety of APIs for searching, mapping, and other purposes. As the world of mashups and related technologies expands, a core set of such APIs seems to be evolving with search and mapping at the forefront. Each vendor's APIs share many common architectural features, and, in general, all the mashups and related APIs have many similarities.

The Google AJAX Search API lets you put Google search on your own pages and in mashups. You can find more information at http://code.google.com/apis/ajaxsearch/, as shown in Figure 14-12.

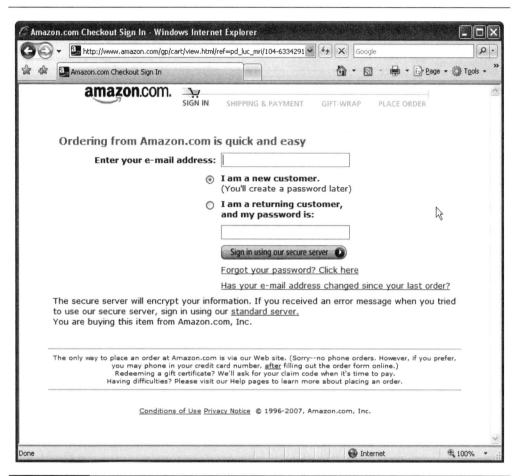

FIGURE 14-11   Using an Amazon shopping cart

The process of using this API is similar to the process of using Google Maps. Begin by clicking Start Using the API (either at the left or at the top of the page). You are prompted to enter the directory for which you want to use the API and you receive a key to use.

To use the API, you include a script in your mashup code that uses the src attribute to load the script from Google's servers. The src attribute includes the URL, as well as the key you obtain when you register for search (not the same as your Google mapping key). In addition to including the script in your code, you need to include a style sheet. Thus, your mashup that will use the Google search API requires these two lines of code:

```
<link href="http://www.google.com/uds/css/gsearch.css"
  type="text/css"
  rel="stylesheet"/>
```

FIGURE 14-12　Find out about Google AJAX Search API

```
<script
  src="http://www.google.com/uds/api?
    file=uds.js&amp;
    v=1.0&amp;
    key=yourKey"
  type="text/javascript">
</script>
```

The style sheet is used to format the search results. Using the API to retrieve search results and to format them yourself is possible, but the simplest use requires the style sheet.

The script element's src attribute contains the URL of the script you are including, the version, and your search key. It also contains a standard type attribute indicating this is JavaScript.

When you register for a Google search key, you can see the most basic search code with your key already included in it. As with the mapping API, immediately copy this code into a new file, save it, place it on your server, and access it with a browser. Make certain it runs before you try to continue.

This code provides a search page, shown in Figure 14-13.

The entire interface is provided by a powerful object called a *GSearchControl*, which includes the data entry field, the Search button, and the graphics. It also manages the search results. This lets you quickly add search to your pages.

Unfortunately, although this is the simplest way of using search, it is not what you often want with a mashup. In a mashup, you frequently are searching for something in Google and also searching for it (or otherwise manipulating it) in another API. In the next chapter, for instance, you enter a keyword or phrase in a form, and then you submit that form, so the mashup performs

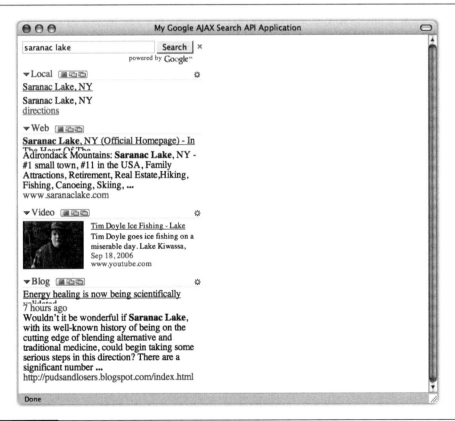

FIGURE 14-13   Run the basic Google search code

a Google search, as well as an Amazon search for products. As a result, the form and the SMALL CAPS: SUBMIT button belong on your starting page, and you do not want them on your mashup page.

There is another issue to note when you are embedding Google search in your mashup. The examples—both for mapping and for search—use the onload handler to perform the search or mapping when the page is loaded. In the architecture of most of the mashups in this book (and in real life), you want to run the components of the mashup on demand when a form is submitted that loads the page and performs the search, map, or whatever.

You can put all of this into the onload handler, but it can quickly become bulky. Using a structure in which the various APIs are run from scripts in the body of the mashup, rather than the onload handler, is easier. This design also has the advantage that each API is self-contained, and you can move the mapping API code to another mashup as easily as moving the searching API code to still another mashup. You do not have to untangle an unload handler.

To create a Google search that works in this way—that is, by searching for a parameter that is passed in, rather than by a phrase typed on the mashup page—you need to create an object that pulls together the pieces of the search API you need without the interactive interface with its Search button. Based on Google sample code, you can create a RawSearchControl. This object, which you define and create in your code, constructs the relevant search objects and executes a search. The search phrase is passed into the object as a parameter, and passed through to the native Google objects.

The constructor for this object has only four lines of code. It takes two parameters: the name of the div in your HTML code into which the results are to be placed and the search string used for the query.

```
function RawSearchControl(divName, searchString) {
  this.results = document.getElementById(divName);
  var searcher = new GwebSearch();
  searcher.setSearchCompleteCallback(
    this,
    RawSearchControl.prototype.searchComplete,
    [searcher]
  );
  searcher.execute(searchString);
}
```

First, it finds a div in your HTML code that it uses for the results of the search. (This is the same architecture as for mapping.) Thus, your HTML code must have something like this in it:

```
<div id="results"></div>
```

Next, it creates an instance of a searcher object. Currently, six search objects exist. Each is a descendant of the abstract class GSearch and each is capable of performing a search in the indicated area.

- GwebSearch
- GlocalSearch

- GvideoSearch
- GblogSearch
- GnewsSearch
- GbookSearch

For the most basic Web search, which is what the sample code developed here performs, you create a searcher object that is an instantiation of GwebSearch in the second line of code.

In the third line of code, you set the *callback routine*—the routine to be called when the search is completed—by calling set Search Complete Callback. This is the routine that processes the results. You can use this code exactly as it is shown here, and, in fact, you should do so. If you want, you can change the name of the callback routine you write, but it is simplest just to use this code without any changes.

The final line of code executes the search based on the parameter passed in for the search string.

You now need to code the completion routine. The code shown here is based on the Google examples. Directly (by calling clearResults) and indirectly (with clearResults calling removeChildren), it calls the functions to clear the previous results. Nothing in any of these routines needs to be changed.

```
RawSearchControl.prototype.searchComplete = function(searcher) {
  this.clearResults();

  if (searcher.results && searcher.results.length > 0) {
    for (var i=0; i<searcher.results.length; i++) {
      var result = searcher.results[i];
      if (result.html) {
        div = result.html.cloneNode(true);
      }
      this.results.appendChild (div);
    } // for loop
  } // if results
}

RawSearchControl.prototype.clearResults = function() {
  removeChildren(this.results);
}

function removeChildren(parent) {
  while (parent.firstChild) {
    parent.removeChild(parent.firstChild);
  }
}
```

14

The last step in the process of using your RawSearchControl is to provide a constructor that creates it. That constructor needs to take two parameters: one is the name of the div in your HTML and the other is the search string. Here is that function:

```
function createSearchControl (divName, searchString) {
  new RawSearchControl(divName, searchString);
}
```

To use your object, you simply add code to the body of your HTML page to call createSearchControl. Assuming the div is named results and the string you want to search for is "Lake Placid," here is the function call:

```
createSearchControl ('results','lake placid');
```

Of course, in your mashup you will probably hard-code the name of the div and use a variable to set the search string. In the following chapter, you see how this is all put together.

Chapter 15

Build a Mashup to Search Amazon and Google at the Same Time

How to...

- Decide on Your Mashup's Objective
- Identify the Data and the Keys
- Get Access to the Data
- Design the User Interface
- Implement the Mashup
- Implement the Starting Page
- Add Debugging and Error-Checking Code

In the previous chapter, you saw how to use the Amazon and Google Search APIs. This chapter shows you how to put them together into a mashup that lets you search both Google and Amazon for references to a word or phrase.

> **NOTE** *The final section of this chapter shows you how to add debugging and error-checking code to your mashup. This information is placed last in the chapter so the flow of the mashup when all goes well can be presented without interruption. In the real world, however, that convenient flow of processing all too often is interrupted, particularly during development. For that reason, references to the debugging and error-checking section are inserted at places in the mashup code where they are most likely to be useful. Debugging and error-checking may be last in the chapter, but they are not extras or options: without them, you may never get your mashup to work properly.*

Decide on Your Mashup's Objective

This mashup is designed to search Google and Amazon for a word or phrase. The basic output is shown in Figure 15-1.

The mashup includes links to the results of the Google search, as well as links to the Amazon store.

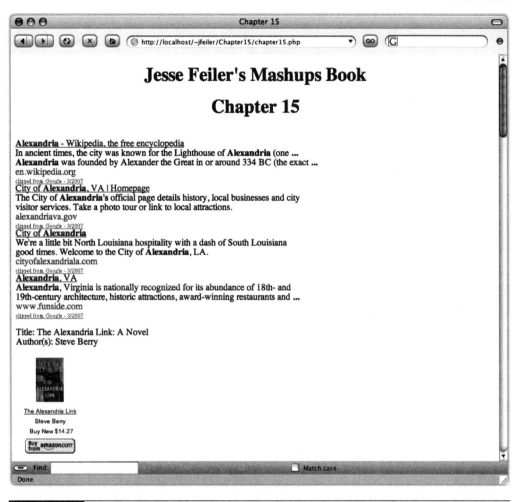

FIGURE 15-1   Search Google and Amazon

Identify the Data and the Keys

In this case, you let the user type in the search phrase. You could enhance the interface by using controls to limit searching to videos, news, books, and so, forth both in the Google search and in the Amazon search.

To modify the Google search, change the RawSearchControl constructor to create a different type of searcher—perhaps GvideoSearch. Likewise, to modify the Amazon search, you can set the searchIndex parameter to Video or whatever other option you choose. The searchIndex and the type of searcher should, obviously, be the same or at least related.

Get Access to the Data

You need both an Amazon access key and an Associate tag, as well as a Google Search API key.

Design the User Interface

The user interface for the example is shown in Figure 15-1. You can vary it so the Google and Amazon search results are next to one another using ordinary HTML code.

Implement the Mashup

Implementing the mashup is just a matter of combining the API code described in the previous chapter. The structure of the mashup (as well as of many mashups) is shown here.

The Basic Mashup Architecture

This is a PHP script, and it uses the conventions described previously in this book. A variable is set for the page title, and then it is used in the included PageTop.html file. PageTop.html opens the head element of the HTML document that will be returned. In the mashup file, you may have scripts placed in the header. The PageTop2.html file then closes the head element and opens the body.

Next, you create any HTML elements (such as div elements) to be referenced by the body scripts. Add the scripts and any final HTML, and then close the document with the PageBottom.html file.

```
<?php
$page_title = "Chapter 15";
include ('./Includes/PageTop.html');
?>

<script type="text/javascript">
  //<![CDATA[
  <!--scripts for head element-->
  //]]>
</script>
<?php
  include ('./Includes/PageTop2.html');
?>
```

```
<!--create div or other elements that will be
  referenced in body script-->

<script type="text/javascript">
  //<![CDATA[
  <!--scripts for body element-->
  //]]>
</script>
<!--other html code (if needed)-->

<?php
  include ('./Includes/PageBottom.html');
?>
```

The include files are the same as those used previously, with the exception of PageTop.html.
It needs your Amazon tag and key, as well as the script element with your Google search key.
The style sheet for Google search is also placed here. This is the code for PageTop.html:

```
<?xml version="1.0" encoding="iso-8859-1"?>
<!DOCTYPE html PUBLIC "-//W3C//DTD XHTML 1.0 Transitional//EN"
  "http://www.w3.org/TR/xhtml1/DTD/xhtml1-transitional.dtd">

<html xmlns="http://www.w3.org/1999/xhtml">
  <head>
    <title><?php echo $page_title; ?></title>
    <meta http-equiv="Content-Type" content="text/html;
      charset=iso-8859-1" />

  <link href="http://www.google.com/uds/css/gsearch.css"
    type="text/css" rel="stylesheet"/>
  <script
    src="http://www.google.com/uds/api?
      file=uds.js&amp;
      v=1.0&amp;
      key=yourKey"
  type="text/javascript">
  </script>

<?php
  define ('amazonAccessKeyID', 'yourAmazonKey');
  define ('amazonAssociateTag', 'yourAmazonTag');
?>
```

Code the Mashup

The code for the mashup uses the same Google search code as in the previous chapter. It also uses the Amazon API described in that chapter, together with the XML parsing, described previously in Chapters 8 and 9.

Code the Google Scripts

The Google search functions are placed in the head of the document. Because the code was just discussed, the bodies of the functions are omitted here.

```php
<?php
$page_title = "Chapter 15";
include ('./Includes/PageTop.html');
?>

<script language="Javascript" type="text/javascript">
    function createSearchControl (searchString) {
      new RawSearchControl(searchString);
    }

    function RawSearchControl(searchString) {
      // code omitted
    }

    RawSearchControl.prototype.searchComplete = function(searcher) {
      // code omitted
    }

    RawSearchControl.prototype.clearResults = function() {
      // code omitted
    }

    function removeChildren(parent) {
      // code omitted
    }

    function createDiv(opt_text, opt_className) {
      // code omitted
    };

</script>
```

Code the Amazon PHP

You now need to create a function to display the results of the Amazon query. You can place it here in the head element to create a structured mashup, which can easily be reused. This PHP code immediately follows the just described script element.

The Amazon search returns an XML document with the results. You parse it using standard XML parsing routines to display the results. The get_subnodes function does that job. This is standard boilerplate code based on two sources: the Amazon examples and the link you can build on the Build Links page, as described in the last chapter. Then, replace the hard-coded asins parameter with the value of a subnode in the list you retrieve.

When you use the Build Links page, you experiment with a known ASIN, ISBN, or UPC until you have a link you like. When you have it, copy the HTML into this function. The entire echo statement is replaced by the HTML you generated. The rest of the function remains the same. You need to make two adjustments in the HTML. Use the amazonAssociateTag define (from PageTop .html) and insert it into the echo string, as shown in the underlined part of this code.

The basic code takes a given node which is passed in as the parameter $theNode, and looks for all subnodes with the name $nodeName (also a parameter). If there are any subnodes, $nodeTitle—such as "Author: "—is echoed back (notice the colon and space in the $nodeTitle string). Then, for each subnode, if the parameter $option is not null, a link is created with your Amazon tag and the asin returned in the subnode. If $option is not present, the value of the text is passed through. Looking at the output shown previously in Figure 15-1, you can see what the results will be.

```php
<?php
function get_subnodes ($theNode, $nodeName, $nodeTitle, $option) {
  $theSubnodes = $theNode->getElementsByTagName ($nodeName);
  echo "<br>";
  if ($nodeTitle)
    echo $nodeTitle;
  $counter = 0;
  foreach ($theSubnodes as $theSubnode) {
    if ($option) {
      $theASIN = $theSubnode->nodeValue;
      echo '<iframe
        src="http://rcm.amazon.com/e/cm?t='
            .amazonAssociateTag.
          '&
          o=1&
          p=8&
          l=as1&
          asins='
            .$theASIN.'
          &
          IS1=1&
          nou=1&
```

```
          fc1=000000&
          lt1=_blank&
          lc1=0000ff&
          bc1=ffffff&
          bg1=ffffff&f=ifr"
      style="width:120px;height:240px;"
      scrolling="no"
      marginwidth="0"
      marginheight="0"
      frameborder="0">
      </iframe>
    ';
  } else {
    if ($counter > 0) {
      echo ", ";
    }
    echo $theSubnode->nodeValue;
  }
  $counter += 1;
}
} //get_subnodes
```

That completes the coding for the head element. PageTop2.html closes the head element and opens the body. The first thing you need to do in the body is to create two div elements to contain the results of the Amazon search and the Google search:

```
<?php
include ('./Includes/PageTop2.html');
?>
  <div id="searchcontrol"></div>
  <div id="results"></div>
```

Now that the get_subnodes function is declared, you can get to work running the query. The starting page contains a form with a field called keywords. You need to pick up that value and store it in a local PHP variable, just as you did before. The one slight difference from previous code is the spaces are replaced with escaped code. You can do this by replacing the spaces or by using the more general urlencode function (if you use the latter, make certain escaped characters that might appear already in the URL are handled properly). Here are your two choices: use one of them.

```
$theKeywords =  str_replace(" ", "%20", $_REQUEST['keywords']);
$theKeywords =  urlencode ($_REQUEST['keywords']);
```

Use heredoc Style as an Alternative

As always, the code shown here is formatted with extra lines and indentation to make its structure clearer. You might want to use the heredoc style, described previously in Chapter 6, instead of the concatenation of strings shown here. That style means you do not have to worry about switching from the building of strings of HTML or JavaScript with interspersed PHP variables and single or double quotation marks. You would, however, need to move the amazonAssociateTag define value into a variable. For example, in the heredoc style, the code in the echo statement that follows would begin as

```
$amazonAssociateTag = amazonAssociateTag;
echo <<<EOT
      <iframe
        src="http://rcm.amazon.com/e/cm?t=$amazonAssociateTag&
        o=1&
        p=8&
        l=as1&
        asins=$theASIN&
        ...more code
EOT;
```

Use whatever style makes the most sense to you as you type, debug, and finalize it for maintenance in the future when other people will need to read it.

You can use the curl routines to open a URL and download a file. This, too, is boilerplate code except for the customization of your own Amazon key, as shown in the underlined text. Nothing else in this code needs to change. (Refer to the previous chapter for more information about the structure of the Amazon URL. Chapter 8 describes the use of the curl library.)

```
$theURL = "http://webservices.amazon.com/onca/xml?
  Service=AWSECommerceService&
  AWSAccessKeyId="
    .amazonAccessKeyID.
  "&
  Operation=ItemSearch&
  Keywords="
    .$theKeywords.
  "&
  SearchIndex=Books&
```

```
    ResponseGroup=Request,Small&
    Version=2007-02-22";
$theURL .= "&Style=xml";

$c = curl_init($theURL);
curl_setopt ($c, CURLOPT_RETURNTRANSFER, 1);
$xml = curl_exec($c);
curl_close($c);

$doc = new DOMDocument();
$doc->loadXML($xml);
$root = $doc->documentElement;
```

The curl code is standard, in all cases, whether you're searching Amazon or accessing another site, but the next few lines are specific to Amazon. First, you get the Item elements of the returned document. Then, you loop through them looking for nodes with names Title, Author, and ASIN. Each of these is then passed into get_subnodes for echoing back for display. If you are using Amazon search, the following lines of code can be used without customization:

```
$theNodes = $root->getElementsByTagName('Item');

foreach ($theNodes as $theNode) {
  get_subnodes ($theNode, 'Title', 'Title: ');
  get_subnodes ($theNode, 'Author', 'Author(s): ');
  get_subnodes ($theNode, 'ASIN', '', "useHref");
  echo "<br>";
}
?>
```

This section of code is sufficient to perform the Amazon search and to display the results. The next script calls createSearchControl with the keywords data from the submitted form. That performs the Google search. Note, the mashup aspect of this is that the same data are passed into the Google and Amazon searches from the submitted form. (The reason the spaces in keywords need to be escaped for Amazon is that the text is embedded in a URL where spaces are not allowed. Here, the text of keywords is passed into a JavaScript function where spaces are allowed.)

```
<script language="Javascript" type="text/javascript">;
<?php
  echo ("createSearchControl ('".$_REQUEST['keywords']."');");
?>
</script>
```

The scripts for the Amazon search and for the Google search are presented in separate PHP code segments. This is for clarity—not just in the book, but in your own mashups. The more you can keep the components of a mashup separate from one another, the easier it will be to reuse them.

Finally, you close the document with the standard include file, and your mashup page is complete.

```php
<?php
include ('./Includes/PageBottom.html');
?>
```

Implement the Starting Page

The last step is to implement the start page, as shown in Figure 15-2.

You can place any graphics, instructions, links, or advertisements on the page. The key is the form that launches the mashup. Here is the HTML for the form:

```html
<form action="chapter15.php"
  method="post"
  enctype="multipart/form-data"
  name="Search Amazon">
  <p>Keywords:
    <input name="keywords"
      type="text"
      id="keywords"
```

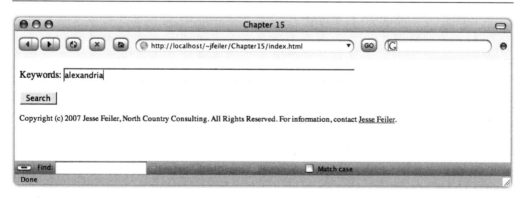

FIGURE 15-2 Create a start page

15

```
      size="60">
  </p>
  <p>
    <input type="submit" name="Submit" value="Search">
  </p>
</form>
```

The only customization you need is to set the form action to the name of the PHP file, and to set the input field name and ID to the name you plan to use in the mashup to extract the data from the request.

Add Debugging and Error-Checking Code

As noted previously, the flow of the example code was not interrupted with debugging and error-checking code, so you can see how it works. In reality, of course, you need that code. Here are two general mechanisms for handling debugging and error checking. They are presented in the context of code used previously in this chapter.

> **NOTE**   *In addition to these techniques, you can also use the approach shown in several chapters of this book, where you begin with a small part of the code and gradually add on new features so, at any given point, you have only a small number of new lines of code. For example, several of the mashups in this book begin by hard-coding items on which to search or even the data to be returned from a query. Once that works, you can add in the interface elements and the actual calls to a database or remote data source.*

Debugging Code

Debugging code is code you use during the development process. In the normal scheme of things, you no longer need debugging code once the mashup is ready to use in production. (In this way, debugging code differs from error-checking code, which may often continue to be used if necessary in production.)

Debugging code for any application normally consists of two components.

1. A mechanism that lets you easily turn debugging on and off. Frequently, this is a compiler option or a global variable. Using a control of this nature lets you leave the debugging code in the application. It is neither compiled nor executed, unless the appropriate switch is flipped.
2. In one or more places in your application, code is placed to let you monitor the processing of the application.

Setting a Global Debug Variable

In the mashup you can download for this chapter, you can find the global debug variable right at the top of the PHP file. Here is the beginning of that file:

```php
<?php $page_title = "Chapter 15";
  $debugMode = "debug";
  include ('./Includes/PageTop.html');
?>
```

The variable *$debugMode* can be set to the string debug to turn on debugging. In a more sophisticated structure, you can use multiple strings for the variable and test for which particular debugging code you want to execute. If you do not want to use debugging, simply omit the line. Then, the variable $debugMode is not set, so the test shown in the next section is not true.

Implementing Debugging

The basic test in this scenario is

```php
if ($debugMode == "debug")
```

If the result is true, then you do something, which, in most cases, displays data or a message indicating where you are in the program and what is happening. In the code described in this chapter, a useful place to use this code is right after you retrieve the XML code from Amazon.

Debugging the XML from Amazon

After you set the URL to be used, you use the CURL routines to attempt to retrieve the data. Here is that section of code with the debugging code added and underlined:

```php
$theURL = "http://webservices.amazon.com/onca/xml?
  Service=AWSECommerceService&AWSAccessKeyId=".amazonAccessKeyID."&
  Operation=ItemSearch&Keywords=".$theKeywords."&
  SearchIndex=Books&ResponseGroup=Request,Small&
  Version=2007-02-22"; $theURL .= "&
  Style=xml";
$c = curl_init($theURL);
curl_setopt ($c, CURLOPT_RETURNTRANSFER, 1);
$xml = curl_exec($c);
curl_close($c);

if ($debugMode == "debug")
  { echo $xml; }

$doc = new DOMDocument();
$doc->loadXML($xml);
$root = $doc->documentElement;
```

15

By echoing this code, you can see exactly what is being returned from Amazon. If all goes well, you should be receiving XML. For that reason, the echo that sends XML to the mashup page as displayed may be misleading. Look at the page source for the raw XML that contains the tags. It is not formatted, but you should be able to see what is being returned. You may want to copy the XML code from the page source and paste it into another application, which either lets you edit it or is sensitive to XML structure and can format it.

Checking the Result

The debugging code is probably not used after you test your mashup. Some error-checking may remain, even after you place your mashup into production. It can be used conditionally, depending on the *$debugMode* variable, or you can execute it at all times.

One prudent step to take is to examine the result codes returned from many procedure calls and from your call to Amazon (or to any other API). Considerable effort has gone into developing this information, so it is amazing how frequently developers ignore it.

In the case of Amazon (and many other APIs), XML elements are used to report on the results of calls. An appropriate place to do the error-checking is right after you execute the curl calls (and after you display the XML, if necessary) and before you start to parse the XML. There is no point parsing the XML if it is not going to have useful data.

Here is how you can add error-checking to that section of the code. The code consists of two strands of processing. The first takes the XML code that has been downloaded and parsed into a new DOMDocument with a $root element. Then, it attempts to find an element called IsValid. If IsValid is found, the value of that node is checked. It should be True.

The second strand sets and resets the variable *$validResult* at each step of the way. It starts by being set to no IsValid node. If getElementByTagName cannot find such a node, $validResult is not updated further in this section of code.

If, on the other hand, the IsValid node is found, then its value is retrieved and placed in $validResult, overriding no IsValid node. In the last section of code, the value of $validResult is checked. If it is True, the IsValid node was found, and that is its value. If it is anything else, $validResult is either left to display its default string (no IsValid node) or it displays whatever value the IsValid element returned—most likely False.

A further test is in this code: the value of $validResult is only echoed back in the case in which it is not True and $debugMode is turned on. You might want to change that section as indicated in the example code, so any unexpected result is displayed.

The underlined lines are the additions.

```
$doc = new DOMDocument();
$doc->loadXML($xml);

$root = $doc->documentElement;
```

```
// error checking
$validResult = "no IsValid node";
$isValidNode = $root->getElementsByTagName('IsValid');
if ($isValidNode != undefined)
{
  $validResult = $validNode->nodeValue;
}
if ($validResult != "True")
{
  if ($debugMode == "debug")// omit to show errors in all cases
  {// omit to show errors in all cases
    echo "IsValid error: ".$validResult;
  }// omit to show errors in all cases
}

$theNodes = $root->getElementsByTagName('Item');
```

Testing Error-Checking Code

Countless hours are spent debugging problems that are reported incorrectly in debugging and error-checking code. Checking out the code before you need to rely on it makes sense.

In the case of debugging code, verifying that it works is simple enough: make certain you see the debugging messages when you set the *$debugMode* variable to debug and that you do not see them when you omit that line of code.

In the case of error-checking, you need to generate an error in the URL you pass to Amazon. The simplest way of testing this is to break the URL. Look for a nonquoted string that is a word Amazon (or any other API) expects, and then change it. For example, here is part of the URL to search Amazon as used in this example:

```
Operation=ItemSearch&Keywords=".$theKeywords."&
```

You can change ItemSearch to NotItemSearch, as shown here:

```
Operation=NotItemSearch&Keywords=".$theKeywords."&
```

The resulting page shows the message, but if you look at the page source, you can see the full XML with its tags. Here is what is shown on the page source page, reformatted for readability. The first section is the XML displayed with the debugging code

```
<?xml version="1.0" encoding="UTF-8"?>

<Errors
  xmlns="http://webservices.amazon.com/AWSECommerceService
  /2005-10-05">
  <Error>
```

```
<Code>AWS.InvalidOperationParameter</Code>
<Message>The Operation parameter is invalid.
Please modify the Operation parameter and retry.
Valid values for the Operation parameter include
ListLookup, CartGet, SellerListingLookup,
CustomerContentLookup, ItemLookup, SimilarityLookup,
SellerLookup, ItemSearch, VehiclePartLookup,
BrowseNodeLookup, CartModify, ListSearch, CartClear,
CustomerContentSearch, CartCreate, VehiclePartSearch,
TransactionLookup, VehicleSearch, SellerListingSearch,
CartAdd, Help.
</Message>
   </Error>
</Errors>
```

Following the XML display will be the message generated in the error-checking code:

```
IsValid error:
```

Chapter 16

Use the Flickr API

How to . . .

- Use the Flickr API
- Get Access to the Flickr API
- Search for Photos
- Display a Photo

Each API you use in mashups has a great deal in common with all the others. Now that you have seen several APIs in action, the remaining ones in this book and in the outside world will seem simpler with each additional one you use. For the penultimate mashup example in this book, you see how to search Flickr and Google simultaneously. The Flickr API is a new addition to the APIs you have already seen. You could use other APIs instead of Google so you could search Amazon, for example, while searching Filckr.

Flickr is the photo-sharing service that lets you upload your photos and view photos others have uploaded. Information about each photo can be added and searched on when you are looking for something. Most important, photos can have *tags*—words the uploader feels can be used to identify the photos. You can search Flickr for photos matching specific tags either interactively or using the API.

Get Access to the Flickr API

The first step, as always, is to get access to the developer API with a key. Then you can explore the API and use API Explorer.

How to ...   Get More Information About Flickr

As with all the APIs discussed in this book, you can use many Web resources to find documentation, as well as to discuss issues with other developers, both novice and experienced. Here are some of them.

- The *Flickr API Group* on Flickr is the official group for discussing API issues: http://www.flickr.com/groups/api/.
- The *Flickr Hacks group* on Flickr is an active forum to discuss less-than-official issues: http://www.flickr.com/groups/flickrhacks/.

FIGURE 16-1   Sign in to Flickr

Getting a Key

If you have not used Flickr for a while (or ever), you may need to get a Yahoo! ID to gain access. As the world of mashup software and the components of Web 2.0 are restructured, mergers and acquisitions have changed the landscape, and Flickr is now part of Yahoo! Figure 16-1 shows the Flickr home page with the sign-in box at the right.

Once you have a key, you can place it in the include file PageTop.html in the same way you placed other keys there. PageTop.html looks like this with a Flickr key in it:

```
<?xml version="1.0" encoding="iso-8859-1"?>
<!DOCTYPE html PUBLIC "-//W3C//DTD XHTML 1.0 Transitional//EN"
        "http://www.w3.org/TR/xhtml1/DTD/xhtml1-transitional.dtd">
```

```html
<html xmlns="http://www.w3.org/1999/xhtml">
<head>
  <title><?php echo $page_title; ?></title>
  <meta http-equiv="Content-Type" content="text/html;
    charset=iso-8859-1" />
<?php
  define ('flickrKey', 'yourFlickrKey');
?>
```

Exploring the API

You can reach the API page by following links to Tools (at the bottom of the home page), to the Developers link at the right of the Tools page that takes you to the Services page, and then to the API link on that page. Or, you can go directly to http://www.flickr.com/services/api/, as shown in Figure 16-2.

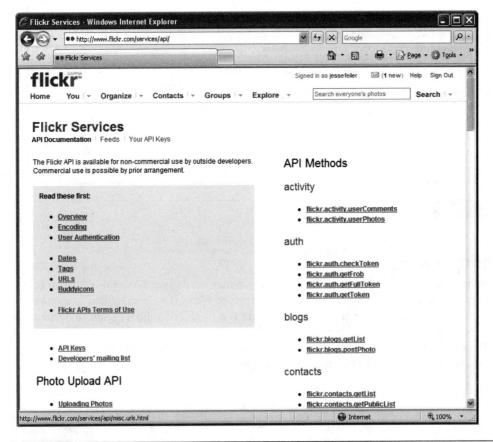

FIGURE 16-2   Go to the Flickr API page

If you do not have a Flickr key, you can get one by clicking API Keys at the left of this page in the Read These First section. If you have one, but have forgotten it, you can find it in the same spot (provided you are signed in with the same Yahoo! ID).

The information at the left side of the page is useful, but it is the API reference at the right side that is most important at this point. The API routines are grouped by category. For the mashup built in the next chapter, you need to scroll down to the Photos section and click on flickr.photos.search, which lets you search for a list of photos.

The flickr.photos.search API page, shown in Figure 16-3, is typical of all Flickr API pages. After a brief description of the routine, the page is divided into several sections.

■ **Authentication**   Calls may require authentication for completion. Some, such as search, require no authentication. Others require one of the currently defined permissions: read, write, and delete. Searching for photos requires no authentication at all, which is one of the reasons it is used in the mashup example in the next chapter (as well as the fact that it is a useful call). The Flickr Authentication API is found at http://www.flickr.com/services/api/auth.spec.html.

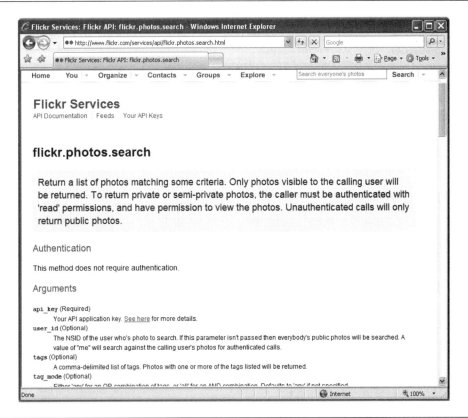

FIGURE 16-3   The flickr.photos.search API

■ **Arguments**   Arguments to each call are listed and defined: each is marked as optional or required. If you are doing anything beyond the basics, you should scan the list of arguments to see what is available and how to use the arguments. However, the API Explorer (described later in this section) may be an easier and faster way of exploring the arguments.

■ **Example Response**   This is a sample of the response you can expect. It is usually a variation on the standard photo list in XML. In its simplest form, this is an XML element called photos that contains any number of photo (note singular form) elements—one per photo returned. Do not bother studying the example too closely, because the API Explorer also provides you with more information.

■ **Error Codes**   These are the possible error codes that can be returned.

■ **API Explorer**   At the bottom of the page is a link to the API Explorer page for each routine. This is described in the next section in the context of searching for photos.

NOTE

Toward the bottom of the Flickr API page, the top of which is shown in Figure 16-2, you see links to the various request and response formats. These are independent of one another. You can send a REST request and get the response back as SOAP. The key to all this is to add the keyword format to the URL you construct as the request. The currently supported values for keyword are rest, soap, xmlrpc, json, and php_serial. A typical request with a format keyword looks like this:

```
http://api.flickr.com/services/rest/?
  method=flickr.photos.search&
  api_key=yourFlickrKey&
  tags=Plattsburgh&
  format=soap
```

Search for Photos

You can use API Explorer to experiment and learn about the method you want to call. Then, it is a relatively simple matter to write the PHP and JavaScript code to implement the call for your own need.

Use API Explorer

Scroll down to the link to API Explorer at the bottom of the API page, as shown in Figure 16-4.

API Explorer provides a list of all the possible arguments for a call and lets you enter data for them. If you click on the API Explorer link in flickr.photos.search, you open the page shown in Figure 16-5.

In this case, data have been entered for the tags argument to search Flickr photos. The Send check box is automatically checked as soon as you type into an argument's data field, but you can uncheck it for testing so it is not sent.

FIGURE 16-4 Use API Explorer

The bottom of the API Explorer page is shown in Figure 16-6. The last two arguments are useful for testing (and for implementation, too). You can limit the number of photo returns per page (that is, in the photos XML element). You can also specify which page to retrieve. Note, the page argument does not specify the number of pages to retrieve, but which of the various computed pages is retrieved.

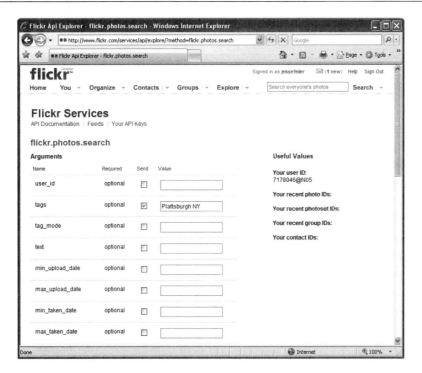

16

FIGURE 16-5 Go to the API Explorer page for flickr.photos.search

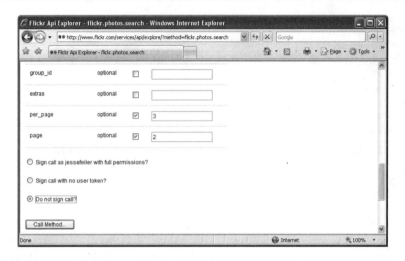

FIGURE 16-6   Set the signing options and call the method

These arguments are specific to flickr.photos.search. At the bottom of the list, you specify how you want to sign the request, and then you can click the Call Method button. If a request does not need authentication, you do not need to sign it, so use the Do not sign call option, as shown in Figure 16-6.

When you call the method, the area beneath the button is updated to show you the results of the call, as shown in Figure 16-7. This is similar to the example response you saw on the basic API page, but this is the actual result of the call you just generated. You can change argument values and call the method over and over to see how it behaves. At the bottom of the page, the actual call to the method is shown. You can copy and paste it into your code or use it as the base of a function in PHP.

Here is a sample function to create a Flickr call, such as the one shown here. It breaks up the construction of the call into several readable lines, which you can use exactly as shown here. As indicated, a variable *$theKeywords* is used—just as it was used in the previous chapters—to pick up data stored in the form's request. This is passed into this function's call. Also, the final link specifies the number of photos per page and the page to display. You can omit this line if you want.

```php
function createFlickrCall ($theKeywords) {
  $theCall = "http://api.flickr.com/services/rest/?";
  $theCall .= "method=flickr.photos.search&api_key=";
  // flickr Key is defined in PageTop.html
  $theCall .= flickrKey;
  $theCall .= "&tags=";
```

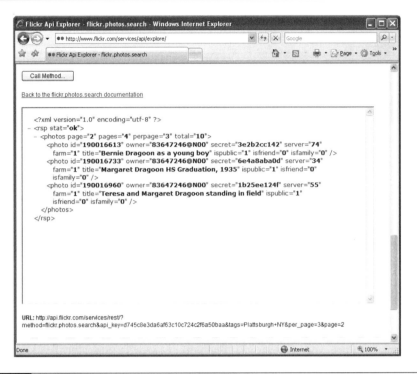

FIGURE 16-7   Results of test flickr.photos.search call

```
    // customize the call with the parameter $theKeywords
    $theCall .= $theKeywords;
    // omit or customize for the amount of data to be returned
    $theCall .= "&per_page=5&page=1";
    return $theCall;
}
```

You can visually parse the results (which is one reason for limiting the number of photos returned, but beware of extrapolating from the minimal list of only one photo—always try to use at least two or three).

The basic element of the response is an *rsp* element with a stat (status) attribute. Within that is the photos element, representing the page requested (or all photos if there is only one). Within the photos element are the photo elements, each representing a single photo.

The structure here begins to differ from the Amazon structure described in the last two chapters. Part of the results of an Amazon search are shown formatted in Firefox in Figure 16-8.

16

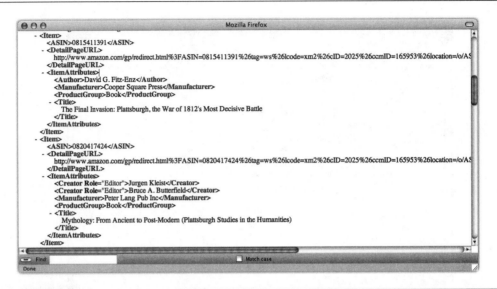

FIGURE 16-8   Results of an Amazon book search

If you compare the two, you can see two different approaches to presenting the data. In Flickr (Figure 16-7), each photo is presented in a single element: attributes specify ID, owner, title, and so forth. In Amazon (Figure 16-7), each item returned (a book in this case) contains subelements such as ASIN, and DetailPageURL. There is even an ItemAttributes element, which, itself, contains subelements for Creator, Manufacturer, and Title. In the case of the Amazon structure, you need to go into the XML tree in a routine such as get_subnodes, as described in the last two chapters. In the case of the Flickr XML architecture, no subnodes are in a photo element, so you merely need to pull out the attributes.

Display a Photo

In the Amazon example, all the information you need to display the results of the query is provided in the XML returned from the method call. You display some of that data directly. In the case of the text, other data are used to display the image and link to buy in an HTML iframe element, adding the amazonAssociateTag and ASIN to the boilerplate HTML.

You do the same thing with Flickr, but the details are different in constructing the URL. You can find the specification at http://www.flickr.com/services/api/misc.urls.html (it is also linked from the API Explorer page). This page is shown in Figure 16-9.

FIGURE 16-9   How to construct a URL for a photo

The code to extract the keywords from the request, call createFlickrCall, and get the resulting XML is shown here (this is the same as the code in previous chapters except for the creation of the specific Flickr call):

```
$theKeywords =  urlencode($_REQUEST['keywords']);

$theURL = createFlickrCall ($theKeywords);

$xml = file_get_contents($theURL);

$doc = new DOMDocument();
$doc->loadXML($xml);
$root = $doc->documentElement;
```

16

file_get_contents relies on fopen_wrappers being enabled in your PHP installation. If this is not enabled, only local files can be opened in this way. The work-around is to replace the line that calls file_get_contents with the same code you saw previously in Chapter 8

```
$c = curl_init($theURL);
curl_setopt ($c, CURLOPT_RETURNTRANSFER, 1);
$xml = curl_exec($c);
curl_close($c);
```

That code sets $xml (in the line just before curl_close). You can then continue with the code, as shown here.

At this point, you need to extract the photo nodes, and then loop through them. You do not need to extract subnodes. Instead, you extract the attributes and build a URL, as shown in Figure 16-9. The only trick here is to note that in the URL syntax, you must differentiate between characters in the URL that appear as is, those that are attributes—enclosed in { and }, and those that represent variable parameters, such as the size of the photo—enclosed in [and], from which you choose one option. For this example, the *m* option is chosen, which is 240 pixels on the largest size. The indicated line is the only one that needs to be customized in your mashup.

Table 16-1 shows the various size options and their meanings.

```
$theNodes = $doc->getElementsByTagName('photo');

foreach ($theNodes as $theNode) {
  $theFlickrURL = "http://farm";
  $theFlickrURL .= $theNode->getAttribute('farm');
  $theFlickrURL .= ".static.flickr.com/";
  $theFlickrURL .= $theNode->getAttribute('server');
```

Option	Longest Side (pixels)
s	Small square (75×75)
t	Thumbnail (100)
m	Small (240)
<none>	Medium (400)
b	Large (1,024)
o <letter *o*>	Original size

TABLE 16-1 Flickr Option Values for Image Size

```
$theFlickrURL .= "/";
$theFlickrURL .= $theNode->getAttribute('id');
$theFlickrURL .= "_";
$theFlickrURL .= $theNode->getAttribute('secret');
// customize the size option by replacing m with another size
// (or with nothing and
// omitting the leading underscore
$theFlickrURL .= "_m.jpg";
```

You can simplify this code with a utility function that builds Flickr URLs. Jim Bumgardner, technical editor of this book, has a function that does this. It has exactly the same result as the code shown previously.

```
function MakeFlickrImageURL($photo, $suffix)
{
  return sprintf("http://farm%s.static.flickr.com/%d/%d_%s%s.jpg",
    $photo->getAttribute(farm),
    $photo->getAttribute(server),
    $photo->getAttribute(id),
    $photo->getAttribute(secret),
    $suffix);
}
```

To call the utility function, rewrite the beginning of the loop as follows:

```
foreach ($theNodes as $theNode) {
  $theFlickrURL = MakeFlickrImageURL($theNode, "_m");
```

Because you know the photo will be 240 pixels on its largest side, you can construct an iframe HTML element that is 240 pixels wide and high: it is guaranteed to display the photo. (If you use other size options, adjust the iframe HTML accordingly.)

```
  echo '<iframe src="'.$theFlickrURL.'"
    style="width:240px;height:240px;"
    scrolling="no" marginwidth="0" marginheight="0"
    frameborder="0"></iframe>';
  echo "<br>";
}
```

That is all you need to access photos from Flickr. You can use many other API calls, not only for photos, but also to query and update other data in the Flickr database. In the next chapter, you build a mashup that searches Flickr and Google for keywords. You also use one of the tags APIs.

16

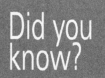

Alternatives to Parsing XML for Flickr

Flickr has recently added support for PHP serialized results for all API calls, which eliminates the need to do an XML parsing pass (the data structures returned are essentially the same as those returned using the JSON option).

Also, some wrapper kits can simplify API use (especially the intricate authentication bits):

```
http://www.phpflickr.com/
http://code.iamcal.com/php/flickr/readme.htm
```

Chapter 17

Build a Mashup to Search Flickr and Google at the Same Time

How to...

- Decide on Your Mashup's Objective
- Identify the Data and the Keys
- Get Access to the Data
- Regroup
- Design the User Interface
- Implement the Mashup
- Implement the Starting Page

As you develop mashups, you can see how the basic processes are the same from one to the other. The list of steps involved in creating a new mashup (or revising an old one) does not get shorter. It does, however, become more and more like a reminder checklist, as you quickly find a way to add your idea of a connection to two or more data sources or representations of data.

This chapter presents a variation on the scenario of Chapters 15 and 16. In that case, keywords were entered and used to search both Amazon and Google. In this case, keywords are entered and are used to search Flickr. Then, instead of using those keywords to search Google, this mashup uses the Flickr API to look up related terms to the entered keywords, and then those terms are used in a Google search. This scenario is one of the most interesting you can discover in the world of mashups, and you can create it for yourself, as long as the first item retrieved returns a value you know can be used in a further call to some API or other.

A major part of the power of mashups is using chains of retrievals such as this to leap from keywords for retrieval to ZIP codes to latitude and longitude, to pictures, and to other data. As long as the endpoint of each link of the chain can share a common retrieval key, with the beginning of the next link, you can combine data to your heart's content.

Decide on Your Mashup's Objective

This mashup uses keywords to search the tags of Flickr photos, as well as a Google search. You can add your own graphics to the mashups page or use it as a starting point for another mashup. The mashup will look like Figure 17-1.

Identify the Data and the Keys

The keys—as is often the case—are keywords. Searches such as Google, Amazon, and Yahoo! use keyword searches all the time to search their various databases. Sites such as Flickr, deli .ci.ous, digg, and many social networking sites let users assign keywords to data. The advantage

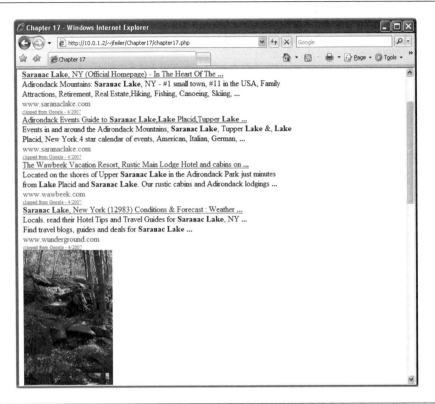

FIGURE 17-1   A mashup to combine Google search and Flickr photo search

of all this is you can search for the same keywords on a variety of sites. The disadvantage is it is loosely structured. Unless you are remarkably careful, you will hit a person, a lake, and a town if you search for Champlain.

When using the various APIs for keyword searches, pay particular attention to the handling of spaces in the search phrase. They may need to be escaped with %20 or replaced with + or another character. The code in this mashup (and others) handles the situation appropriately. Note, the substitution is done to the data that were entered just before they are sent to a query. In this mashup, spaces are escaped for the Flickr call, but they are left intact when creating the Google search object that uses related terms returned from Flickr, which may or may not include spaces.

Get Access to the Data

You need access keys for Flickr and Google, as described in the previous chapters.

17

Design the User Interface

The user interface here is simple: a div element that contains the results of the Google search and iframe elements for each photo returned.

Implement the Mashup

This mashup uses the same architecture and include files as the others presented in this book. You need to change PageTop.html to include the keys for Google and Flickr, as shown here. This is the entire PageTop.html file:

```
<?xml version="1.0" encoding="iso-8859-1"?>
<!DOCTYPE html PUBLIC "-//W3C//DTD XHTML 1.0 Transitional//EN"
          "http://www.w3.org/TR/xhtml1/DTD/xhtml1-transitional.dtd">
<html xmlns="http://www.w3.org/1999/xhtml">
<head>
  <title><?php echo $page_title; ?></title>
  <meta http-equiv="Content-Type" content="text/html;
    charset=iso-8859-1" />
  <link href="http://www.google.com/uds/css/gsearch.css"
    type="text/css" rel="stylesheet"/>
  <script src="http://www.google.com/uds/api?file=uds.js&amp;
    v=1.0&amp;
    key=yourKey"
    type="text/javascript">
  </script>
<?php
  define ('flickrKey', yourKey);
?>
```

This mashup is particularly simple because the Goggle half of it is almost unchanged from the Google search code in Chapters 14 and 15. The only difference is a loop used to construct the follow-on query from related tag values returned from Flickr.

The code for the createFlickrCall function was shown and described in Chapter 16. A new function that looks up related tag values is added here, but its structure is much the same as createFlickrCall. To clarify the code, createFlickrCall is renamed createFlickSearchCall, and the new call is named createFlickrGetRelatedCall.

These calls could be combined into one with a set of parameters, but because they take different sets of parameters, making them into separate functions is easier.

Here is the basic structure of the top of the mashup. The bodies of the functions are omitted except for the two Flickr routines. Because all these routines use parameters, you can use the code shown here exactly as is with no further customization.

```php
<?php
$page_title = "Chapter 17";
include ('./Includes/PageTop.html');
?>

<script language="Javascript" type="text/javascript">

  function createSearchControl (divName, searchString) {
    // code omitted
  }

  function RawSearchControl(divName, searchString) {
    //code omitted
  }

  RawSearchControl.prototype.searchComplete = function(searcher) {
      // code omitted
  }

  RawSearchControl.prototype.clearResults = function() {
    // code omitted
  }

  function removeChildren(parent) {
    // code omitted
  }

</script>

<?php
  function createFlickrSearchCall ($theKeywords) {
    $theCall = "http://api.flickr.com/services/rest/?
      method=flickr.photos.search";
    $theCall .= "&api_key=";
    $theCall .= flickrKey;
    $theCall .= "&tags=";
    $theCall .= $theKeywords;
    $theCall .= "&per_page=5&page=1";
    return $theCall;
  }
```

17

```
    function createFlickrGetRelatedhCall ($theKeywords) {
      $theCall = "http://api.flickr.com/services/rest/
        ?method=flickr.tags.getRelated";
      $theCall .= "&api_key=";
      $theCall .= flickrKey;
      $theCall .= "&tag=";
      $theCall .= $theKeywords;
      return $theCall;
    }
?>


<?php
include ('./Includes/PageTop2.html');
?>
```

Begin the body of the page by declaring a div into which the Google search control will be placed:

```
  <div id="results"></div>
```

Now comes the PHP code to unload the keywords from the submitted form, encode the URL with urlencode, call createFlickrSearchCall, and get the XML result:

```
<?php
$theKeywords = urlencode ($_REQUEST['keywords']);

$theURL = createFlickrSearchCall ($theKeywords);

$xml = file_get_contents($theURL);

$doc = new DOMDocument();
$doc->loadXML($xml);
$root = $doc->documentElement;
```

Remember, if file_get_contents is unavailable in your server's PHP environment, you can substitute the following code for file_get_conents:

```
$c = curl_init($theURL);
curl_setopt ($c, CURLOPT_RETURNTRANSFER, 1);
$xml = curl_exec($c);
curl_close($c);
```

Once you have the root of the returned XML document, you need to pick up all the photo nodes, as described in the previous chapter. Then, it is a matter of a loop to go through each node, extracting the relevant attributes to build a URL to use in the iframe element to display the photo:

```
$theNodes = $doc->getElementsByTagName('photo');

foreach ($theNodes as $theNode) {
  $theFlickrURL = "http://farm";
  $theFlickrURL .= $theNode->getAttribute('farm');
  $theFlickrURL .= ".static.flickr.com/";
  $theFlickrURL .= $theNode->getAttribute('server');
  $theFlickrURL .= "/";
  $theFlickrURL .= $theNode->getAttribute('id');
  $theFlickrURL .= "_";
  $theFlickrURL .= $theNode->getAttribute('secret');
  $theFlickrURL .= "_m.jpg";
  echo '<iframe src="'.$theFlickrURL.'"
    style="width:240px;height:240px;" scrolling="no"
    marginwidth="0" marginheight="0" frameborder="0"></iframe>';
  echo "<br>";
}
```

After having created the iframe elements to display the photos, you call the new createFlickrGetRelatedCall function to create the keywords for the Google search. This is one of the Flickr tags functions. It takes a single parameter, which is the tag value to look up, and it returns an XML tags element with individual tag elements containing related tag values. Here is a sample return value from a lookup of related values for Plattsburgh (the XML was formatted for readability here):

```
<rsp stat="ok">
  <tags source="plattsburgh">
    <tag>lakechamplain</tag>
    <tag>newyork</tag>
    <tag>lake</tag>
    <tag>ny</tag>
    <tag>water</tag>
    <tag>landscape</tag>
    <tag>ferry</tag>
    <tag>adirondacks</tag>
    <tag>usa</tag>
    <tag>champlain</tag>
  </tags>
</rsp>
```

17

The code to generate this call, and then combine all the result tag strings into a single variable, is comparable to the code for handling the createFlickrSearchCall. The only differences are the name of the call used to generate $theURL and the name of the tag elements to retrieve.

```
    $theURL = createFlickrGetRelatedCall ( $theKeywords);
    $xml = file_get_contents($theURL);
    $doc = new DOMDocument();
    $doc->loadXML($xml);
    $root = $doc->documentElement;
    $theNodes = $doc->getElementsByTagName('tag');
?>
```

Having retrieved the tag elements, you can create a loop to concatenate them. Notice the concatenation inserts spaces between the tag values. After the loop, you call createSearchControl with the concatenated text to perform the Google search on the related terms.

```
<script language="Javascript" type="text/javascript">;
<?php
   $theRelatedTags = '';
foreach ($theNodes as $theTag) {
    $theRelatedTags .= $theTag->nodeValue. ' ';
  }
 echo ('createSearchControl ("results", "'.$theRelatedTags.'");');
?>
</script>
<?php
include ('./Includes/PageBottom.html');
?>
```

NOTE *If you use this as a model, consider the data with which you are working. You will probably not know what keywords people use to launch the process, but you may want to build in some controls, so the volume of data retrieved is not enormous. The more you know about your users and what they might be looking up, the more you can customize the logic of your mashup. For example, if you refer to the XML sample previously shown in this chapter, you will note "usa" is one of the related tags. It may be that such a tag is so prevalent that you might want to screen out the most frequently found (and not needed) tags for the domain of knowledge you are dealing with.*

Implement the Starting Page

For the last step, you need to implement a starting page, which is almost identical to the preceding starting page. The key element is a form that specifies an input field for the keywords (which must be named keywords) and the action to perform (which is the name of the PHP document to be executed). Here is the code with the customized items underlined:

```
<form action="chapter17.php" method="post"
  enctype="multipart/form-data" name="Search">
  <p>Keywords:
    <input name="keywords" type="text" id="keywords" size="60">
  </p>
  <p>
    <input type="submit" name="Submit" value="Search">
  </p>
</form>
```

Chapter 18

Use the eBay API

How to...

- Get Access to the eBay API
- Use the API Test Tool
- Use the REST Interface
- Use the SOAP Interface
- Parse the XML Results

The eBay API is the most complex one described in this book. There are many reasons for that, not the least of which are that it has been open to third-party developers for a long time and the process (auctions) is more complex than the relatively simple process of buying and selling for a fixed price.

This chapter presents the basics of the API and shows you how to search for items using both the SOAP interface and the REST interface. In the next chapter, eBay searches are displayed on a Google map based on the location of the seller.

> **NOTE**
> *The SOAP protocol can be more powerful and complex than the REST protocol. For some applications, the additional power and complexity are not only useful, but also desired. Among these applications where SOAP may be preferred are many, such as eBay, where security is a primary concern. Because this chapter shows both the SOAP and REST APIs, you can compare them in action.*

Get Access to the eBay API

The basic steps for getting access to the API are the same as with other APIs, but in the case of eBay, you have more keys to worry about. You begin by going to the eBay Developer Center at http://developer.ebay.com. You register as a developer through that page, and then sign in, as shown in Figure 18-1.

You can use two environments in testing your access to eBay: the Sandbox and Production. The *Sandbox environment* is a protected environment for developers where you can experiment with listing items and entering transactions without fear of corrupting the live database. If you are developing a mashup that searches eBay, but does not update the database with new items or bids, you may prefer to use the *Production environment,* so you can see more data in your test mashup.

When you register as a developer, you receive two sets of three keys, one set for each of the two environments. The three keys are a *Developer ID*, an *Application ID*, and a *Certificate ID*. The Developer ID identifies you uniquely in each environment. If you develop more than one application, then you have separate Application ID keys for each application, but you normally share the Developer ID, so all your applications can be linked together. The Certificate ID provides authentication of the application when calls are made. These keys are long strings of

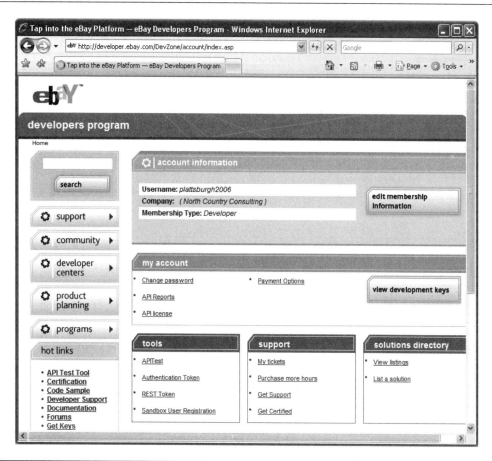

FIGURE 18-1   eBay Developer Sign In

numbers, letters, and certain characters. You can always retrieve them from the Developer Sign In page shown in Figure 18-1.

Use the API Test Tool

The *API Test Tool* lets you test API calls from a Web page. To use it, you need your keys as described in the previous section, as well as an eBay User ID. You also need Internet Explorer (IE) running on Windows, because that is the only browser currently supported. (This is for the API Test Tool only. The API itself works with other browsers and on other platforms.)

18

Two steps are needed to use the API Test Tool. First, you need to create a token that links together your three keys (for either the Sandbox or Production environment) with a specific eBay User ID. Then, you provide all this information to the API Test Tool and execute a call.

Generating the Token

To generate the token, go to http://developer.ebay.com/tokentool, as shown in Figure 18-2.

If you are using REST, make certain to check the box that returns a specific REST token. Do not bother to type in your keys: you can return to the Developer Sign In page to retrieve them, and then copy and paste them here. They are too long and complex to type. When you click the Continue link, you see the standard eBay User ID Sign In page, shown in Figure 18-3. Sign in with your own eBay User ID—not a developer ID.

The person signing in must confirm this action is desired, as you can see in Figure 18-4.

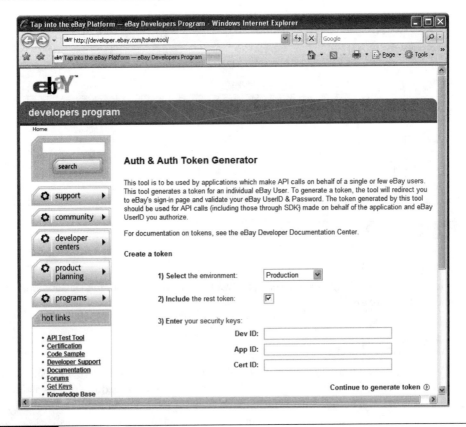

FIGURE 18-2   Generate the token

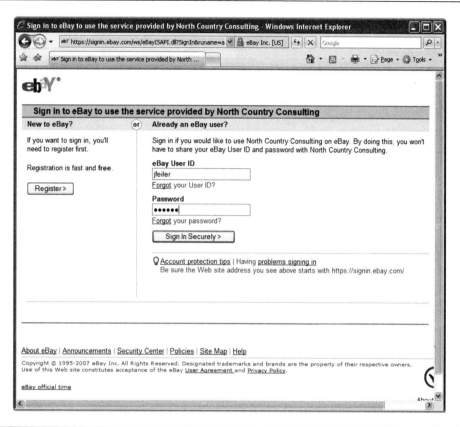

FIGURE 18-3   Sign in to eBay

You then receive the token linking your three keys with the eBay User ID. You are now ready to make calls. This token is even longer than the keys you already received. Move the window that displays the token aside, so you can copy and paste it in the next step.

 This basic process is repeated when you grant access to your code to an eBay user. However, you can program the code so the sign in for the user is done as part of your application, not as part of this interactive tool, which is designed primarily for testing.

Making the API Call

The actual API Test Tool is linked from the Tools section in the lower part of the Developer Sign In page, shown previously in Figure 18-1. (It is also linked from a number of other places on the site.) The API Test Tool runs only in IE on Windows at this time. Figure 18-5 shows the API Test Tool with the keys and token obscured.

18

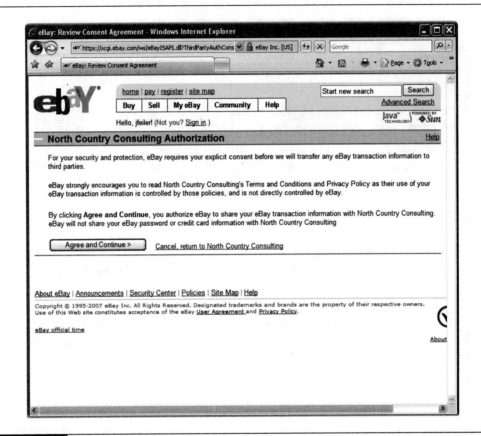

FIGURE 18-4   The user confirms the request

Choose either Sandbox or Production, and then copy and paste the three appropriate keys into the form. Also, paste in the token you generated in the previous step. The Compatibility Level is preset with a current version, and the default Site ID is 0 (the United States). You can change these if you want.

On the next page, you can select the API call you want to test from the pop-up menu. You select a template for the SOAP call, which is shown in the large text area you see in Figure 18-6. Your token is automatically placed into the call in the appropriate place. If you are using GetSearchResults to do a search of eBay, you can see the Query element. Type in whatever you want to search for, and then click Submit. The call is then submitted and the results are displayed. (You will see the results later in this chapter.)

The next three sections provide details of the calls for REST and SOAP, as well as the XML results returned in both cases.

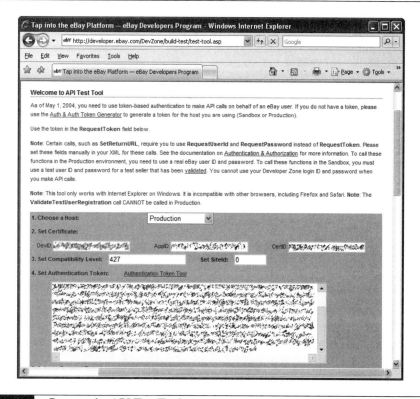

FIGURE 18-5 Prepare the API Test Tool

NOTE *The Documentation link at the left of the Developer Sign In page, shown in Figure 18-1, provides you with the details of all the eBay calls. Many details are available and you have many options. Many mashups use the eBay data as a source for information to be mashed up. If this is what you are doing, you can safely ignore the bulk of the documentation because it is involved with the actual updating of the database with listings, bids, and so forth. Retrieving data is far simpler.*

Use the REST Interface for GetSearchResults

Using the REST interface from PHP takes four steps:

1. Define your token and user ID.
2. Set up variables for the call.
3. Put the variables into an HTTP request.
4. Execute the request.

These are the same basic steps shown in most of the calls you have already seen.

18

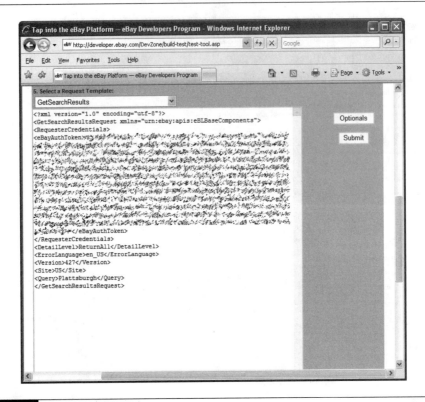

FIGURE 18-6 Seleect the template

Define Your Token and User ID

For a REST call, you need an eBay User ID and a REST token. The REST token is generated in Step 2 of the Token Generator, if you have the checkbox selected shown previously in Figure 18-2. Your three keys for Sandbox or Production are used internally in creating that tool. Remember, you must use the appropriate keys for the environment you are using. One of the reasons for using a specific REST token is this: the request you send is visible at various points, so the more secure set of three keys should not appear in it.

As is the case with the other examples in this book, the needed keys are placed in defines in PageTop.html. Here is an example:

```
define ('requestToken', 'yourRESTToken');
define ('requestUserId', 'youreBayUserID');
```

Set Up Variables

Your code is more readable and easier to maintain if you place values into variables, which are then incorporated into the actual request. Here is a set of variables to use for a call to GetSearchResults:

```
$theCall = "GetSearchResults";
$theSite = "US";
$SiteId = '0';
$Version = '427';
$EntriesPerPage = '4';
$PageNumber = '1';
$theQuery =  str_replace(" ", "+", $_REQUEST['keywords']);
```

These use the US site (0), and version 427 of the software and the GetSearchResults call. The page parameters are similar to the Amazon page parameters: the number of entries per page, and the specific page to be shown (not the number of pages). All these are placed in local variables, as well as the contents of the keywords field in the submitted form. Note, spaces are replaced with the + character as you saw in previous calls.

Create the Request

Now that the variables are filled and the defines created, you can build the request. This is the same process that has happened in each example so far. If you created the variables in the previous step, you can use this code without any changes.

```
$theURL = "http://rest.api.ebay.com/restapi?"
  ."CallName=".$theCall
  ."&RequestToken=".requestToken
  ."&RequestUserId=".requestUserId
  ."&SiteId=".$SiteId
  ."&Version=".$Version
  ."&Site=".$theSite
  ."&Query=".$theQuery
  ."&EntriesPerPage=".$EntriesPerPage
  ."&PageNumber=".$PageNumber
  ."&UnifiedInput=1"
;
```

Execute the Request

Finally, execute the request as in the previous examples.

```
$xml = file_get_contents($theURL);
```

18

Use the SOAP Interface for GetSearchResults

The SOAP interface requires the same four steps.

Define Your Token and User ID

For a SOAP call, you need your three keys (Developer, Application, Certificate) and the token you created with the Token tool.

As is the case with the other examples in this book, the needed keys are placed in defines in PageTop.html. Here is an example:

```
define ('DevID', 'yourDevID');
define ('AppID', 'yourAppID');
define ('CertID', 'yourCertID');
define ('UserToken', 'yourToken');
```

Set Up Variables

You can set up exactly the same variables as you did for the REST request, although this example uses a slightly different version number. The one difference is the SOAP request does allow spaces, so you do not need to substitute the + for space characters in the keywords field.

```
$theCall = "GetSearchResults";
$theSite = "US";
$SiteId = '0';
$Version = '433';
$EntriesPerPage = '4';
$PageNumber = '1';
$theQuery = $_REQUEST['keywords'];
```

Create the Request

A SOAP request is packaged as an XML document. The document you want to construct will look like this if it is formatted for readability and if the contents of the keywords field is movies.

All the elements in the XML request are defined in the documentation, but these are the ones you can use most easily in searching for eBay listings. Note, the values are the same as in the previous REST example.

The entire request is placed within an element with the name of the call—GetSearchResults, in this case. Two elements with subelements are here. RequesterCredentials contains your eBayAuthToken. The Pagination element contains both EntriesPerPage and Page Number. Each of those has the same meaning as in the REST call.

```
<?xml version="1.0" encoding="utf-8" ?>
<GetSearchResults  xmlns="urn:ebay:apis:eBLBaseComponents">
```

```
<RequesterCredentials>
  <eBayAuthToken>
    yourToken
  </eBayAuthToken>
</RequesterCredentials>
<Query>
  movies
</Query>
<Pagination>
  <EntriesPerPage>
    4
  </EntriesPerPage>
  <PageNumber>
    1
  </PageNumber>
</Pagination>
</GetSearchResults>
```

If you set up the variables shown in the previous section, you can construct the relevant XML document with the following code:

```
$requestXmlBody = '<?xml version="1.0" encoding="utf-8" ?>';
$requestXmlBody .= '<';
$requestXmlBody .= $theCall;
$requestXmlBody .= ' xmlns="urn:ebay:apis:eBLBaseComponents">';
$requestXmlBody .= "<RequesterCredentials><eBayAuthToken>";
$requestXmlBody .= UserToken;
$requestXmlBody .= "</eBayAuthToken></RequesterCredentials>";
$requestXmlBody .= "<Query>";
$requestXmlBody .= $theQuery;
$requestXmlBody .= "</Query>";
$requestXmlBody .= "<Pagination>";
$requestXmlBody .= "<EntriesPerPage>";
$requestXmlBody .= $EntriesPerPage;
$requestXmlBody .= "</EntriesPerPage>";
$requestXmlBody .= "<PageNumber>";
$requestXmlBody .= $PageNumber;
$requestXmlBody .= "</PageNumber>";
$requestXmlBody .= "</Pagination>";
$requestXmlBody .= '</';
$requestXmlBody .= $theCall;
$requestXmlBody .= '>';
```

18

Execute the Request

Finally, execute the request. The XML request requires a little more handling than the REST call because you need to use the curl routines. However, if you package them together in a function such as this one, you can use it unchanged in your mashups. Here is the general function:

```php
function sendHttpRequest(
  $userRequestToken,
  $developerID,
  $applicationID,
  $certificateID,
  $useTestServer,
  $compatabilityLevel,
  $siteToUseID,
  $callName,
  $requestBody) {
    $headers = array (
      'X-EBAY-API-COMPATIBILITY-LEVEL: ' . $compatabilityLevel,
      'X-EBAY-API-DEV-NAME: ' . $developerID,
      'X-EBAY-API-APP-NAME: ' . $applicationID,
      'X-EBAY-API-CERT-NAME: ' . $certificateID,
      'X-EBAY-API-CALL-NAME: ' . $callName,
      'X-EBAY-API-SITEID: ' . $siteToUseID,
    );

    if(!$useTestServer)
      $serverUrl = 'https://api.ebay.com/ws/api.dll';
    else
      $serverUrl = 'https://api.sandbox.ebay.com/ws/api.dll';

    $connection = curl_init();
    curl_setopt($connection, CURLOPT_URL, $serverUrl);
    curl_setopt($connection, CURLOPT_SSL_VERIFYPEER, 0);
    curl_setopt($connection, CURLOPT_SSL_VERIFYHOST, 0);
    curl_setopt($connection, CURLOPT_HTTPHEADER, $headers);
    curl_setopt($connection, CURLOPT_POST, 1);
    curl_setopt($connection, CURLOPT_POSTFIELDS, $requestBody);
    curl_setopt($connection, CURLOPT_RETURNTRANSFER, 1);
    $response = curl_exec($connection);

    curl_close($connection);

    return $response;
}
```

When called with the following line of code, your function does all the work:

```
$responseXml = sendHttpRequest(UserToken, DevID, AppID, CertID,
   true, $Version, $SiteId, $theCall, $requestXmlBody);
```

Parse the XML Results

With the API Test Tool, you can generate a call as described previously. A good idea is to use it to test any call you plan to code in a mashup. Figure 18-7 shows the results of a call to GetSearchResults.

In the scrolling pane at the top of the window, you can review the call that was sent. In the lower pane, you can examine the results. There are many elements in the results, but the basic structure of the document is the following elements:

- Timestamp

- Ack. You want to make certain its value is Success.

- Version

- Build

- SearchResultItemArray. The SearchResultItemArray contains SearchResultItem elements. Each of those has some subelements that will be useful in the mashup in the next chapter.

- ViewItemURL. This is the URL of the eBay page for the item.

- Title

- CurrentPrice

- PostalCode. This is the code where the item is located.

You can use getElementsByTagName to find these elements. Remember, the routine starts from a given node and searches within it. If you search for Item elements starting from the root of the document, you can find the Item elements that are subnodes of SearchResultItem and of SearchResultItemarray. Likewise, searching for the ViewItemURL subnode within an Item element will find it, even though the ViewItemURL subnode is inside an intervening ListingDetails element. You can see this structure in Figure 18-7.

This is all there is to searching eBay with REST or with SOAP. In the next chapter, these techniques are put together with others described previously to create your mapped mashup of locations of eBay items for sale.

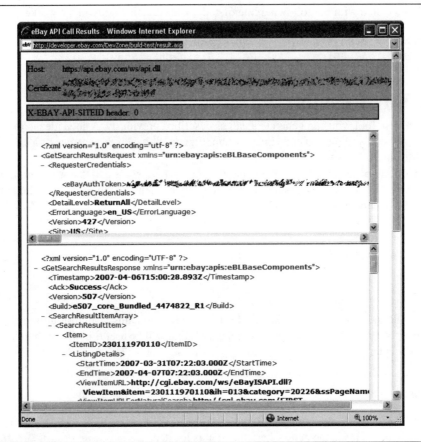

FIGURE 18-7   Results of GetSearchResults call

Chapter 19

Map the Locations of eBay Items

How to...

- Decide on Your Mashup's Objective
- Identify the Data and the Keys
- Get Access to the Data
- Design the User Interface
- Implement the Mashup
- Implement the Starting Page

This last chapter brings together two complex APIs: Google mapping and eBay searching. It has the same structure as all the mashups you have already seen, and the APIs were already discussed. Creating mashups is just a matter of deciding what specific insight you have about how to combine or display information, and then applying the standard mashup structures to that idea.

Decide on Your Mashup's Objective

This mashup lets you search eBay for items using keywords. When it finds results, it returns them in an XML document. From that document, it extracts the title of each item and its price, as well as the location of the seller. These items are then mapped on a Google map with markers providing that information, as well as a link to the actual eBay listing page for the item.

Identify the Data and the Keys

The data come from eBay and use the Google mapping API. This is an example, and it makes some assumptions that are not valid in real life. For example, the mapping API is relying on U.S. ZIP codes. Other postal codes (as well as items with incorrect postal codes) should be omitted or shown in a separate table. Also, you might want to trap errors in processing by checking the Ack element of the returned XML.

Get Access to the Data

As noted in the previous chapter, you need various keys to access the eBay API. You also need your Google access key for the mapping API.

Design the User Interface

The mashup is shown in Figure 19-1. The eBay data are only displayed inside the markers. If you want, you could add another section to the page, so the text of the listings is displayed above or below the map.

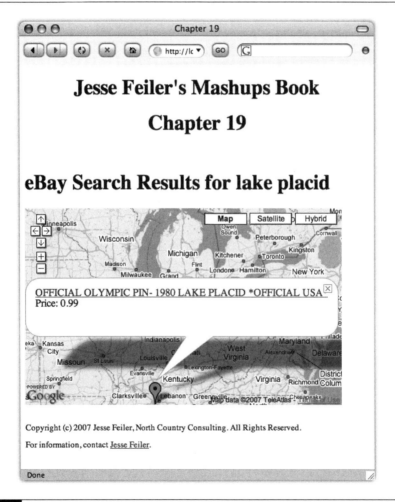

FIGURE 19-1   The eBay/Google maps mashup

19

Implement the Mashup

This is the major part of this chapter and it is short because so much code is being reused.

Implement the Page Top Include

This include file needs your Google mapping key, as well as either REST or SOAP keys for eBay. Here is the REST version:

```
<?xml version="1.0" encoding="iso-8859-1"?>
<!DOCTYPE html PUBLIC "-//W3C//DTD XHTML 1.0 Transitional//EN"
  "http://www.w3.org/TR/xhtml1/DTD/xhtml1-transitional.dtd">
<html xmlns="http://www.w3.org/1999/xhtml">
<head>
  <title><?php echo $page_title; ?></title>
  <meta http-equiv="Content-Type" content="text/html;
    charset=iso-8859-1" />
  <script src="http://maps.google.com/maps?
    file=api&amp;v=2&amp;
    key=yourKey"
    type="text/javascript"></script>
<?php
  define ('requestToken', 'yourRESTToken');
  define ('requestUserId', 'youreBayUserID');
?>
```

And, here is the SOAP version:

```
<?xml version="1.0" encoding="iso-8859-1"?>
<!DOCTYPE html PUBLIC "-//W3C//DTD XHTML 1.0 Transitional//EN"
  "http://www.w3.org/TR/xhtml1/DTD/xhtml1-transitional.dtd">
<html xmlns="http://www.w3.org/1999/xhtml">
<head>
  <title><?php echo $page_title; ?></title>
  <meta http-equiv="Content-Type" content="text/html;
    charset=iso-8859-1" />
  <script src="http://maps.google.com/maps?file=api&amp;v=2&amp
    key=yourKey"
    type="text/javascript"></script>
<?php
  define ('DevID', 'yourDevID');
  define ('AppID','yourAppID');
  define ('CertID', 'yourCertID);
  define ('UserToken', 'yourToken');
?>
```

Implement the PHP Code

The code from Chapter 12 is reused here for the mapping. That code is presented with the bodies of the functions removed.

Create the Top of the File

This is the beginning of the PHP file:

```php
<?php
$page_title = "Chapter 19";
include ('./Includes/PageTop.html');
?>

<!--from Chapter 12-->
<script type="text/javascript">
    //<![CDATA[

  var map = null;
  var geocoder = null;

  function createMap () {
  }

  function setMarkerAndText (mapPoint, text, icon) {
  }

 function showAddress (latitude, longitude, address, addressText, icon) {
 }  //showAddress
//]]>

</script>
<!--end Chapter 12-->
```

Create get_subnodes to Parse Returned XML

The XML to be returned has subnodes of the returned items. A variation of the get_subnodes function is used here. When used with Amazon data, the function checked to see if it needed to create a link to the item. Here, a more generalized form is used. The chief architectural difference is this: the function receives a string ($returnString) to which it adds the data it finds. Then, the function returns the string.

The function searches $theNode for a subnode named $nodeName, just as before. It then adds $nodeTitle (if that string exists) and the values of all the found subnodes and returns the string.

```php
<?php
function get_subnodes ($theNode, $nodeName, $nodeTitle, $returnString) {
  $theSubnodes = $theNode->getElementsByTagName ($nodeName);
  if ($nodeTitle)
    $returnString .= $nodeTitle;
  foreach ($theSubnodes as $theSubnode) {
    $returnString .= $theSubnode->nodeValue;
  }
  return $returnString;
}
?>
```

Create sendHttpRequest for SOAP

Following this, the PageTop2.html file is included, and there are some slight variations for the REST and SOAP versions. In the case of SOAP, the sendHttpRequest function, described in the previous chapter, is added.

```php
<?php
function sendHttpRequest($userRequestToken, $developerID,
  $applicationID, $certificateID, $useTestServer,
  $compatabilityLevel, $siteToUseID, $callName, $requestBody) {
}
```

Do Nothing for REST

In the case of the REST version, you simply open this section of PHP code:

```php
<?php
```

Set Variables for the Calls

In both versions, you continue with identical code to set the variables:

```php
$theCall = "GetSearchResults";
$theSite = "US";
$SiteId = '0';
$Version = '433';
$EntriesPerPage = '4';
$PageNumber = '1';
```

Adjust Keywords for REST and SOAP

For REST, you replace spaces in the keywords text with + as in the following line of code:

```
$theQuery =  str_replace(" ", "+", $_REQUEST['keywords']);
```

For SOAP, you do not need to replace blanks, as you see here:

```
$theQuery = $_REQUEST['keywords'];
```

Add H1 and DIV HTML Elements

Close this section of PHP code, and then enter the HTML header and div elements:

```
?>

<h1>eBay Search Results for
  <?php echo $_REQUEST['keywords']; ?>
</h1>
<div id="map" style="width: 500px; height: 300px"></div>

<?php
```

Create the REST Call

For the last time, the two versions diverge. You create the REST call with this code:

```
$theURL = "http://rest.api.ebay.com/restapi?"
  ."CallName=".$theCall
  ."&RequestToken=".requestToken
  ."&RequestUserId=".requestUserId
  ."&SiteId=".$SiteId
  ."&Version=".$Version
  ."&Site=".$theSite
  ."&Query=".$theQuery
  ."&EntriesPerPage=".$EntriesPerPage
  ."&PageNumber=".$PageNumber
  ."&UnifiedInput=1"
;

$xml = file_get_contents($theURL);
```

Create the SOAP Call

You create the SOAP call with this code:

```
$requestXmlBody = '<?xml version="1.0" encoding="utf-8" ?>';
$requestXmlBody .= '<';
$requestXmlBody .= $theCall;
$requestXmlBody .= ' xmlns="urn:ebay:apis:eBLBaseComponents">';
$requestXmlBody .= "<RequesterCredentials><eBayAuthToken>";
$requestXmlBody .= UserToken;
$requestXmlBody .= "</eBayAuthToken></RequesterCredentials>";
$requestXmlBody .= "<Query>";
$requestXmlBody .= $theQuery;
$requestXmlBody .= "</Query>";
$requestXmlBody .= "<Pagination>";
$requestXmlBody .= "<EntriesPerPage>";
$requestXmlBody .= $EntriesPerPage;
$requestXmlBody .= "</EntriesPerPage>";
$requestXmlBody .= "<PageNumber>";
$requestXmlBody .= $PageNumber;
$requestXmlBody .= "</PageNumber>";
$requestXmlBody .= "</Pagination>";
$requestXmlBody .= '</';
$requestXmlBody .= $theCall;
$requestXmlBody .= '>';

$responseXml = sendHttpRequest(UserToken, DevID, AppID,
  CertID, true, $Version, $SiteId, $theCall, $requestXmlBody);
```

Parse the Returned Document

You parse the XML results just as you did before. The revised get_subnodes function lets you
construct the string that will appear in each marker:

```
$doc = new DOMDocument();
$doc->loadXML($xml);
$root = $doc->documentElement;

if ($root) {
  $results = '';

  $theNodes = $doc->getElementsByTagName('Item');

  foreach ($theNodes as $theNode) {
```

Construct the marker string for each item returned. The only piece of this code that was not presented previously is the link in the marker. You do that by constructing the HTML, as shown here.

NOTE *Constructing the HTML in the marker can be tricky with all the quotation marks. For debugging, add an echo statement to echo $theString, so you can see what you created. Errors are usually easy to spot visually.*

```
$theString = '';
$theString =
  get_subnodes ($theNode, 'ViewItemURL',
    '<a href="', $theString);
$theString =
  get_subnodes ($theNode, 'Title', '">',
    $theString);
$theString .= "</a><br>";
$theString = get_subnodes ($theNode, 'CurrentPrice',
  ' Price: ', $theString);
```

Set the variable for the postal code of the seller. Note, you must set it to an empty string first because it is inside a loop and the new get_subnodes function adds on to whatever text is already there.

```
$thePostalCode = '';
$thePostalCode = get_subnodes ($theNode,
  'PostalCode', '', $thePostalCode);
```

Finally, echo out a script to call the showAddress JavaScript function with the variables you just created:

```
echo ('<script type="text/javascript">');
    echo ("showAddress(0, 1, '"
      .$thePostalCode.
      "', '"
      .$theString.
      "');");
    echo ('</script>');
  }
}
```

Close the Script

Add the standard closing of the script and you are finished:

```
?>

<?php
include ('./Includes/PageBottom.html');
?>
```

Implement the Starting Page

You can use the same starting page you used previously. All you need to remember is to set the form action to the name of this PHP file and to make certain you have a keywords field.

What's Next?

This chapter shows you how to map the results of an eBay query, placing information about the items into the markers you place on a map. You can use it as the basis for further adventures.

For example, remember the text in a Google Map marker is, in fact, HTML. This means you could pull the PictureURL out of the PictureDetails block in the eBay search results and display a product photo in the Map marker (reducing or enlarging it in size with the width and height attributes). As you have seen, mashups bring together a lot of technologies, each one of which is simple (or at least used simply) in the world of mashups.

Few things are more basic in the world of HTML than inserting an image into HTML. That simple procedure, when combined with the eBay API and the Google mapping API, can provide you with an exciting mashup. The only thing to remember is this: your space can be somewhat limited inside the marker, so you might want to use a link instead of (or in addition to) an image.

As you saw in this book, mashups use a few pieces of many technologies to accomplish their goal of displaying multiple data sources or multiple presentations of the same data. You've seen how mashups start from a simple search term and use it to search Google, Flickr, eBay, or Amazon. You've seen how you can chain queries so that, for example, a search term to Flickr uses the Flickr API to find related terms, which, in turn, are sent to Google search.

As long as you understand the data involved (particularly common values that can be used to match data from two sources), you can use the basic techniques here to create an infinite number of mashups. In fact, once you create a few mashups using the code in this book, the basics become almost second nature to you. Then, the fun part begins: working with the data and the people who are interested in it. A basic knowledge of HTML helps you to create Web pages, but a few hours in the world of mashups (and using examples in this book) can help you know where to go to convert among various geographical locations—latitude/longitude, counties, ZIP codes, and the like.

You can also push beyond the basics of mashups that start from a given query that is typed in. Wherever you can find text that is useful for a search, you can begin to build a mashup. And text is everywhere.

For example, you can use Image Functions in PHP (http://se2.php.net/manual/en/ref.image.php) to retrieve the metadata stored in the headers of JPEG and TIFF files. While many people access that information to find the original size of the image, many other fields can tempt the mashup designer. You can find more information about some of the data available at the International Press Telecommunications Organization page (http://www.iptc.org/).

If you want to explore this area, there is little to do beyond what you have already seen. All you do is replace the search text field used on so many of the mashup start pages with a field that either contains an image or a URL (possibly local to the user's computer) that locates the image. If the image contains metadata, you can retrieve it in your PHP code. Digital cameras provide exposure, date, and other data, but many programs let you enter additional data.

You can get the IPTC data as a byproduct of a call to getimagesize, where you pass in the image as the first parameter and, optionally, receive information to parse in the second parameter:

```
$size = getimagesize("yourimage.jpg", $info);
```

Then, you check to see if you have data to parse:

```
if (isset($info["APP13"])) {
  $iptc = iptcparse ($info["APP13"]);
```

You now have an array with the various data fields available from the image. Two that might be of interest are the caption and the headline:

```
$headline = $iptc["2#105"][0];
$caption = $iptc["2#120"][0];
```

At that point, you close the if statement:

```
}
```

With either (or both) of those strings, you are ready to launch the same kind of searches you saw in the examples in this book. Just use $headline or $caption where you have used variables such as $keyword, and away you go.

NOTE   *The standards are under development at press time, so check out the IPTC Web site and the PHP link shown here to get the latest info and examples.*

Keep your eyes open for the mashup opportunities in the data to which you have access. One of the most important aspects of the Web as it is evolving is that not only does it contain vast stores of data (such as the population, statistical, and campaign contributions data used in this book), but it also contains localized and specific data, either as parts of these large databases or as stand-alone resources. The mashup developer understands such a specific dataset. The developer who can create a mashup to help friends, neighbors, and colleagues understand the data they deal with every day on a superficial level is a valuable addition to a corporation, a community, or any other group.

Designing mashups lets you help people to move beyond the minutiae of data points to an understanding of the realities the data suggest. Few technologies today have such far-reaching possibilities.

19

Index